The Japanese Nation

The
JAPANESE NATION
A Social Survey

JOHN F. EMBREE

GREENWOOD PRESS, PUBLISHERS
WESTPORT, CONNECTICUT

Library of Congress Cataloging in Publication Data

Embree, John Fee, 1908-1950.
  The Japanese nation.

    Reprint of the ed. published by Farrar & Rine-
hart, New York.
    Bibliography: p.
    Includes index.
    1. Japan--Civilization. I. Title.
DS821.E53 1975   952   75-8766
ISBN 0-8371-8117-8

Originally published in 1945 by Farrar & Rinehart, Inc.,
New York

This edition is published by arrangement with Holt, Rinehart
and Winston.

Reprinted in 1975 by Greenwood Press,
a division of Williamhouse-Regency Inc.

Library of Congress Catalog Card Number 75-8766

ISBN 0-8371-8117-8

Printed in the United States of America

TO

E L L A

without whom . . .

Acknowledgments

NO man writes alone. The present book is the result not only of personal observation during three trips to Japan (1926, 1932, 1935–36) but also of conversations with others and the reading of previous writings on Japanese society. All I can do here is to acknowledge specific quotations and direct recent advice. The following persons have been kind enough to read and comment on the book in manuscript form: my wife, Ella Embree, Henry Bloch (University of Chicago), D. H. Buchanan (Department of State), Fred Eggan (Director, Civil Affairs Training School, University of Chicago), Captain Clarence Glacken (Civil Affairs Training School, Northwestern University), Miwa Kai (Oriental Section, Columbia University Library), Alexander Lury (War Department), Ryusaku Tsunoda (Columbia University), W. Lloyd Warner (University of Chicago), Chitoshi Yanaga (Federal Communications Commission), and my father, Edwin Embree.

Special acknowledgments are due to the following for permission to make quotations: Doubleday Doran for permission to quote from Wilfred Fleisher's *Volcanic Isle,* J. B. Lippincott for permission to quote from Helen Mears' *Year of the Wild Boar,* and Mr. Joe Mickle for permission to quote from his privately distributed paper *Letters from Japan.*

The cartography of Figures 2, 4, 5, 6, 7, 8 and 10, as well as of the end-paper map, is by Alfred Harris of the University of Chicago.

Contents

x CONTENTS

List of Maps and Charts

The Japanese Nation

Introduction

JAPAN THE UNKNOWN

THE attack on Pearl Harbor caught the United States off guard. Even more serious, perhaps, than the terrible loss in lives and ships, was the complete psychological unpreparedness of this country for a war in Asia.

Our first reaction naturally was one of outrage. But righteous indignation was not of much help as Japan's army spread all too rapidly over the Philippines, Thailand, Malaya, the East Indies, and finally into Burma and New Guinea. Within a few months Japan had gained all her primary objectives, while America was still arguing as to whether Germany or Japan should be listed as Enemy Number One. In the meantime, a spate of books and articles on Japan and the Japanese began to appear to make up for the void in our knowledge. Some writers seemed to have swallowed whole Japan's official mythology of a sacred emperor, robot soldiers, and a meek populace, while others indulged in gory tales of Asiatic atrocity. Only a few attempted to outline the social organization of Japan, or to point out some of the historical and economic factors which lay behind the development of the present conflict.

It is difficult for an American to understand the nature of Japanese culture. It is an Old-World Asiatic culture in contrast to the United States, a New-World, machine-age culture, with a population just now being fused into a single people. The peasant background, the age-old traditions and cultural homogeneity characteristic of Asiatic and European nations alike are notably absent from modern America. For these reasons one must frequently turn to recently industrialized Old-World European cultures such as France and Germany for meaningful comparisons with Japan, rather than to the immigrant-settled, machine-age culture of the United States. Japanese feudalism had its earlier European parallel; the closeness of family ties and arranged marriages of Japan can be found also in France; the emphasis on the state as against the individual is as characteristic of Germany or Soviet Russia as of Japan.

There is, however, one interesting parallel between Japan and the United States: the dramatic changes which have taken place in both countries during the past hundred years. In 1853, the United States was still only half integrated as a nation with a bloody civil war ahead before true national unity could be achieved. At the same time feudal Japan was made up of a number of rival provinces, some of them envious of the ruling group in Tokyo. A civil war also lay ahead before a unified Japan could develop. Both nations have been transformed from rural, almost subsistent, peoples to manufacturing, industrial nations within the space of two generations. And most important of all, so far as Americans are concerned, when Japan broke out of feudalism and when the United States grew to maturity, both nations became powers and rivals in the Pacific. On the whole, it is probably safe to say that Japan realized this rivalry before we did. She was less secure, her industrialization was more recent, her land and natural resources were less abundant than those of America, so that she was more self-consciously concerned with her future in the world.

Japan made it a point to learn about America and Europe, but the average American gave little heed to Japan and the Japanese beyond the interests of a few traders and missionaries. Belatedly, we are setting to work to learn something of the nature of Japan, primarily as a means of achieving victory in the war and ultimately, it is to be hoped, in order that through a better awareness of the nature of Japanese society, as well as of other Asiatic cultures, future Pearl Harbors may be avoided.

This book is primarily a study of the social organization of a nation. Anthropologists have often outlined the social structure of small preliterate societies; the present author, who happens also to be an anthropologist, has attempted to apply the methods of social anthropology to a social survey of a modern nation, viewing its social structure as a functioning whole with each of its parts having meaning only in relation to all other parts. Being primarily a *social* survey, the book pays little attention to the material aspects of Japanese culture such as art and architecture, while it devotes considerable attention to government, religion, schools, and the network of social relations making up the national structure. Thus it is hoped to give a context for the interpretation of the behavior of Japanese and some basis for an understanding of future developments in Japan.

GEOGRAPHICAL SETTING

Geography rarely determines culture but always exerts an influence upon it. Japan's island setting made possible a long period of political isolation; her climate made possible a wet rice agriculture. On the other hand, the fact that the Japanese grow rice rather than some other crop is the result not of geography but of cultural diffusion from Southeast Asia.

Japan proper, with a population of over seventy million, is composed of an archipelago of four main islands and hundreds of smaller ones. The large islands are Kyūshū, the original home territory of Japan's semihistorical founder Jimmu Tennō; Honshū, the main island on which is located Tokyo; Shikoku, a land of double rice crops; and, in the north, the recently settled Hokkaidō. The total area of Japan proper (including the Ryūkyūs) is 147,707 square miles, somewhat less than that of California. By including the empire as of 1941 (Formosa, Korea, Karafuto),

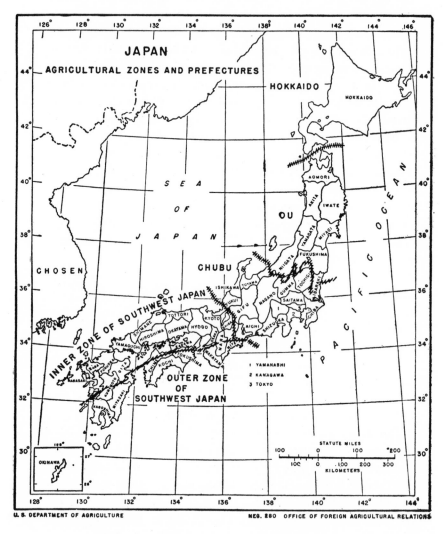

FIG. 1.—Agricultural Zones and Prefectures.

6

the area is raised to 260,769 square miles, about the size of Texas.

One cannot travel far in Japan without coming upon volcanic peaks and picturesque inlets—scenes of striking.natural beauty. The cost of this inspiring scenery is that only about 20 per cent of the countryside is arable and the farmers of the land must concentrate their efforts on the small plain areas scattered here and there along the seacoasts or between mountains. The very volcanic forces and rifts which give to Japan much of her beauty also cause devastating eruptions and earthquakes.

Geographers divide the four large islands of Japan into four major divisions: Hokkaidō, Ōu, Chūbu, and Southwest. (Fig. 1.)

Hokkaidō, the northern island, has cold winters, rugged mountains, and extensive forests. It is the most recently settled area of Japan and despite the encouragement of the government it is still underpopulated as compared with the rest of the nation. The few aboriginal Ainu left in Japan live mostly in small settlements on this island. Some rice agriculture has gradually developed, but, as a result of the influence of American agricultural advisers, farming techniques in Hokkaidō bear marked resemblances to American rural areas with cattle raising and separate homesteads in contrast to the village clusters characteristic of intensive wet rice agricultural regions elsewhere in Japan. Fisheries are also important in the Hokkaidō region.

Ōu, or Tōhoku, is that part of Honshū lying north of the thirty-seventh parallel, a mountainous region with a temperate climate. It is largely an agricultural area, principally devoted to rice growing with a little tea and mulberry in the south. In neither Ōu nor Hokkaidō has manufacturing development been very extensive so that large urban centers are not found in these areas.

Chūbu is the central Honshū region with broad alluvial plains along the coastal areas and high mountains in the interior. The Tokyo or Kwantō plain alone supports over fourteen million people both as farmers in the rich paddy land and as workers in the highly industrialized centers. Nagoya, at the head of Ise Bay, is another manufacturing center in the Chūbu area.

Southwestern Japan includes Shikoku, Kyūshū, and southern Honshū. The inner zone of this area, centering about the Inland Sea, taken together with the Chūbu region, forms the heart of modern Japan. The lowlands comprise the Kinki District, including Osaka, Kyoto, and Kobe, three of Japan's largest cities. Formerly famous for textiles and ceramics, this region is now a center for metallurgical and chemical industries. It is also a region of intensive agriculture and fishing. Another industrial center is that of northern Kyūshū centering in Yawata, an iron and steel center located near native coal deposits.

The climate of Japan proper resembles that of the American Atlantic coast from Maine to Georgia. The southwest is characterized by mild winters where two crops of rice may be grown in some parts, while Hokkaidō has winters characterized by heavy snows and bitter cold. There is adequate rainfall for agriculture throughout Japan, but it varies according to season, and serious crop losses may result from drought, flood, or windstorm.

The Kuroshio current from the south warms the southern half of Japan, especially in the east from Kyūshū to north of Tokyo, giving this region a pleasanter climate than on the western shores. Cyclonic storms may strike Japan, coming across the water from the Asiatic mainland, or up from the south especially in the fall, bringing with them damaging winds, rains, and high seas. In some parts of Honshū gentle, steady, and depressing monsoon rains fall from about the middle of June to the middle of July and are called by the Japanese "plum rains" because they set in with the ripening of plums.

Since the Japanese have lived traditionally on the basis of a rice economy and since the seasons vary markedly in temperature, humidity, and windiness, all of which fundamentally affect the rice crop, the seasons play an important role in Japanese religion and cultural life. Much of Shinto ceremonial is concerned with the elements, and in rural areas there are not only different occupations but also different social activities according to season.

By way of natural resources Japan has fair soft coal deposits and is rich in gold, copper, and sulphur. Hydroelectric power is also plentiful. However, for a modern industrial nation Japan is poor in the essential resources of iron and petroleum.

An island people, the Japanese are fishermen as well as farmers so that while mountains preclude the growing of rice in much of the area, the sea provides fish to make up for this loss. Today the mountains with their rapid streams are of inestimable value to Japan as a source of water power for industrial development. The mountains and the seas have also influenced artistic and religious developments, providing Japanese artists with stimulating art motifs and the people with a sacred world of mountain and forest spirits and deities of land and of sea.

Today Japan is an industrial nation with great manufacturing cities which depend for their existence on natural resources such as oil from Southeast Asia and coal from Manchuria as well as on free access to markets. This has led to the situation of a newly industrialized independent nation in the midst of an area dominated by Occidental colonial and economic interests—a situation which was bound, sooner or later, to lead to a war of survival.

RACIAL ORIGINS

The origins of the Japanese are in part determined by the fact that Japan is an island archipelago lying off the large mainland continent of Eurasia. In this geographical position she resembles Great Britain and, like Britain, she has received immigrants and cultural influences from various parts of the near-by continent from prehistoric times up to the present day.

The oldest historical native inhabitants of Japan, the aborigines, were the Ainu and Kumaso. "Kumaso" is a term used to refer to the early inhabitants of the southern island of Kyūshū, while

"Ainu" is generally used to refer to the aborigines of the main island of Honshū and their modern descendants in Hokkaidō. "Kumaso" and "Ainu" are probably two terms for a single type of people or two varieties of a closely related type. The type appears to be a survival of an early Caucasoid stock in Northeast Asia and probably came into Japan from there, but the exact route taken is unknown. The most conspicuous Caucasoid trait of this group is the heavy facial and body hair of the men. This hair is usually black, like that of the Mongol, but it is also sometimes wavy; and while Ainu eyes are usually brown, there are occasional individuals with hazel eyes. The epicanthic fold (which gives the appearance of "slant eyes" to Mongoloids) is not characteristic. In contrast to the traditional round-headed Mongol, Ainu are, as a rule, medium- or long-headed, and their skin color is, on the average, somewhat lighter than that of the Japanese.

Although the Ainu were the aborigines of the islands, they exist today as a separate ethnic group only in small numbers (15,000 or so) in the north, where they still speak the Ainu language and follow Ainu customs. Many modern Japanese show the effects of racial mixture with Ainu and Kumaso in bearded faces and hair on the chest.

From the south have come, at one time or another, appreciable numbers of southern Mongoloids from Malaysia and Southeast Asia. One may see an occasional kinky-haired individual in southern Japan, a fact which indicates either a small number of one-time aboriginal Negritos similar to those found in parts of the Philippines today or simply a Negrito strain in some of the early immigrant Malaysian groups.

The predominant Mongoloid types have come to Japan over a long period of time mostly via Korea, a peninsula which has been a channel of racial and cultural influence on Japan for thousands of years.

Modern Japanese, then, as a result of their varied origins, are of mixed racial stock with a predominant Mongoloid strain.

In general, it may be said that modern Japanese are short in stature (averaging about five feet four) with straight black hair, a relatively hairless face and body, and legs relatively short in proportion to trunk. However, the stature varies from a little under five feet to over six feet; wavy hair is not uncommon because of the racial mixture with Ainu types and wavy-haired peoples from Malaysia, and head shape varies from long to round. By popular tradition, the slightly built, narrow-faced types are of the noble and upper classes, while the stocky, round-faced people (Satsuma type) are of peasant stock, but there is too much variation of physical type in all classes for any such easy generalization to hold. The wide variation of individual physical types in both Japan and China makes it impossible to set up foolproof criteria for identifying a Japanese as against a Chinese on the basis of physical traits alone.

Chapter I

Historical Background
The Tokugawa Shogunate

THE ERA OF SECLUSION BEGINS

THE social organization and cultural values of modern Japan cannot be understood without some knowledge of the Tokugawa feudal era, a long period of peace and national seclusion which was inaugurated by Tokugawa Ieyasu after the battle of Osaka in 1615 and which ended with the arrival of Commodore Perry in 1853. Much of the form and spirit of modern Japan was shaped during this long period of isolation and cultural consolidation.

During the latter part of the sixteenth century the first important European contacts with Japan occurred with the advent of Portuguese missionaries and Dutch and British traders. St. Francis Xavier came in 1549, and in 1600 a remarkable English ship captain, Will Adams, arrived and was made official shipbuilder to the Tokugawa government. At the same time, Japanese traders and pirates were going overseas, especially in the direction of Southeast Asia. In 1582, for example, a group of four Japanese visited Lisbon, Madrid, and Rome. As a result of these numerous Asiatic and European cultural contacts, the times seemed ripe for a great cultural revival or renaissance in Japan comparable to that of Elizabethan England.

Missionaries and other foreigners who came to Japan at this time were at first well received and a number of feudal lords became converted to Christianity, but as time went on the activities of some of the Jesuit and Franciscan priests who were in Japan seemed to indicate a desire on their part to overthrow the Tokugawa government and even to pave the way for European conquest of the country. In addition to the disorganizing activities of the missionaries within Japan, Ieyasu learned from agents he sent to Europe many things that must have caused him grave concern for the future of his government and country. This was the period of religious intolerance in Europe, the Inquisition, extensive aggression in the cause of Christianity, and a religious head who claimed authority to confiscate the countries of non-Christian rulers.

Danger of civil strife as a result of the political activities of the missionaries and anxiety concerning the possibility that Western powers might attempt to take advantage of such strife by stepping in with colonial aspirations led the Tokugawa government to pass a number of edicts against the Spanish and Portuguese priests.

Just previous to the rise of the Tokugawa family as rulers of Japan there had been a long period of wasting feudal wars, so that one of the primary concerns of Tokugawa Ieyasu was the consolidation of his government and the bringing of law and order to the realm. The persecution of the Jesuits and their converts that eventually developed was thus not so much an oppression of religion as it was a political move, undertaken for national security. The culminating event was the Shimabara revolt of 1637-38, probably caused by local tyranny and economic distress but carried out under the banner of Christianity. This revolt against authority by an estimated thirty-three thousand people ended in a dreadful massacre of the rebels. The Dutch traders who gave assistance to the government were the only foreigners (other than

Chinese) allowed to remain in Japan after this time and even they were restricted in their movements to a single island in the harbor of Nagasaki. Thus it came about that the potential cultural revolution of the early seventeenth century was put off for over two centuries.

THE SHOGUNATE CONSOLIDATES ITS POSITION

The Tokugawa government was a nonaggressive government by dictatorship. Feudalism, which had existed in Japan before the Tokugawa rose to power, was now organized into a relatively centralized and stable political system. The political capital was set up in Yedo (the old name for Tokyo) while the emperor continued to reside in Kyoto, the imperial capital. The imperial court in Kyoto was the final authority in priestly affairs, court etiquette, and the bestowing of titles, but the military ruler or *shōgun,* while receiving his title from the emperor, held the economic and political reins of government. One purpose in setting up the political capital in Yedo was to avoid the softening effects of court life and the dangers of court intrigue. The city soon became not only the military and administrative capital but the economic and cultural capital as well with a few softening effects of its own.

In the Tokugawa struggle to gain control of Japan, certain feudal lords or *daimyō* served as allies while others had to be overcome by force of arms. Those lords, the majority, who sided with Tokugawa before the critical battle of Sekigahara (1600) were called the *fudai* or hereditary vassals. They numbered 176 at the beginning of the period and all important functions were reserved for them as men whose loyalty to the shogunate could be depended upon. The other lords, 86 in number, were called *tozama* or Outside Lords and were not given the honor of being called vassals of the *shōgun.* The most powerful of these Outside Lords were Maeda (Kaga), Date (Sendai), Shimazu

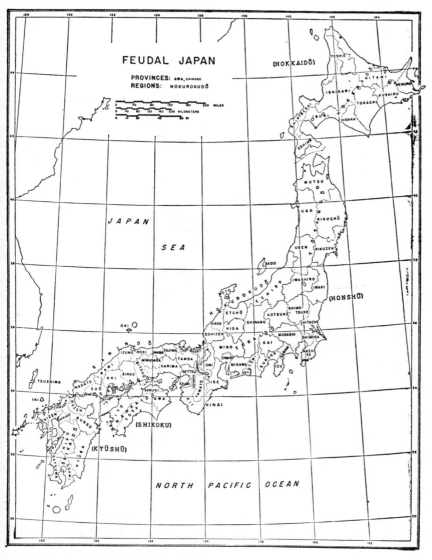

FIG. 2.—Feudal Japan.

15

(Satsuma), and Mori (Chōshū). These last two families never became fully loyal to the Tokugawa and were the spearhead of the revolt which occurred two centuries later.

One of Ieyasu's first steps to insure the security of his regime after the battle of Sekigahara was to have all *daimyō* sign an oath of loyalty to the Yedo government. Ieyasu made it a point to split the main bodies of Outside Lords from one another and to place two families of equal power next to one another in order that they might become rivals. Furthermore, it was required of all lords that they reside six months or a year in the capital, and when not in the capital to leave their wives behind as hostages. This rule, which had economic as well as administrative effects, was called *sankin kōtai,* or alternate attendance. While communications between the loyal *fudai* were facilitated, barriers between fiefs were maintained in order to guard against the development of subversive plots. As an additional guarantee of safety, the Tokugawa government maintained in each fief representatives to keep the Yedo government informed as to local developments. Such agents were even maintained in the imperial court in Kyoto. In this way the central government was able to keep its fingers on the social and political pulse of the country and to govern accordingly.

The unified feudalism thus established by Ieyasu lasted over 250 years, a remarkable record. This was made possible in part by able government administration, especially by the early Tokugawa, and in part by the policy of national seclusion which retarded the development of commercial and industrial capitalism —a development which, when it finally came in the nineteenth century, spelled the doom of feudal society in Japan.

THE SHŌGUN CREATES A BUREAUCRACY ...

The government of the shogunate being evolved from that of the Tokugawa house law, its administrative structure was not very different from that of a feudal lord.

As advisors to the *shōgun* in all matters of high policy such as relations with the court and the feudal lords, there was a Council of Elders (*toshiyori*), four or five in number, presided over by one of its members called the Great Elder, an office which rotated among the members on a monthly basis. This council came to be the most influential policy-making group and as time went on the *shōgun* usually accepted its final recommendations without question. If the *shōgun* were a minor, a member of the council served as regent. Beneath the council came the four to six Junior Elders concerned with the supervision of the *shōgun's* direct vassals below the rank of *daimyō* (*hatamoto* and *gokenin*). Attached to the boards of elders were censors and secret agents (*metsuke*) who served as intelligence officers for the shogunate.

Below the councils came a fairly sizable civil service of executive, administrative, and judicial officers termed collectively *bugyō*. These were, for instance, the treasury officials, the city magistrates and police officials, and the officials in charge of shrine and temple affairs. In general, high government positions were held by the loyal vassals (*fudai*) on a hereditary basis, and only exceptionally by members of families of the Outside Lords.

These various officials had functions which were not clearly defined and high offices were often duplicated or their functions carried on by councils. Frequently, official duties were carried out by a system of rotation which led to considerable shifting of responsibility and red tape. Part of this lack of individual responsibility was traditional and part a deliberate governmental policy to guard against a monopoly of power by any one person.

Boards and councils were not only characteristic of the higher bureaucracy, but the system extended right down to the *goningumi* or five-man groups of peasants, the smallest rural administrative units. The five-man group as a whole was responsible for the behavior of each of its constituent members. Group, not individual, responsibility was fundamental to the Tokugawa administration.

Local fief government followed the same general pattern as the national administrative organization. Within their own fiefs, *daimyō* exercised almost complete autonomy as to local affairs, including taxation and lawmaking, while shogunate officials, the *bakufu,* were stationed only in certain large cities and the direct Tokugawa domains. However, if a given lord was in danger of becoming too wealthy and strong, the Yedo government could order him to construct expensive public works.

The important political units were the district, the town, and the village. Officials such as judges and tax collectors of the feudal lords or the *shōgun* were stationed in each district office as well as in the larger towns. Villages were governed by a people's representative (*nanushi* or *shōya*) who was, however, subject to the *shōgun's* district officer (*gundai* or *daikwan*). The village headman was assisted in his administration by locally elected village councilors (*toshiyori*). Below the rural headman were the neighborhood heads (*kumigashira, kumichō*). These village officials were not *samurai* but were as a rule from old landed farm families. The village head was on the one hand responsible for the good conduct of his villagers and on the other was expected to make any necessary representations to the *shōgun's* officials on behalf of the farmers.

. . . AND LAYS DOWN THE LAW

The law of Tokugawa, a martial law carried on in times of peace, was largely repressive in nature. It was based on a rigid division of the classes headed by the soldier and aimed at maintaining the social and political *status quo*.

The backbone of this law is found in Ieyasu's code which lays down rules of conduct for the military class, exhorting them to maintain their military arts and at the same time devote themselves to literature. Loose living and luxury are specifically warned against. The code outlines broadly the proper relations between fiefs, and warns against combinations between *daimyō* against the shogunate, such as through marriages arranged for political purposes. The proper costumes, retinues, and general behavior of each class are provided for and *samurai* are specifically exhorted to be frugal and lords to avoid favoritism in their local administrations. This code was regarded by the shogunate as essentially unchangeable and it was reaffirmed by each *shōgun* on his succession in a solemn ceremony in the presence of all the vassals.

The laws of the Tokugawa, like those of preceding Japanese lawmakers, had a strong moral flavor with Confucian exhortations to virtue, loyalty to superiors, and right conduct. In practice the Tokugawa rulers avoided the compiling of unified codes because of a feeling that each case should be judged on its merits and judges should not be too closely bound by precedents and rules which might not fit the case in hand.

Punishments were calculated to strike terror into possible offenders and included various gruesome methods of death depending on the crime. (The treatment of prisoners and cruel punishments were, however, no worse than those in seventeenth-century England.) Punishments also varied according to the social class of the offender, *samurai* receiving lighter sentences than merchants or peasants. If a lord did not obey the laws laid down by the shogunate, he might be exiled, have his fief confiscated, or even be condemned to death. Ieyasu did not hesitate to apply such penalties even to lords who were related to him. Some crimes for which they were punished included (1) contracting a private marriage without prior approval of the Tokugawa (thus possibly establishing a dangerous political alliance), (2) rebuilding or improving a feudal castle without permission, (3) not visiting the capital as prescribed, (4) allowing conditions in a fief to become out of hand because of negligence.

As a rule disputes between individuals were settled by arbitration and the man who appealed to courts of law was looked upon with suspicion. For groups of villages and urban wards there were district courts, with special courts having jurisdiction over temples and priests. A magistrate often referred minor cases back to the village headman while important criminal cases might be referred to a higher court in Yedo. This high court was under the general supervision of the Council of Elders.

As time went on unification of law and custom developed in the various domains inasmuch as all but the strongest Outside Lords tended to adopt the laws of the Tokugawa as their own house law.

In addition to the censors who served as eyes and ears of the Yedo government, and who were respected men, there was a loose organization of police or "thief catchers" and secret police or spies. The police were often priests or innkeepers, while the spies were men of low class whom the government could employ secretly and for whose safety they need assume no responsibility.

THE CLASS SYSTEM MAINTAINS SOCIAL STABILITY

A class system, already in existence before 1600, became more elaborate and rigid during the long peaceful period of Tokugawa rule. It was a system encouraged and legally sanctioned by the shogunate to maintain the *status quo* and in the name of national law and order. The hierarchy included five main categories.

The Court Nobility (*Kuge*)

The Imperial Family and the Emperor's immediate vassals, the court nobles, made up a special class, the *kuge*. At the top of this group was the court at Kyoto. Only the Emperor had the right to bestow titles of nobility, including the supreme title of *shōgun*. However, except for foreign relations—largely an academic subject until the end of the period—the Emperor had no governmental functions. The Emperor was granted land and income by the Yedo government, but, while his family and vassals were extremely high socially, they were very poor financially and none of them received as much income as the smallest feudal lord.

The Warriors (*Samurai*)

The warrior or *samurai* group included everyone from the *shōgun* down to the humblest foot soldier. The *shōgun* and high-ranking officials of the *shōgun's* court in Yedo were at the apex of this social pyramid and below them came the feudal lords, about 270 in number, in order of rank (based largely on rice income).

A *daimyō* was any feudal lord whose income was ten thousand *koku* or more of rice—the more powerful had incomes of hundreds of thousands of *koku*. Direct retainers of the *shōgun*, with incomes of less than ten thousand *koku* and in general ranking below *daimyō*, were of two kinds: *hatamoto* and *gokenin*. These direct retainers of the *shōgun* were required to live in Yedo. Some were civil officials, others military, and they varied in rank according to family and income.

Daimyō and *hatamoto* had retainers called *baishin*. High-ranking *baishin* acted as government advisors, lower ranks as administrative officials, and lowest as foot soldiers (*ashigaru*). These foot soldiers, who came last in the train of a *daimyō*, constituted perhaps the largest single group belonging to the *samurai* class. A joint cause of their increase in numbers was the development of castle towns and the use of firearms. The total number of *samurai* (*daimyō* and their vassals) was almost two million in a national population of about thirty million.

Unemployed warriors not connected with any particular *daimyō* were called *rōnin* and numbered about four hundred thousand. This large number was in part the result of the confiscation of the lands of *daimyō* defeated by Ieyasu. Some of these *rōnin* or masterless *samurai* played an important role in maintaining education by becoming teachers in temple schools and elsewhere, some became outlaws after the manner of Robin

Hood, and still others drifted to urban areas and developed into or joined lawless groups, prototypes of the modern thug or *sōshi*.

Below *samurai* and *rōnin* came *gōshi* or *samurai* who dwelt in agricultural villages and were really farmers but who became active combatants in time of war. All *samurai* except *gōshi* and *rōnin* lived in Yedo and the castle towns, thus clearly separating the functions of *samurai* and farmer. The duties of the *samurai* were administrative and military and none was supposed to enter into any sort of trading or business activity. This separation of soldiers from the land created a heavy burden directly or indirectly on the farmer groups, who had to raise food for their support.

Scholars, including priests, nuns, and physicians, occupied a rather low social position, higher than the common people (*heimin*) but lower than *daimyō* and *shōgun*. They gained a livelihood from court and feudal lord patronage on the one hand and offerings of poor peasants on the other.

The Farmer and the Artisan

Below the *samurai* came, in order, the farmers, the artisans, and the merchants. The farmers were of three main groups: (1) village headmen and officials, (2) landowning farmers, and (3) the poor peasantry. These last were very poor and were by far the most numerous. The farmers were required by law to practice frugality in living and were subjected to heavy taxes both in rice and in conscripted labor. As their economic position grew more difficult, many peasants deserted their homes and became part of a growing urban low-class group. For all practical purposes, the artisans or small handicraftsmen were in the same social level as the farmer groups.

The Merchants

The merchant or *chōnin* class was divided into two categories: (1) those who owned their own houses and lands and (2) those who were landless. While of low social status at the beginning of the era and technically ranked below the peasant, the economic position of the merchant class improved steadily until, by the end of the period, successful merchants were in a position of considerable social influence. Members of the low ranks of *samurai* sometimes joined the *chōnin* class, but there was, as might be expected, considerable resentment of the rising merchant group on the part of the *samurai* who were losing ground.

The Outcastes

At the bottom of the social ladder was a pariah group, the *senmin*. This lowly group was in turn divided into two subclasses: the *hinin* and the *eta*.

The *hinin* were a pariah group under the jurisdiction of their own local chiefs who were responsible for their good behavior. *Hinin* were not allowed to trade so that they had to beg for money and rice in return for entertainments including puppet shows, animal performances, storytelling, juggling, and acrobatics. Executioners, beggars, and some brothel keepers also belonged to this class. Special laws restricted the headgear and clothing permitted to *hinin*, and their women were not allowed to shave their eyebrows or blacken their teeth as commoners could. One became a *hinin* either by birth or by edict as a result of committing some crime.

The *eta*, even lower than *hinin*, were largely artisans engaged in the manufacture and sale of leather goods, sandals, clogs, lamp wicks; they were also employed for slaying animals and disposing of dead animals. In general, these occupations were connected with the various processes of preparing leather and making leather goods. *Eta* were also meat eaters so that both in occupation and diet they were set off from other and higher social classes. They were required to marry *eta* and had to live in special ghettos or villages under the jurisdiction of special *eta* chiefs. They were not even allowed to enter the service of commoners (farmers and merchants) as servants. *Eta* were not included in the census, were not allowed to wear clogs, and were counted with the numerals used to count animals. They could not sit, eat, or smoke in the company of commoners.

There is a popular belief in Japan today that the *eta* are descendants of Korean prisoners, but a study of Japanese social history points rather to a gradual occupational degradation associated with the Buddhist tabus on the killing of animals. At the beginning of the Tokugawa period, *eta* and *hinin* were not too badly off and some were even rich. But as time went on, special discriminatory laws increased, the relative value of their products decreased, and their numbers increased both through births and through additions in the form of stragglers and criminals from above, so that their state became, by the end of the period, one of degradation and misery. At the same time the Tokugawa government, in line with its policy of keeping society stable, respected their bodies of self-government and protected them in their special trades, not allowing farmers or merchants to encroach upon their spheres of activity.

This whole class organization was calculated to maintain the superior position of the warrior class, and the careful regulation of behavior proper to each class and of relations between classes was an integral part of the feudal organization. The grants of land and rice made by the *shōgun* to *daimyō* and *hatamoto* and by them to their retainers formed part of the feudal relationship of master and retainer and the whole body of ethics of loyalty which went with it. The *daimyō* and *hatamoto* were under the obligation to render military assistance to the *shōgun* before all else. The vassals of the *daimyō* were under similar obligation to their lords and so on down the line. The *shōgun* and the lords in their turn were expected to govern the country for the collective welfare of the vassals and to give them protection in the event of attack, and relief in the event of fire, flood, and famine.

These principles of loyalty and paternalism also applied to

other relationships in Tokugawa days—between masters and apprentices, shopkeepers and their employees, the head of a family and his wife and children. The social classes were part of this hierarchial system of human relations and their duties and privileges were recognized by law.

THE FARMER FEEDS THE WARRIOR

Agriculture formed the economic base of the Tokugawa feudal society. At the same time manufacturing industries were carried on by manual workers with a connection with agriculture but such connections often became rather thin as separate crafts and industries arose and privileged guilds of manual workers were formed. Commerce, at first combined with manual industry, also came eventually to be separated with the formation of special trading guilds. The problem of the nation under the Tokugawa policy of exclusion was how to conserve and increase its own resources without benefit of foreign trade, a problem complicated by this gradual transition from an agricultural to a mercantile economy.

During this period the farming population constituted about 80 per cent of the population. Most farmers were nearly self-sufficient, making or providing their own fertilizer, agricultural implements, food, and houses while purchasing only a few things such as salt, fish, medicines, and a few metal necessities.

Taxes, largely assessed by the local lord, who was guided to some extent by custom, were usually paid in rice and in the form of periodic compulsory labor which could sometimes be converted into rice or cash. The annual tax rate usually amounted to 40 or 50 per cent of the crop yield. For tax purposes, the village was the unit and every five household heads became jointly responsible for a share of the payments. Such taxes left little if any surplus over and above daily needs for the farmers for their year's work.

To maintain such a system it was necessary to place restrictions on farmers' activities. There were laws against farmers' leaving the villages to become townspeople, the choice of crops raised was restricted, and an ordinary farmer was not allowed to build a fine house or to wear silk clothing. There were also laws against the buying and selling of farmers' lands. In general it was assumed that the farmer had little intelligence of his own and so must have his life regulated for him, and that it was desirable to see that he had just enough to eat but no more. Fundamentally, all such rules were intended to maintain the social and economic *status quo*, but as time went on they became more and more difficult to enforce.

On the positive side, encouragement was given to improved agricultural techniques and agricultural productivity increased during the period. Programs of cattle breeding, afforestation, and sericulture were carried out under the auspices of the government as were also special agricultural studies. The use of marine products and rape-oil cakes as fertilizer came into general use at this time as well as a number of new crops, including sweet potatoes, Irish potatoes, tobacco, and pumpkins. Sweet potatoes, especially, came to be a valuable insurance against starvation among the peasants. The shogunate also encouraged the reclamation of new land for agricultural purposes by remitting or reducing taxes on such lands for a number of years.

As time went on taxes became heavier because of the growing expenses of the national and provincial governments, so that the position of the farmer did not improve despite technical improvements in agriculture. The government policy was more concerned with the condition of agriculture than with the plight of the agriculturalist.

There were also general economic trends adverse to the farmer. While a "natural economy" was basic to the farm villages, with the development of commerce in the urban centers the use of money eventually found its way into rural areas. The buying, selling, and mortgaging of land developed despite laws to the contrary and there was a tendency for poor farmers to become tenants or employed laborers. A number of severe famines in which hundreds of thousands died did not add to the farmer's happiness and simply increased the differences between rich and poor. The shogunate attempted to insure against famine by providing for the storage of grain against lean years.

Farmers themselves reacted to these conditions in a number of different ways. Since the ordinary farm family could afford to maintain only two or three children, infanticide and abortion became common. The shogunate legislated against infanticide and even offered partial grants in aid to prevent it, but without success. Evidently, the closed economy of the nation simply could not support a larger population. (In view of the Japanese love of children it is not to be assumed that the Tokugawa farmers were more hardhearted than others simply because they practiced infanticide. Similar economic distress leads to similar results among the Chinese farmers today and has led to it in Europe during periods of economic privation.)

Another reaction of the farmer to his plight was to desert the farm—sometimes individually, sometimes by families. Such wandering peasants went to the cities and castle towns to join the ranks of day laborers or servants and in a few cases to become themselves artisans and small merchants. Those unable to find work became gamblers or beggars or died by the roadside. Such migrations sometimes led to the neglect of cultivation and a decrease in tax revenue and hence threatened the security of the *daimyō*. Various laws were passed against farmers' migrating but these were never fully effective.

Finally, as the most extreme reaction, farmers openly revolted or rioted as a form of protest. Such riots tended to increase as time went on and the farmer's position became more acute. They may be divided into three general types: (1) The farmers, after making a petition concerning grievances to the *daimyō* through proper channels and such petitions being ignored, would band together and threaten the *samurai* with force and commit outrages on village officials and rich men. (2) A group of farmers might petition directly to a *daimyō,* ignoring channels; then, such a petition being intercepted and so not reaching the feudal lord, a riot would ensue. (3) Passive resistance in the form of wholesale desertion of villages, thus demonstrating the social solidarity of the aggrieved group.

Very often the riot and passive-resistance techniques of the farmers were successful in achieving the immediate ends they had in view though, as a matter of decorum, the *daimyō* usually punished severely or even executed the leaders of such revolts. Government the world over must provide some channels for grievances to move upward and adjustments to move downward if it is to avoid internal trouble. The system of censors and spies was in part a provision for this by the Tokugawa, but it was not always adequate as demonstrated by the occurrence of peasant revolts.

MERCHANTS RISE TO POWER

Manufacturing was for the most part in the handicraft stage, much of it in the form of part-time work carried on by farmers. Artisans usually made their products to order though there was some production in anticipation of orders: i.e., of ready-made products. This last form was most characteristic of urban artisans.

The various craftsmen were organized into guilds, e.g., of carpenters, stone masons, dyers, and weavers, similar to those of the European craft guilds. These guilds acquired monopoly rights in given trades and were protected in these rights by the government.

A commercial development of the period was that of the wholesale dealers or *tonya* who purchased the products manufactured by farmers and sold them in Osaka and other centers to middlemen or retailers. Frequently the wholesaler would make advance loans to certain farmer producers and so have prior rights to their products. In the spinning industry industrialists bought cocoons from farmers and had them reeled by specialists on commission, on early form of methods followed more recently in the silk industry.

The beginnings of a factory system also grew up whereby a capitalist employed a number of people and provided them with raw materials to be processed. Sometimes the workers carried out their labors in their own homes under the supervision of the capitalist and sometimes they worked together under one roof.

The increasing productivity of agriculture and manufacture led not only to developments in trade but also to the growth of cities and improvements in communication. All of this was, of course, interfief and intranational since foreign trade was strictly limited and travel abroad forbidden.

The roads between such commercial centers as Yedo, Osaka, Kyoto, and Nagasaki became well-traveled highways. These highways were in charge of special Road Magistrates, and relays of men and horses were maintained at regular intervals for the use of *daimyō* and others. These relay stations were also responsible for the transport of official letters and freight. Hotels and *geisha* houses sprang up along the way to cater to the travelers—a colorful and varied lot of people as depicted in Japanese art and literature of the period.

While land communication thus made progress, it was at the same time restricted by certain policies of the government. A system of barriers was established at key points where strict control of all travelers was maintained as an aid to police control and the maintenance of law and order. (This system has since been perfected to the point where today no one can travel in Japan without registering at every hotel at which he stops, such registration papers then going to the local police office.) For strategic purposes, bridge building was prohibited over important rivers intersecting main roads.

Water transport between the chief ports also made progress but it was legally restricted to coastwise navigation. Shipping guilds developed in such centers as Yedo and Osaka together with special rules in regard to such things as shipping rates and demurrage charges.

Cities grew in population during this period as a result of the growth of castle towns and large commercial centers. The large numbers of retainers and foot soldiers attached to the organization of daimyoates in castle towns such as Nagoya did much to create large concentrations of population.

Yedo, the capital, became the largest city not only in Japan but in the world with a population of well over one million. (London had less than a million during the same period.) Its great expansion was due to its being the political capital and to the regulation that *daimyō* (which meant, in practice, *daimyō* and numerous retainers) had to spend half their time in the capital. Most of the retainers of the *shōgun,* the *hatamoto,* and their retainers also lived in Yedo. Thousands of artisans and workers were needed to supply the needs of this large administrative group.

Kyoto was next to Yedo in population with more than half a million inhabitants. This old city, the imperial capital, was a religious and commercial center as well as headquarters for artistic handicrafts such as the making of brocades, cloisonné, and lacquer ware.

Osaka, older than Yedo, developed as a great trade and commercial center, attaining a population of half a million. It was in Osaka that rice and other products came from the various fiefs to be redistributed by middlemen throughout the nation.

Castle towns such as Nagoya, Sendai, Hiroshima, and Oka-yama became population centers with tens of thousands. Nagasaki, the only port open to foreign trade, had a population of about forty thousand.

The growth of cities and improved transport went hand in hand with the growth of commerce and the rise in power of the merchant class. The *daimyō*, obliged to lead expensive lives in Yedo, had to send their provincial products, the chief of which was rice, to central markets in Osaka and Yedo. City merchants and brokers controlled great rice warehouses and would buy rice from the *daimyō*, later reselling it at considerable profit. Such large quantities were handled that rice exchanges were opened and speculation in grain began—speculation which seriously affected the security of both *daimyō* and farmer.

Merchants grew in strength, prices of commodities in castle town and remote province were equalized and the unorganized *daimyō* were no match for the organized traders, no matter what legal restrictions were made by the feudal lords. With their growth in economic power, it was inevitable that the merchants should rise in social position, and it was not long before they attained a higher position than the farmer, being on occasion called into the presence of men of rank.

Together with the developments in production and trade, the need arose for money and credit. Gold, silver, copper, and brass coins were minted by the shogunate and paper money was issued by some of the *daimyō*. All of the gold, silver, and other coins of various mintings were used concurrently and there were constant fluctuations in their relative values. Credit was given by special financiers who lent money even to *daimyō*, by pawnbrokers, by moneylenders, and through mutual-aid associations (*mujin* or *kō*).

The big financiers of the period engaged in a form of business resembling banking in present-day Japan. Financiers held on deposit gold and silver coins of merchants, issuing bills of exchange which could pass from hand to hand in much the same way as convertible notes today. The money so deposited was lent to *daimyō* and ordinary merchants.

In Osaka, the financiers consisted of ten families who had charge of the government revenue and expenditure and were privileged to wear swords and were exempted from taxation. In Yedo, there was also a group of financial houses, the most powerful of which was the house of Mitsui. Eventually, the financiers of Kyoto, Osaka, and Yedo entered into business relationships with one another, formed regulations for market prices of gold and silver and for the drawing of bills of exchange. Thus a large-scale credit organization came into existence within the limits of the feudal social structure.

The primary source of government revenue was in taxes collected from people under the direct control of the shogunate— taxes consisting of 40 to 50 per cent of the total yield of agricultural land plus miscellaneous taxes on forests and commercial enterprises as well as compulsory labor on public works. There were special taxes on the people of Yedo and on the *hatamoto*. The government collected land rents in large cities, maintained a monopoly on minting and reminting coins, and received gifts from *daimyō* and forced loans from merchants in the name of benevolence. The shogunate kept exclusive control of most of the important ports, of large centers of commerce and industry, and of the mines.

Out of a total national income estimated at twenty-eight million *koku* at the beginning of the period, the shogunate owned eight million, adequate for the government expenses of the time. But government expenses gradually increased until by the end of a century of peace it became necessary to increase the government income by debasing the currency and increasing the number and amount of forced loans. The bulk of the government's income being fixed, the shogunate became gradually worse off financially as a result of the rising costs of government and the support of tens of thousands of *hatamoto, gokenin,* and other dependents.

The *daimyō* in turn depended on the agricultural resources of their domains, income from which was also more or less fixed. Life in the capital and in castle towns gradually became more expensive with increased standards of living during two centuries of peace. More than half a *daimyō's* expenses went to the upkeep of his Yedo establishment and most of the lords had to borrow money from the big city merchants. Such debts tended to drain off their profits from rice crops and so *daimyō* found themselves becoming deeply indebted to the merchants.

The *samurai* classes, in general, dependent on the shogunate and *daimyō* for their incomes, largely given in rice, also gradually declined in economic status. The poverty of the *samurai* was due to the fact that they were living a complex urban economic life on a fixed income based on the rice produced in rural communities. During the latter half of the period, many poorer *samurai* took to trade and manufacturing and many married their sons to daughters of wealthy traders or, conversely, adopted the sons of merchants desirous of acquiring *samurai* rank. Some were even reduced to selling their swords or entering into the company of swindlers and thugs.

TOWNSMEN HUMANIZE THE ARTS

As the merchants grew wealthy and the capital city grew in population, many frivolous developments occurred in art and literature in contrast to the Spartan beginnings of the Tokugawa regime and the enforced frugality of the provinces. This condition gave indigenous Japanese popular art forms a chance to develop in drama, in plastic arts, and in Japanese screens and color prints. One special center where the arts flourished was in the Yoshiwara, at that time a glamorous community centering around professional and talented courtesans. It was in this feminine environment that many of the famous color print artists and popular novelists did much of their work. (There is an interesting parallel here to the Heian period—794–1192—which was also characterized by a predominance of feminine society including such great writers as Murasaki Shikibu; the chief difference was that while artists of the mid-Tokugawa era were men, those of Heian were mostly women.)

The Yoshiwara at this time was not, as at present, simply a district of prostitution but a place where lived the courtesans, attendants, dancing and singing girls, and a varied collection of tradespeople catering to their needs. Not only did wealthy young townsmen (chōnin) visit the Fuyajō or Nightless City, as it was called, but also samurai in disguise and officers of the shōgun. Within the area, there developed an elaborate etiquette and social hierarchy. It was here that "social life" as Westerners understand the term was carried on since the family life of the period made no provision for the commingling of men and women to exchange either conversation and ideas or banter and gossip.

The shogunate, in an attempt to restrain these social trends in the city, issued special edicts to restrain the clothing, activities, and general mode of life of merchants as well as of farmers, but since the merchants had money and usable economic power while the farmers did not, the repressions affected chiefly the rural folk. The rising urban middle classes gave superficial obedience by, for instance, wearing clothing of dull exterior but with brilliant silk linings.

The reaction of the upper samurai classes to the luxurious life developing in Yedo and Osaka was to scorn such frivolities and follow their traditional pursuits such as Zen Buddhism and the maintenance of Bushidō, the Way of the Warrior. Much of this samurai way, being in a sense artificially maintained, tended to become stiff, formal, and meticulous as in the elaborate tea ceremony. While the merchant class was looked down upon socially by the warrior class as of low origin and taste, the wealthier merchants nevertheless also developed strict standards of their own in literature and art as well as in the field of social etiquette.

RELIGION SUPPORTS THE SOCIAL SYSTEM

In the previous era of civil wars Buddhist sects had not been above taking up arms for one faction or another. Because of this, Ieyasu split the great Buddhist sect called Shinshū into two branches, East and West Hongwanji, in order to break its political power. Buddhism in general, which had been the great religious force of earlier ages in Japan, fell into a state of suspended animation. There were no new developments. The old sects simply continued the old rituals; Buddhist priests served at funerals and memorial services, and recited sutras to cure the sick. From being the chief inspiration in Japanese art and scholarship, Buddhism became a routine set of beliefs and practices concerning death and burial. Its organization and teachings were calculated to maintain the *status quo* and as such Buddhism was encouraged by the government.

Confucianism, more as an intellectual than a religious influence, was important during this period. Much of the government was conducted along Confucian lines and there were numerous schools headed by Confucian scholars who, while often disagreeing violently as to detail, agreed on the fundamental concepts of a public and private ethic based on the duties of loyalty and service. Even the dramas and novels of the period showed Confucian influences. In general, the Japanese of this period, as today, have been concerned not so much with heaven and hell, with abstract good and evil, grace and sin, as with problems of behavior, and questions of man's duty to others and to the society of which he is a member.

A special code of morals and behavior for the *samurai* class developed early in the Tokugawa period, known today as *Bushidō* or the Way of the Warrior. The concepts involved in this code included the traditional and indeed necessary loyalty of warrior to his overlord in a feudal society, Confucian ideas of virtuous conduct in familial and social relations, and the virtues of mental and physical self-discipline as honored in Zen Buddhism. The ideals of *Bushidō,* while practiced by many of the better class of warrior, were by no means generally practiced any more than the ideals of English feudal chivalry were a matter of common practice in the days when knighthood was in flower.

During the long period of peace, much of the real basis for the concepts of *Bushidō* disappeared and *samurai* developed highly elaborate and artificial points of honor to be upheld in duels to the death somewhat in the eighteenth-century European manner. Confucian ethics upheld the revenge idea whereby one should avenge the death of one's brother or one's lord. *Samurai* and *rōnin* acting on these precepts in time of peace sometimes upset law and order so that the shogunate had to take strong measures to suppress *samurai* brawls and vendettas, as for instance in the sentence of honorable suicide passed on the famous forty-seven *rōnin* who took the law into their own hands to avenge the death of their lord.

It is quite possible that the gradual impoverishment of the warrior class because of economic developments together with the *samurai* tradition did much to develop and strengthen the Japanese cultural values of frugality, lack of ostentation, and self-discipline. Proud warriors were forced to maintain social standards of gentility on increasingly meagre incomes while less meticulous merchants and lower *samurai* took to moneylending and trade and so could afford to indulge in such worldly things as theaters and the society of courtesans.

SHINTO SCHOLARS BECOME SUBVERSIVE

During the middle ages Buddhism had come to be the predominant form of religion in Japan, and under the name of

Ryōbu Shinto in the ninth century the thesis was developed that the native Japanese deities were simply transmigrations of Buddhist divinities. Buddhism thus became virtually the national religion until Tokugawa times, when Confucian philosophy also became important. Confucian scholars, in their enthusiasm for their doctrines, often became intolerant of many old Japanese ideas and this led eventually to a reaction in favor of things and ideas Japanese.

The Tokugawa encouraged the maintenance of libraries and the researches of scholars, little realizing that in so doing they provided one of the weapons for their own destruction. Motoori (1730–1801) and his student Hirata (1776–1834) were among the anti-Confucianist scholars whose writings gave sanction to the later movement to restore the Emperor to temporal power. These men had but little use for Confucian philosophy, contending that it might be necessary for Chinese, who were naturally immoral, but that it had no applicability to the Japanese. Rather, Japanese should study ancient Japanese books such as the Kojiki and the Nihongi to learn of the origin of things and the essence of the Japanese way, the way of the gods. And, since in those ancient times government was always administered by the Emperor and his court, the contemporary rule of the shogunate was in direct conflict with the Japanese way.

THE ERA OF SECLUSION ENDS

A combination of three developments — economic, literary, and political — brought about the eventual downfall of the shogunate. The economic development was a gradual shift in the internal economy of the country whereby the merchant classes were gaining power at the expense of the *samurai* classes including the shogunate itself. In the literary field the researches of the Shinto scholars Motoori and Hirata showed the rule of the *shōgun* to be a usurpation of imperial power. The political development was the opening of the country as a result of expanding Occidental pressures, both European and American. The final capitulation of the *shōgun* to Perry and his warships lowered the prestige of the Tokugawa government in the eyes of the nation.

The first official attempt—an unsuccessful one—by the United States to open diplomatic and trade relations with Japan was in 1846 when Commodore Biddle anchored off Uraga for that purpose. The American government sent a ship on this mission because of the dual problem of American whalers and others shipwrecked off Japan, and of the Japanese fishermen swept by hurricanes to the Aleutians and the northwest coast of America. Usually any attempts to repatriate such castaways were repulsed. Another American motive for establishing relations with Japan was that the French, British, and Russians for commercial reasons were becoming actively interested in opening up the country, and New England traders did not wish to be beaten to a new commercial field by foreign merchants.

In 1847, Commodore Glynn anchored his brig, *Preble,* off Nagasaki and threatened to bombard the city if fifteen foreign seamen being held for shipment to Batavia were not handed over. The Japanese authorities bowed to this show of force.

The Dutch government sent official warning to Japan of American plans to force the opening of the country and recommended a peaceful opening rather than a resistance that might lead to war. The shogunate did not act on these advices immediately but it realized that agricultural Japan's position was indeed precarious in an industrial nineteenth-century world of aggressive colonial powers. Japan knew that the Dutch held the Indies and Formosa; the Spanish, the Philippines; the British, India; and that there were designs on the part of the powers to slice up China into "spheres of influence" for economic exploitation.

But the shogunate also had a home front to deal with, an antiforeign home front by no means generally familiar with these developments abroad, and with attitudes increasingly critical of the Tokugawa regime. At the same time, the court nobles were beginning to take an active interest in politics, and the possible overthrow of the Yedo government was being discussed in Kyoto. Soon after his coronation, the Emperor Kōmei (1846–67) formally instructed the *shōgun* that, in accordance with ancient tradition, all questions of foreign policy must be submitted to the court before the final decision.

So matters stood when, in 1853, Commodore Perry of the United States Navy appeared off Uraga Bay near Tokyo with four warships. In the face of this emergency, the shogunate went to the unusual length of calling a council of the *daimyō*. At this juncture the *shōgun* died and the government asked Perry to permit postponement of an answer to America's demand that trade relations be opened. Meanwhile President Fillmore's letter brought by Perry was circulated among the *daimyō* for their opinions. In general their opinions may be summarized thus:

The aim of the foreigners is to have access to Japan in order to reconnoiter it (such a design seems actually to have been planned by some of the Catholic missionaries of the sixteenth century and a recent case of Russian surveying had just occurred in the north); what has been done to India and China will be done to Japan if the Western powers get a chance; foreign trade would only impoverish the country, giving to Japan unnecessary luxuries and draining from her her precious metals; the proposal to open Japan to foreigners for trade would revoke the time-tested policy of exclusion begun by that able administrator, Ieyasu.

There were, however, a few men in favor of opening Japan, men who realized the nation's weakness against foreign ships. They recommended that Japan make some show of opening her ports to trade in order to appease the Western powers and thus gain time to equip the country with modern naval construction and weapons of war; that on the basis of past experience, care should be taken not to admit Christianity in the train of foreign trade; that strict economy should be exercised by all classes in order to provide funds for the building of a navy and the fortification of Japan's coasts.

Meanwhile the shogunate, the funds of which were running low and which was at the same time mortally afraid of a disgraceful defeat for Japan by Perry's ships on their return, issued a decree ordering the people to treat the foreigners gently in order to avoid arousing them to anger. "It is imperative that everyone should practice patience, refrain from anger, and carefully observe the conduct of the foreigners. Should they open hositilities, all must at once take up arms and fight strenuously for the country."

So when Perry returned in 1854, he was peacefully received and a treaty was signed providing, among other things, that American ships could anchor at the ports of Shimoda and Hakodate. Russia, Holland, and England soon obtained similar treaties.

An American, Townsend Harris, was the first man to negotiate an actual commercial treaty with Japan after much careful and patient negotiation on the part both of himself and of the shogunate. The *shogun's* government promised a treaty and lived up to its promise at the ultimate expense of its life. Most of the *daimyō* had expressed themselves as opposed to such a treaty and, with the firm refusal by the Emperor to sanction it, the shogunate faced a serious internal crisis. At the same time, aside from the desire to keep their word to Harris, the high Yedo officials realized, as the reactionary and isolated court group in Kyoto did not, that the alternative to persistent refusal to negotiate a treaty peacefully would be the national shame of having to sign one under direct threat of Western warships. So, despite the refusal of the Emperor to sanction the action and in the face of criticism by conservative *daimyō*, the government concluded the treaty.

Representatives of foreign nations now began to appear in Yedo under the protection of the *shōgun*, but in Kyoto conservative patriotic men plotted against the Tokugawa government under the slogan *"Sonnō jōi"* ("Revere the Emperor, expel the barbarian"). The economic decline of the farmer and warrior toward the latter part of the period was one cause of the bitterness of many *samurai* against the *shōgun* and the newly arrived foreigner. The latter, especially, was a convenient scapegoat so the new slogan, "Revere the Emperor and expel the barbarian," fell on fruitful soil.

One result of all this was the assassination of Ii Kamon no Kami, one of the farsighted statesmen who had advocated opening Japan for the nation's own good. This was but one of a number of such acts against Japan's more progressive leaders on the part of patriots who regarded these men as traitors to the national security.

Just as the demands that the government actually expel all the newly arrived foreigners were being pressed by the court there occurred the Namamugi incident. A group of British subjects met at Namamugi the procession of the Satsuma *daimyō* as he was returning home from Yedo. Not being familiar with the strict Japanese etiquette on such an occasion, the foreigners attempted to ride through the procession with the result that one Englishman was killed and two were injured. When the British government were refused their demand for the surrender of the *samurai* responsible, they sent a naval squadron to bombard the city of Kagoshima, capital of Satsuma. This bitter humiliation demonstrated to the Satsuma men the helplessness of their old weapons and methods of warfare and so put a sudden quietus on their propaganda for expelling the foreigner—though it by no means made them love him more.

Meanwhile court nobles in Kyoto had issued in the Emperor's name a number of anti-alien rescripts which they demanded that the shogunate carry out but which it was unable and unwilling to do. One such edict named May 11, 1863, as the day for foreigners to be expelled. The Chōshū (Yamaguchi) *daimyō* thereupon opened fire on (but did not damage) American,

French, and Dutch merchant ships passing through Shimonoseki Strait. In retaliation, a squadron of warships of the offended nations plus English vessels destroyed the Chōshū forts and later demanded an indemnity of three million dollars.

The Chōshū and Satsuma *daimyō* soon saw the dangers of conflicting governmental policies issuing from Kyoto and Yedo in the face of the current national emergency and joined forces in opposition to the *shōgun* and in the name of national unity. The Tosa *daimyō* of Shikoku addressed a memorial to the *shōgun* outlining the helplessness of the Yedo government and advocating that administration be turned over to the Emperor in order that the nation might put up a united front. Keiki, the new *shōgun* in office, actually agreed with the conclusions of this memorial and on October 14, 1867, handed in his resignation to the Emperor.

Because of attacks on the *shōgun's* character by the Satsuma and Chōshū *daimyō*, a number of his followers put up armed resistance to the surrender of Yedo; a rival candidate for the throne was set up and the *shōgun's* admiral went north to Hokkaidō, where he attempted unsuccessfully to set up a republic. Thus suddenly and ingloriously ended the Tokugawa regime which, for all its administrative genius, was unable to stem the tide of social change.

HERITAGE OF THE TOKUGAWA

Just as the nature of modern America cannot be understood without a knowledge of puritan New England, the slave economy of the South, the westward-moving frontier, and the general political ideal of individual freedom of conscience and action, so Japan cannot be understood without a knowledge of the feudal governmental system based on loyalty to overlord, on careful checks on the growth in power of Outside Lords, and on a general faith in Confucian principles of government and society which stress the interests of the social group rather than that of the individual. The two and a half centuries of peace and cultural consolidation under the Tokugawa regime produced the foundation on which modern Japanese social organization is based, and the roots of practically all modern Japanese cultural values and social attitudes can be traced back to the days of the *daimyō*.

The feudal lords are gone today but the old provincial allegiances have been transferred to the nation and in particular to the Emperor as the head and father of the great Japanese national family. Economically great changes have come about since Tokugawa times, but rice, the old staple, is still the central article of diet and of drink, and the honest farmer is sentimentally regarded as more virtuous than the money-grubbing merchant.

The ever-present agents of the shogunate in village, castle town, and the very precincts of the Imperial Palace have developed today into the extensive intelligence system of modern Japan whereby dossiers are compiled on every individual, high and low, and the government keeps careful tab on the development of various social groups within the nation which might grow strong enough to challenge the power of the Tokyo government.

Philosophical concepts of government had been inherited from the Tokugawa era where a man was punished because he was upsetting the relations between classes or trespassing against filial piety. The Tokugawa regulation of personal matters such as dress, housing, and occupation set a precedent in Japan for extreme government regulation of the individual for the good of the society.

The tendency to resort to group or rotated responsibility is still to be found in both local and national government together with overlapping functions making possible such developments as the dual foreign policy in regard to Manchuria in the 1930's.

The *samurai* virtues of Spartan living and mental discipline for its own sake are still very much alive and the government still struggles to instill such virtues in young urban moderns who, like the rich youth of the Yedo period, tend to engage in frivolous pastimes. Sentimental phonograph records are suppressed and university students are prohibited from visiting bars, while ardent patriots full of the old *samurai* spirit often take matters into their own hands in ways reminiscent of incidents from the Tokugawa period.

Attitudes toward foreigners, especially Occidentals, at first friendly in the sixteenth century, turned to suspicion on the discovery of supposed imperialist plottings and missionary preachings which condemned honorable ancestors to hell. This attitude of suspicion and dislike has never died, partly because the grounds of the suspicions—fear of economic exploitation and fear of theological or political concepts upsetting to Japanese social solidarity—have never disappeared.

The Tokugawa regime was essentially a feudal military dictatorship. The forcing open of the country by Western warships has done nothing to change the Japanese administrators' views as to the essential role of the military, and today the power behind the throne still rests with military men.

Chapter II

Modern Economic Base

THE MEIJI TRANSITION

IMMEDIATELY following the Tokugawa collapse there set in a period of rapid change and reorganization in which the nation transformed itself from an old feudal peasant economy to a modern industrial state with a centralized government. This transition period is known as the Meiji Era (1868–1912), from which term the then reigning Emperor's posthumous name was derived.

The traditional economic base of the Japanese nation had long been one of wet rice agriculture. Upon this foundation the Tokugawa feudal system could thrive, but when the economy became more complex the feudal structure crumbled. A fairly advanced money and credit system and the beginnings of industrial specialization had developed toward the end of the Tokugawa, but with the coming of Perry and the opening of the country to foreign trade the whole economy underwent drastic change. A more or less closed economy gave way to one dependent on foreign trade. Foreign cash balances accumulated as a result of the export of handicrafts and silk, and funds procured through credit were used for the purchase of foreign raw materials and machinery. The government subsidized new industries such as

45

spinning factories which in turn brought further income. A large proportion of government and private funds went into the construction of new industrial developments such as railroads, a telegraph system, and the strengthening of national defenses and the building of a modern army and navy.

The initial stages of this new development were carried out by the Meiji government with the aid of loans from the great financial houses, such as Mitsui, which had developed in Tokugawa times. In the early years of Meiji the government controlled almost all large-scale industrial enterprises somewhat after the precedent of the Tokugawa who owned or controlled all important mines and ports. However, as time went on, this early national control gave way to a form of private enterprise, large firms such as Mitsui and Mitsubishi being allowed to enter the banking business, shipbuilding, and other industries. The operation of the telegraph system and the railroads, however, remained as functions of the government. The old salt and tobacco monopolies of Tokugawa times have also remained in government hands.

In the course of the first fifty to seventy years after Perry's visit, Japan took over and adapted to her own purposes all the important developments of the industrial revolution so that by 1941 Japan was no longer basically an agricultural country but had become instead a nation dependent on manufacturing and trade. This drastic change in the course of two generations brought the country into repeated conflict with the nations around her as a result of her attempts to gain national security in a world of competing economies.

POPULATION CHANGES

Together with the economic changes following the Tokugawa period there came marked increases in population. At the end of the Tokugawa period Japan was largely an agricultural nation of thirty million or so, with a few big concentrations of population in cities such as Osaka, Kyoto, and Tokyo (Yedo). Each of these centers was characterized by trade, by cultivation of the arts, and by the presence of innumerable artisans to supply the material needs of the people. With the industrialization of Japan beginning in the Meiji period Japanese population doubled in a period of seventy years. (When England became industrialized her population doubled in a period of fifty years from 1801 to 1851.) Today Japan has a population of seventy-three million of which about 50 per cent is urban in nature. Many of these urban centers are industrial areas with mines and factories in contrast to the handicrafts of 1870. The rate of population increase rose steadily from 5 per cent in the decennial period of 1871–81 to 15 per cent in the decennial period of 1920–30. The greatest annual growth was in 1932, when the population increased by one million. There has been a slight decline in the rate since then and it appears that, quite aside from the factor of war deaths, the population of modern industrial Japan proper is in the process of stabilizing itself.

RECENT GROWTH OF JAPAN'S TEN LARGEST CITIES, 1935 AND 1940

City	Population		Per Cent Increase
	1935	1940	
(Total Population of Japan Proper)	69,254,148	73,114,308	5.6
Tokyo	5,895,882	6,778,804	15.0
Osaka	2,989,874	3,252,340	8.8
Nagoya	1,110,314	1,328,084	19.6
Kyoto	1,080,593	1,089,726	0.8
Yokohama	796,581	968,091	21.5
Kobe	912,179	967,234	6.0
Hiroshima	310,118	343,968	10.9
Fukuoka	305,793	323,217	5.7
Kawasaki	191,700	300,777	56.9
Kure	259,584	276,085	6.4

A notable fact about Japan's great increase in population since 1868 is that it has nearly all occurred in urban centers while the rural populations have remained relatively unchanged; as industrialization made possible larger urban populations, the increase in the rural areas migrated to the urban and industrial centers. An indication of the extent of more recent urban growth may

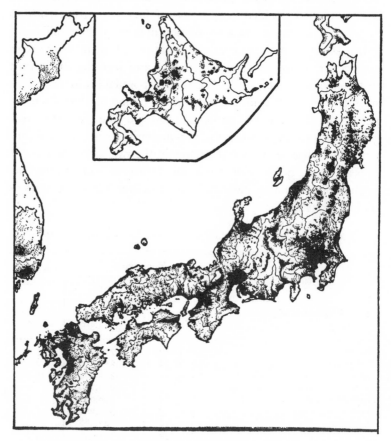

FIG. 3.—Population Density in Japan.

(Data for 1935 from Nihon Chiri-Fuzoka Taikai. 1 dot = 1000 persons.)

be seen from the figures for the population of Japan's ten largest cities.

According to the Japanese census of 1940 the total population of the Japanese Empire is 105,226,101 with 73,114,308 people living in Japan proper. The present distribution of this population can best be seen from looking at the population map (Figure 3). The heavy densities are in the plain areas such as Kwantō and certain industrial centers such as Fukuoka. As one goes north the population thins out. Lightly populated areas in Honshū, Shikoku, and Kyūshū are mountainous areas not suitable for agriculture.

Over 99 per cent of the inhabitants of Japan proper are of Japanese stock. There are over a million Koreans, many of whom have been brought in as cheap factory workers, and twenty to twenty-five thousand Chinese, mostly from Formosa and Manchuria. In 1940 there were about ten thousand other foreigners (including two thousand Americans) but many of these have since left. The 1940 population was almost evenly divided as to sex, with 36,566,010 males and 36,548,298 females.

With relatively few Japanese overseas—there are, for instance, more Koreans in Japan than Japanese in Korea—and the Japanese birth rate beginning to decline from a high of thirty per thousand, the Japanese argument of overpopulation is scarcely adequate as a reason for aggressive warfare. What *is* a real factor is that to support the larger population the industries of the nation must be furnished with raw materials and markets and that most newly industrialized nations in the past have spread out to acquire or control such raw materials and markets.

AGRICULTURE

In 1941 about half the population of Japan was engaged in agriculture and fishing. Japanese farmers are, for the most part, small operators holding scattered fields totaling two to three acres. About a third of these farmers are peasant proprietors, a quarter tenants, and the remainder farmers who own some land and rent the rest.

Only a small proportion of the land in Japan is suitable for agriculture. The total cultivated area is about fifteen million acres, but because much of the land is used twice and sometimes even three times a season, the yearly crop area is more like eighteen to twenty million acres. Cultivation is thus very intensive and requires much hard labor. The small plots of paddy land prevent the use of large agricultural machinery, so that most of the tools used in planting and harvesting are simple, age-old hand tools. Horses and oxen are used to some extent in heavy tilling.

The basic crop is paddy-field rice, which accounts for about 50 per cent of all cultivated farm land. Rice is a money crop with a high yield (up to eighty bushels) per acre and so forms the main source of income for the average farmer. Lesser crops, sometimes sown in rotation with rice, are wheat and barley. Another important secondary crop is mulberry, grown on upland fields. Until 1941 all the farmers who had any upland to spare planted it in mulberry to feed silkworms during summer months. The sale of cocoons during good years sometimes made the difference between sending a daughter to high school or keeping her at home. Since the beginning of the present war farmers have been encouraged by the government to plow under mulberry and plant food crops.

The intensive agriculture of the Japanese farmer requires equally intensive fertilization of the soil. All human waste is carefully saved as well as that of domestic farm animals. This is supplemented by the use of marine products and chemical fertilizers, the cost of which is an important item in the raising of paddy-field rice.

Some agricultural areas are specialized, such as the truck gardeners in suburban villages, the tea growers of Shizuoka, and tobacco growers in parts of Kagoshima.

Because of taxes and economic developments beyond their control, such as the fall in silk prices in the 1930's, most farmers are chronically in debt to the tune of seven or eight hundred *yen*. Land rents amount to as much as 50 per cent of the yield, about the same as the old feudal taxes. In some areas where there are large numbers of tenants there have arisen disputes between them and the landlords from time to time, but on the whole a rural landlord is often himself in debt as a result of special taxes on his lands and income. The real distinction in Japan is not so much between agricultural landlord and tenant as between farmer and urban merchant and financial interests. Because of this, and as a result of pressures for agricultural reform by the military, the government has been active in sponsoring agricultural cooperatives which serve to give the farmer a better bargaining position vis-à-vis big business.

Many items of consumption, such as tea, vegetables, and basketry, are home grown and prepared in rural Japan. In the burial of the dead or the building of a house a farmer may count on the assistance of his hamlet so that in many ways a farmer's family may live without laying out much cash. In peacetime, at any rate, farmers, even though they had relatively low incomes, had time for frequent banquets and festivals, and in their daily work could always knock off for a smoke and some gossip.

While the basic crop is paddy-field rice, there are considerable differences in farming according to differences in climate. In Hokkaidō, where the population is relatively sparse and dry farming is the rule, farmers are less dependent on traditional paddy field agriculture. Dairying and cattle breeding, occupations new to Japanese farmers, are to be found in this newly settled region. Even the house types are different, the homestead-like settlements being made up of Russian- or American-style log and frame houses.

In mountainous areas where the people make a living at forestry, charcoal making, and mushroom raising, they grow for home consumption millet, beans, and potatoes.

In general the standard of living of the farmer has improved considerably since Tokugawa times. Today a farmer can purchase chemical fertilizers instead of traveling miles to the hills to collect loam; he owns individually or on a group basis numerous small machines for threshing and hulling grain; practically every house is equipped with electric light in place of oil lamps. The bicycle and rural bus lines provide improved transportation, and in the social sphere farmers may and do indulge in things forbidden them under Tokugawa law such as silk *kimono* and family crests. Every child receives six years of schooling.

Because the general wants of a Japanese farmer are few compared with those of an American traveler (usually well-to-do) and because he lives in the traditional (and efficient) thatch-roofed dwelling rather than a frame house with wasteful flush toilets, there has been a tendency among Westerners to underrate the Japanese farmer's material progress and present economic position. While the war has undoubtedly altered many things and while farmers in certain depressed areas such as Tōhoku in the north have lived under miserable conditions, it is safe to say that the general position of the farmer was remarkably stable and secure when Japan embarked on her present war.

INDUSTRY

A lack of raw materials and industrial inexperience handicapped Japanese industry at the beginning of the Meiji period, and many European and American economists thought that it was not possible for Japan to compete with the cheap labor of China and India on the one hand and the efficient production of Western countries on the other. However, after an initial period of study and adaptation of Western techniques Japan began to launch out on her own and during the past few decades has made remarkable industrial progress. Although the shortage of raw materials has continued, Japan is today industrially far ahead of any other country in Asia.

The production units of Japanese industry, like those of Japanese agriculture, are small. Almost half the people in Japanese industry operate in work places with under five persons and two-thirds in work places with under fifty persons. Many of these small-scale industries are concerned with the making of articles necessary to the Japanese way of living—floor mats, sliding screens, lacquer trays—things which require a high standard of workmanship. Various common foods such as bean-curd (*tōfu*), soybean paste (*miso*), and noodles (*soba* and *udon*) are also prepared by small producers.

The distribution system for some of these goods manufactured in small establishments is often centralized in the hands of city merchants. A silk piece-goods merchant in Kyoto, the center of the trade, obtains most of his supplies from various small-scale producers, parcels them out to other establishments for further processing such as dyeing and embroidery, and then distributes the finished products to retailers in towns and cities throughout the land.

A variation of this principle is seen in the practice of the large-scale silk companies which provide farm families with eggs and expert advice and then purchase the silk cocoons spun by the silkworms hatched from the eggs. In this way the company insures good genetic stock, but takes no risks in the "processing," purchasing only such finished products as come up to standard.

The production of Western-style manufactured goods such as bicycles is often adapted to this same system. In Osaka hundreds of small workshops specialize in preparing some part—the frame, the hub, the rim. These small producers work on contract for a merchant who may supply materials and machinery. He then farms out once more the manufactured parts to other workers for enameling and plating, before finally assembling whole units in a central plant. Here again the central industrialist takes no risks on rejects. The economist Allen, in his *Japan: the Hungry Guest*, has compared this system to that of Great Britain fifty years ago, thus indicating that it may be a step in the industrial evolution of a nation rather than something distinctively Japanese. Changes since 1940 tend to verify this view. Incidentally, the silk and textile industries have been sharply reduced, and strict governmental control has changed some of the methods of distribution.

There is in Japan something of the personal closeness between master and servant in the home and employer and employee in the shops which existed in the England of Charles Dickens. Domestic employment is not lightly undertaken but, when a decision is reached, employment is on a yearly rather than a monthly or weekly basis and the employer assumes the role not only of master but also of protector. The servant on his part is expected to be loyal to his master and look out for his interests. There is also a notable social closeness in the relation of master and servant whereby advice may be exchanged and even joking comments indulged in when strangers are not present. In farm villages the manservant and the maidservant work together with the family in the field and share the family meal at home. Even in modern factories something of the traditional relationship remains, the employer often undertaking to house and look after the morals of his workers. The benefits of this paternal arrangement in modern industry are most likely to accrue to the employer, and it serves as an effective damper on the development of strong labor unions.

This system is also related to the existence of a plentiful labor supply and a narrow diffusion of capital. Before 1941 the small workshops were often family affairs and included more workers than necessary for the job on hand. It would not pay a man to risk capital in setting up a factory when he could obtain his supplies so cheaply from small independent suppliers.

On the whole, the small-scale industrial system produces finished consumer goods. The heavy industries and some trades dealing in semifinished goods are organized on a centralized factory system similar to that of modern England or the United States. Such industries as iron and steel, shipbuilding, rayon and cotton spinning are characterized by large factory units. The heavy industries have been assisted in their development by government subsidies or even government ownership as a part of the government program of building up national defense. The great cotton-spinning industry, on the other hand, has grown up independently.

Japanese industry is notable for the concentration of economic control in a few large business houses. Large-scale manufacturing, mining, finance, transport, and foreign trade are all dominated by a few great family corporations—the *zaibatsu*—each with an immense range of economic interests. Each of the four greatest *zaibatsu*—Mitsui, Iwasaki (Mitsubishi), Sumitomo, and Yasuda —owns a great bank, most of them own or control trust companies, insurance companies, and trading companies. A large share of the ocean-going ships and the companies that make them are Mitsui- and Mitsubishi-owned or -controlled. Most heavy industry is in the hands of the *zaibatsu*. The small scale of much of Japan's industry is of a technical nature—financially the small enterprises are often part of and dependent on a great organization.

Japan's large industrial plants are engaged in a wide range of production which originated with the growth of the industrial system; as shipbuilding was established, or as mining was being reorganized on a modern pattern, the companies had to produce the necessary machinery and parts for their own plants. Eventually they began to produce these items for the market. When a new industry, such as automobile manufacture, arose, it would naturally be taken over by the existing engineering plants and the concentration of capital in a few large firms would lead to the centralization of large plant ownership.

Other industries which have grown tremendously and which now operate on a large scale are the producers of rayon, cement, glass, paper, canned fish, flour, sugar, beer, and confections. Most of these are controlled by a few large firms. Oji Paper Company produces about four fifths of the foreign type of paper, the Asahi Glass, the Nippon Sheet Glass, and the Shoho Glass Company produce all of the sheet glass. The Meiji Company and the Morinaga control about one third of the candy output (this applies only to the foreign style of candy, canned milk, and chocolate; the Japanese type of candy and cookies are made in small shops of the old family type where the candy is sold as it is made). In some cases the modern mechanization of production has extended to typically Japanese products such as soybean sauce or Japanese socks (*tabi*) which are produced on a large scale.

An important development in Japanese industry is a concentration on light metals and chemicals. Because of Japanese military restrictions not too much is known of progress in this direction, but the development of the Zero plane which broke out of its shell of secrecy in 1941 is one reflection of it. Another is the intensive development of electric power facilities. Japan may well have once counted on her own skillful development and use of a light metals economy to bring a Western heavy metals economy to self-defeat.

Many of the great financial corporations gained strength in Meiji days when the government was in need of commercial, industrial, and financial assistance. The government, through subsidy and other privileges, enlisted the services of the important commercial houses to serve its ends. The abler and stronger houses absorbed smaller ones and great monopolies grew up. These houses have lent large sums to the government in time of war and supplied capital for the development of new territories or new enterprises favored by the government in the interests of national security.

Thus the interests of government and *zaibatsu* are interdependent. The business houses have often risked their fortunes in support of the government, especially in Meiji days when the future of the new regime was uncertain; at the same time they have made great profits through their government affiliations.

Since Japanese industrial development depended to a large degree on the work of farmers and since all national surpluses from foreign trade went into industrial development much of which involved profits to the *zaibatsu* in proportion to their gigantic capitalistic girth, many Japanese have come to resent them. Opponents of the *zaibatsu* were interested not so much in breaking monopoly per se as in distributing profits more evenly through greater government control and ownership. One of the objects of attack of reactionary national societies has been the *zaibatsu*. Army factions, contending for political power with the *zaibatsu* and interested in effective national mobilization policies have done little to discourage such attacks and have done much to help national socialistic measures favoring workers and especially farmers.

Japan achieved her industrial revolution several decades later than Europe and America, but today she stands in the lead so far as Asia is concerned. The mass production of manufactured articles, ready-made goods and fixed prices (in contrast to custom-made goods and individual prices set up as a result of separate bargaining for each purchase) have all become standard in urban Japan.

The fact that Japan had her industrial revolution later than the Western powers is steadily losing its significance in the economic development of the country. The preparation for the military program in the 30's required considerable industrial expansion and was accompanied by modernization of the economic production and distribution machinery. The antidepression monetary program in the 30's required considerable industrial expan-just prior to the real beginning of an anticyclical fiscal policy in the United States. An anti-inflationary program, which included both administrative and fiscal control, started in the late 1930's about simultaneously with that of Great Britain. The modern war economy generated economic changes second only to those created during the industrial revolution, and it is important to realize that Japan kept pace with the Western nations in the revamping of her economic policies during the 1930's and early 1940's.

While the industrial revolution brought an increase in the standard of living, the wartime industrialization brought about a decrease in this standard, with a consequent need for new distributional controls—i.e., price control and rationing. It may be attributed in part to this increasing necessity for economic controls that Japan had a total financial reform in 1940 which coordinated her national and local fiscal systems to a degree higher than that of the United States in pre-Pearl Harbor days.

Chapter III

Government Structure

AFTER the fall of the shogunate in 1867 the need arose for a reorganization of the governmental structure. The form of government that has eventually developed is a combination of the old Tokugawa structure and European forms adapted to this old structure, together with a special emphasis on the central position of the throne. There are a number of traditional Japanese concepts of government which underlie the whole structure, such as the idea that society is more important than the individual, the idea that the patriarchal family is the ideal basis for a governmental structure, and the old Confucian principle which equates ethics and politics. The general principles of rotating and group responsibility are also characteristic. This means that no one person is long the responsible head of a government. European forms of governmental structure which were borrowed during the Meiji Era have all been adapted to these basic Japanese principles of social order. This gives the new government a firm base in forms and concepts characteristic of an old, well-integrated social organization.

DEVELOPMENT OF THE CONSTITUTION

In form, the Japanese civil government is a constitutional monarchy. There is a constitution, a parliament, and a monarch.

This constitution, however, is a relatively new development, having been promulgated by the Emperor Meiji in 1889. Furthermore, the monarch has a much more important role in Japanese government than in the ordinary constitutional monarchy, and he exercises religious and military as well as civil authority. To be accurate one should describe the government in the terms of the eminent Japanese jurist Hozumi as a theocratic-patriarchal-constitutional monarchy.

The Japanese constitution is the final result of a long period of agitation from 1867 to 1889 among Japan's post-Tokugawa leaders for some new form of government. These men, clan leaders, court officials, and *samurai* who had risen to power during a period of social flux through intellectual ability plus indomitable will power, were by no means in agreement as to just what form of new government they desired. Some were for a liberal representative government, others for a strictly limited form of representation. There was general agreement that the new Japanese government should be one of imperial rule in conjunction with "public opinion widely collected." The dispute between the liberals and conservatives was largely as to the width of this public opinion to be recognized: Should it be only lords, *samurai*, and nobles in general, or should it include the masses of the people?

The extreme degree of division of opinion on various domestic and foreign issues in the 1870's is exemplified by the counter-revolutionary movement of Saigō Takamori, a conservative *samurai* leader, in 1877 which ended in the decisive defeat of his Satsuma *samurai* forces by a newly organized imperial army of conscripts. Later there was an attempt made on the life of Itagaki, one of the men pressing for a liberal form of representative government. A number of parties which agitated for more liberal action by the government were suppressed in 1884 and 1885, and the response of a newly organized Tokyo government to criticism of its policies was to make use of "Peace

Preservation" ordinances to expel from Tokyo 570 leaders of the opposition.

Special motivation for the organization of some form of representative government was given by the existence of a number of unequal treaties which the Western powers had imposed on Japan shortly after Perry's visit and which she wished to be rid of at the earliest possible moment. A governmental structure with some Western touches, in addition to the building up of an adequate army and navy, would hasten the day when these treaties could be changed. On the basis of studies at home and in Europe, influential opinion tended to favor the German form of constitutional monarchy as best suited to Japan's needs because of the controlling position given to the king.

In 1880 elective assemblies in prefectures, cities, and villages were established as a preliminary step in representative government. In 1885 a cabinet was formed made up of government department heads to replace a court council which had been formed immediately after the fall of the Tokugawa.

A number of leading statesmen, such as the liberal Ōkuma and the conservative Iwakura, drew up preliminary suggestions for a constitution, and Prince Ito, a disciple of Iwakura, was specifically authorized by the Emperor to draw up a draft of a constitution. In 1888 the Privy Council was created, largely in order to function as a deliberative body to discuss this proposed draft. Many of its members were conservatives who were determined that traditional Japanese concepts of governmental structure and the supreme position of the Emperor should receive proper emphasis. It is interesting to note that one of its more liberal members, Count Ōkuma, hardly attended the meetings. He is said to have refrained from attendance in order to avoid face-to-face controversy with Ito. Ito, on his part, is said to have promised to include in the constitution certain clauses favored by Ōkuma. Another member of the council held out for certain clauses based on ancient Chinese precedents.

Thus the Japanese constitution is, like most constitutions of the world, the result of extended planning and compromise. It was officially promulgated by the Emperor on February 11, 1889, on the coronation anniversary of Jimmu Tennō, the first "historical" ruler of Japan.

The text of the Japanese constitution is given as Appendix I. The preamble and Chapter I stress the supreme position of the Emperor. "The rights of sovereignty of the State we have inherited from our ancestors. . . . The Empire of Japan shall be reigned over and governed by a line of Emperors for ages eternal. . . . The Emperor is sacred and inviolable. . . . The Emperor has the supreme command of the Army and Navy. . . . The Emperor declares war, makes peace and concludes treaties. . . . The Emperor confers titles of nobility. . . ."

However, there is also provision for a parliament or Diet, and its prerogatives are outlined in the constitution. While the Emperor convokes, opens, closes and prorogues the Diet, any imperial ordinances issued by the Emperor during a time when the Diet is not in session are subject to approval by it when next in session. Furthermore, "no Imperial Ordinance shall in any way alter any of the existing laws." The preamble closes with the statement that "Our ministers of state, on Our behalf, shall be held responsible for the carrying out of the present Constitution, and Our present and future subjects shall forever assume the duty of allegiance to the present Constitution." This paragraph has proved a strong bulwark against pressures from the military in recent decades to eliminate such branches as the Diet from Japanese government.

The rights and duties of Japanese subjects are set forth in Chapter II of the constitution and include such rights as equal opportunity to hold public, civil, and military office, liberty of abode and changing of residence, of trial by judges according to law, secrecy of personal letters, right of private property, freedom of religious belief, of petition, and of speech. Most of these rights are modified by the clause "within the limits of the law" and the whole body of them is subject to change in time of war or national emergency. The duties of Japanese subjects include the payment of taxes, and service in the army or navy.

Then follow separate chapters giving constitutional sanction to and outlining the functions of the Imperial Diet, Ministers of State, the Privy Council, and the Judicature. The two final chapters are Finance and Supplementary Rules. The absence of anything resembling a bill of rights in response to popular agitation is in accordance with the long and careful planning of the constitution for promulgation by the Emperor as a gift to his people.

At the same time that the constitution was issued five other important laws and ordinances were promulgated by the Emperor: the Imperial House Law, regarding the succession to the throne, three special laws concerning the composition and procedures of the Diet, and a Law of Finance. Thus the constitution, while an important document and one which gives imperial legal sanction to the present form of government, is by no means the sole document to do so—nor is it the first. The provincial legislatures, the Cabinet, and the Privy Council were all in existence before the constitution itself was finally promulgated. Since 1889, however, the constitution has been recognized as the supreme law and as such it serves as a strong unifying force in the government. Since the constitution is a gift of the Emperor only he has the power to initiate an amendment to it, a power he has never exercised.

In addition to the constitution as basic law there are the Imperial House Law, imperial ordinances, statutes, and international treaties and agreements. The Imperial House Law is concerned with matters of the Imperial Family. The imperial ordinances make up a vast and important body of law supplementary to the constitution. They are issued in the name of the Emperor, approved by the Privy Council, and countersigned by a minister of state. Statutes are laws passed by the Diet, usually after being introduced to it by some minister of state. Treaties are ratified by the Emperor and cannot be altered by ordinances or statutes; they must not, however, conflict with either the constitution or the Imperial House Law.

THE ROLE OF THE EMPEROR

The Emperor (*Tennō Heika*) reigns over and governs the state as head of the great Japanese family. As the divinely descended governor of the nation he is a powerful symbol of national unity. This strong central position of the Emperor is a post-Tokugawa development and one consciously fostered by the statesmen of Japan as a means of transforming feudal loyalties into national loyalties. According to present-day Japanese interpretation the Emperor is the state.

Succession to the throne is in the male line, though before the constitution of 1889 there had been a number of reigning Empresses in Japanese history. In the event that the male heir is under age, a regency is established by the Imperial Family Council and the Privy Council which carry on in the name of the Emperor.

The prerogatives of the throne fall into five main categories: (1) Imperial Household Affairs, (2) General Affairs of State, (3) Supreme Command of the Army and Navy, (4) Ritualistic Affairs, and (5) Conferment of Honors.

In regard to Imperial Household Affairs, there is an Imperial House Law to govern the conduct of the internal affairs of the Imperial Family of which the Emperor is the head. Through its numerous landholdings, vast financial investments, and large annual income, the Imperial Family is today one of the richest in the nation—a condition vastly different from that of some centuries ago when Emperors lived on a pittance. The House Law also provides rules in regard to succession to the throne and the institution of a regency. The Emperor is assisted in his government of Imperial Household Affairs by the Imperial Family Council, the Privy Council, and the Lord Keeper of the Privy Seal. The Imperial Court is almost an autonomous unit within the Japanese state.

The Emperor is the central authority of the civil government. He may dissolve the Lower House of the Diet subject only to the limitation that it must be convened at least once a year. All laws passed by the Diet must be sanctioned by him, but this sanction has never been withheld. According to the constitution, the Emperor determines the organization of the various branches of administration and fixes the salaries of all civil and military officers.

There are, however, some important limitations on the executive powers of the Emperor. The organization of courts of law can be determined only by laws, and the Privy Council cannot be abolished or deprived of its constitutional powers. Furthermore, the Diet through its budgetary control can render a new organization inoperative by refusing to vote funds for its maintenance. In practice the Cabinet usually obtains prior unofficial consent to financial appropriations before setting up a new government function.

As commander in chief of the army and navy the Emperor serves as the supreme military leader of the nation. This supreme military command is exercised by the Emperor not through the Cabinet but directly through the general staffs of the army and navy who in turn are directly responsible to the Emperor. This independence of the supreme command from general affairs of state has been recognized ever since the establishment of the general staff in 1878. Thus His Majesty's government and His Majesty's high command are independent of each other. It is worth noting that this arrangement has no express sanction in the written constitution and that a new system of civilian control of military affairs could be instituted without amending the constitution.

The Emperor is head of the system of State Shinto and personally carries out rituals for the benefit of the nation. As with military affairs, so with ritualistic ones, the prerogatives of the Emperor are outside the domain of civil government.

The Emperor's prerogative of conferring honors is expressly recognized in the constitution and is exercised with the advice of the minister of the Imperial Household and the director of the Bureau of Decorations. This function of the Emperor is also outside the scope of ministerial responsibility.

Finally, the Emperor has supreme powers in regard to foreign affairs. The declaration of war, the making of peace, and the concluding of treaties are all done in the name of the Emperor.

The ritualistic and decoration-conferring functions of the Emperor were about the only ones that the court had in Tokugawa days, since his powers over foreign affairs meant little until the advent of Perry. Today the ceremonial functions of the Emperor are overshadowed by the role of the Emperor as chief of the military forces and head of the civil government.

THE EMPEROR'S ADVISERS

The Emperor, while the supreme head of the nation, does not in actuality initiate policy but acts only on the basis of advice from a number of important men in the government. Being "inviolable," the Emperor cannot be held responsible for any of his acts. (The responsibility for an imperial ordinance, for instance, falls upon the man who countersigns it.) The real policy makers of the nation thus become the advisers to the throne and any pressures or struggles for power between factions take place behind the scenes, final compromise agreements on policy being presented by a strong and unassailable Imperial government.

The Lord Keeper of the Privy Seal (*Naidaijin*), as an official of the Imperial Household, is a person whose influence can be very great. He holds the seals which must be affixed to state documents. As a court official he tends to be conservative and to favor policies likely to maintain national stability, and as a member of the Imperial Household he is independent of direct military and party pressures.

The Minister of the Imperial Household (*Kunaidaijin*) is another special adviser. He is responsible for matters concerning the Imperial Family. While called a minister he is not a member of the Cabinet, so is unaffected by Cabinet changes. Together with the Lord Keeper of the Privy Seal he provides a strong upper-class influence in advice to the Emperor. All appointments to see the Emperor must be made through one or another of these two Imperial Household officials. A third court official of importance is the Grand Chamberlain (*Jijūchō*).

The Genrō, or elder statesmen of Meiji's day, were important advisers of the Emperor, controlling the nomination of new prime ministers and exercising strong influence over government policy. With the death of Saionji, the last of the Genrō, this important extraconstitutional body has gone out of existence. The concept of elder statesmen still lives, however, and on important occasions the advice of respected statesmen is often sought.

The Privy Council (*Sūmitsu In*) gives advice to the Emperor upon request. It resembles the Council of Elders of the Tokugawa Shogunate except that the person it advises is today the Emperor rather than the *shōgun*. It consists of a president, a vice-president, and twenty-four councilors all appointed for life by the Emperor. Cabinet ministers are also members so long as they are in office. A privy councilor is appointed by the Emperor on the recommendation of the prime minister, but the prime minister makes such a recommendation only after consulting with other privy councilors so that no one becomes a permanent member who is not acceptable to the rest. Its members include important

civil and military officials and a few men chosen for their eru-
dition.

The Council is an organ of both the Imperial Household and
of the State. It deliberates with the Imperial Family Council on
such matters as succession and regency. It plays an important
role in civil government since it has authority to advise on draft
amendments to the constitution, draft laws, and ordinances, and
questions of interpretation of the constitution and of laws and
ordinances which may be submitted to it. When the Diet is not
in session the Privy Council may carry out certain of its functions
such as approving emergency imperial ordinances. It also must
be consulted on matters such as international treaties and the
declaration of martial law.

The Privy Council is an advisory body, final decisions lying
with the Diet in matters of laws and with the Emperor in matters
of ordinances and treaties, but it possesses a moral influence and
functions to restrain the government from hasty or ill-conceived
action.

The prime minister as head of the Cabinet is an important
adviser of the court in matters concerning domestic government.
He is one of the few imperial advisers, in peacetime at least, who
is in any way responsible to the nation at large. His backing—
nobility, big business, or military—gives some indication of the
dominant political group of the period. In military and naval
matters the chiefs of the general staffs and the war and navy
ministers act as imperial advisers.

In times of national emergency an Imperial Conference may
be called when all important advisers gather in the presence of
the Emperor. Full and final responsibility for the collective decisions arrived at in such a conference is assumed by each individual present. The Conference met just before the Manchurian Incident, just before the signing of the Tripartite Pact and just
before the recognition of the Wang Ching Wei regime in Occupied China.

Many of these imperial advisers are of the nobility. Immediately after the Restoration the men of Satsuma and Chōshū were leaders of the new government, but of recent years other men have come to the fore and no one province has a monopoly of influence. The big capitalists, despite their great economic power, have been less important as direct determiners of governmental policy than might be expected. This is undoubtedly due to old feudal tradition which placed the merchant below the farmer in social rank. The military—its leaders from old *samurai* families—have great traditional prestige and since the 1930's have been perhaps the most influential single force among the Emperor's advisers. Nevertheless all these groups—old nobility, financial, and military—must be considered in assessing government action, and even in wartime it is false simplicity to consider the military as being solely responsible for national policy.

THE CIVIL GOVERNMENT

The Emperor is the sanctioning fountainhead of control for all aspects of the national government. Under the Emperor there are three distinct forms of social control within the governmental structure—civil, military, and religious.

The civil government includes, on the national level, the Cabinet, the Diet, and a vast civil service. Administratively the country is subdivided into eight regions within each of which there are a number of prefectures.

The Cabinet (*Naikaku*)

The Cabinet consists of the heads of the various government departments and some members without portfolio. Army and navy ministers must be active generals and admirals and they have the privilege of direct access to the Emperor. A new Cabinet is formed on the request of the Emperor by a prime minister whom he designates.

The function of the Cabinet is to formulate the general policies of the government; it also serves as the channel through which the Emperor exercises his prerogative over civil affairs. The primary responsibility of the Cabinet is to the Emperor, and its advice, together with that of the Privy Council, is, as a rule, decisive.

All important matters of state must be submitted to the Cabinet for discussion and recommendation, as, for example, drafts of laws, treaties, and imperial ordinances concerning administrative organization. Cabinet meetings are secret and the discussions are for the purpose of coming to general agreement on the matter at hand. As a rule no formal vote on the subject under discussion is taken but the matter is left open until some compromise is reached. The Cabinet is expected to present an outward unanimity.

The prime minister as head of the Cabinet is responsible for maintaining its unity, advising the Emperor on affairs of state, and exercising general supervision over all branches of civil administration. While not directly responsible to the Diet, the prime minister usually accepts responsibility for government policy. In the event of a sharp difference of opinion among Cabinet members, or criticism by the Diet or the public at large, the prime minister may resign to make way for a new "government." If either the army or the navy disapproves the policies of a particular Cabinet, it may be wrecked by the resignation of the minister of war or navy.

Originally the prime minister was a government official having no particular connection with any political party; then, as parties gained in strength, it became necessary for the prime minister to work with the majority party as a means of gaining cooperation between Diet and Cabinet. Since the dissolution of political parties in 1940 and the organization of the single-party Imperial Rule Assistance Association, the position of the prime minister has become stronger since he is no longer dependent on party affiliations for the backing of his policies.

The Diet (*Gikai*)

The Diet consists of two houses, a House of Peers and a House of Representatives. The House of Peers is composed of six classes of members, as follows: (1) Princes of the Blood who by tradition take no active part in the discussions of the House; (2) princes and marquis; (3) counts, viscounts, and barons who are elected from among their respective ranks for seven-year terms; (4) men appointed by the Emperor as lifetime members because of meritorious service or great learning; these men are appointed on the recommendation of the Cabinet and may include prominent government officials, businessmen, or, until 1940, political party members; (5) four members of the Imperial Academy elected by the Academy for seven-year terms; (6) wealthy men elected for seven-year terms by and from the highest national taxpayers. All these persons except Imperial Princes, who become members on coming of age at eighteen, must be over thirty years of age. Out of a total of almost four hundred members, about half are of the nobility, and a fourth are imperial appointees. They exert, as might be expected, a strongly conservative influence on legislation.

The House of Representatives is composed of some four hundred and fifty men elected by the people (i.e., men over twenty-five years of age) for a term of four years. It may be dissolved at any time by the Emperor, whereas the House of Peers cannot; otherwise the legislative powers of the two are about equal.

Two primary functions of the Diet are to pass laws and serve as a sounding board for public opinion. Its powers in both respects are limited. The Diet has no power over dynastic affairs, it cannot initiate a constitutional amendment, nor may it convene of its own accord. Matters of foreign affairs, being part of the Emperor's prerogatives, are outside its domain. The budget is prepared by the Cabinet for Diet approval but its amending power is restricted to reducing or rejecting estimates—it cannot increase a budget or insert new items; if Diet approval is not forthcoming, the budget of the previous year automatically goes into effect.

The passing of general laws pertaining to the internal affairs of the nation are within the province of the Diet but most bills are introduced by Cabinet ministers in whose selection the Diet has no choice. Statutes require a majority vote in each house. The Diet also has the power to approve or not approve imperial ordinances which are themselves a form of law. An amendment to the constitution would also require the consent of the Diet.

While the Diet has few direct controls, budgetary or otherwise, over the policies developed by the Cabinet, it does have certain indirect means of exerting pressure. It may address the throne or make representations to government departments, though neither of these powers is very important and neither the Emperor nor any department head is under obligation to respond to representations of the Diet. One important means of expressing disapproval of some policy of the Cabinet is through interpolations and questions from the floor which require some sort of answer from the Cabinet minister concerned. While ministers may refuse to answer on grounds of military security or may give vague replies, critical interpolations can embarrass the Cabinet and serve as an important check on its actions.

The Diet may also pass resolutions which serve to express its opinion. Before the war a resolution of no confidence in the government meant the dissolution of the House of Representatives followed by a general election or a resignation of the Cabinet or the ministers thus criticized.

As a means of forestalling criticism on really important matters the Cabinet may come to its decisions without consulting the Diet. No special session was called when the Peace Preservation Law was amended to provide the death penalty, nor on such matters as concluding the London Naval Treaty or undertaking the invasion of Manchuria.

Political Parties

Political parties developed early in the Meiji Era over such issues as the nature of parliamentary government and when it should be introduced in Japan. The parties took various names and suffered various vicissitudes until the 1930's, when two major parties, the *Minseitō* and the *Seiyūkai,* controlled most affairs concerning elections. Political parties came to wield sufficient power to make it necessary for Cabinets to include party members; and at the height of their power even prime ministers were party leaders.

The two major parties tended to be pretty much financed and controlled by big business interests and were subject to considerable corruption. One of the weaknesses of the political party system and of the House of Representatives was the shyster character of many of the politicians—some of them having no political principles, being in politics simply for what they could get out of it for their financial backers and from the spoils of office. This made the parties an easy target for army criticism. An exception was the Social Mass party (*Shakai-Taishūtō*), members of which were strong in their allegiance to principles. This party was gaining in power before the war, but it ran into opposition not only from the older parties but from the army as well. All political parties were disbanded in 1940 to make way for the Imperial Rule Assistance Association in which the army plays an important role. Most of the older party members joined the new organization and a committee was formed to advise the Diet.

Civil Service

The actual work of carrying out the administrative functions of government is done by a vast body of civil servants who man the various departments, the heads of which compose the Cabinet. These departments are as follows:

Department of War and Department of Navy, whose functions

are military and whose ministers have direct access to the Emperor.

Department of Home Affairs, an important department including among its functions local government, shrine affairs, the police organization, and public works. The control of press and radio are also within its jurisdiction. Prefectural governors are appointed by the Minister of Home Affairs. Since the war the Department of Home Affairs has become responsible for civilian defense.

Other regular departments are: Foreign Affairs, Welfare (Public Health, Social Welfare, Labor), Transportation and Communications (Telegraph and Telephone, Postal Service, Railroads, Merchant Marine), Agriculture and Commerce, Education, Justice, and Finance (which includes both tax collecting and budgetary functions).

Two new departments which have come into existence since the conquest of Malaysia are the Department of Greater East Asia, concerned with overseas administration in areas acquired since 1941, and the Department of Munitions, concerned with coordinating the economic and industrial resources of the nation. The Department of Greater East Asia is an especially important innovation since it overshadows the once-powerful Foreign Office in matters concerning the Asiatic area. It has four bureaus: General Affairs, Manchurian Affairs, China Affairs, and Southern Affairs.

In addition to the department and coordinating agencies there are also a number of special bureaus responsible to the Cabinet. These include an Information Bureau, a Statistics Bureau, a Pension Bureau, and a Decorations Bureau.

This vast bureaucracy has a definite *esprit de corps* of its own and its upper brackets are definitely identified with the upper classes. The service draws to it many of the best brains of the country, an official career being regarded as one of the highest to which a young man may aspire. Since able young men are ad-

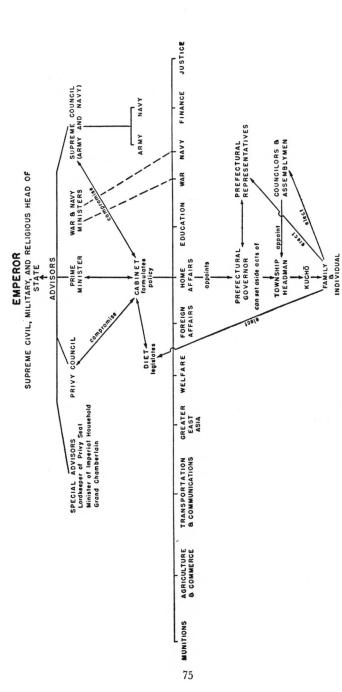

FIG. 4.—Outline of Japanese Government.

75

mitted to the service by means of graduation from a university and passing of civil service examinations without regard to wealth or rank, the general level of governmental personnel is high. Most of the classified ranks are filled by college graduates and many of the more liberal men of the country are in the civil service. A characteristic skepticism about governmental forms and official pronouncements exists among them as with civil servants in any large governmental organization.

It is possible to rise in the hierarchy to vice-ministerial positions and frequently able men who reach the top ranks are then appointed to the House of Peers, the Privy Council, or some other high office. The civil service provides a path for men from middle-class and merchant backgrounds to rise in the governmental—and also the social—system. Civil service jobs in Tokyo and in the foreign service are much sought after because of the high prestige attached to them. The broad educational and urban middle-class background of much of the bureaucracy makes it a stabilizing force in government and at the same time accounts in part for the secular, pragmatic outlook on life of many civil servants.

There is a hierarchy of four major classes in the service. The highest rank of civil service, *shinnin,* includes the premier, Cabinet ministers, privy councilors, governors general of Korea and Formosa, ambassadors, and high judicial officers. They receive their appointments directly from the Emperor. The second grade, *chokunin,* includes vice-ministers, judges and procurators, directors of bureaus, prefectural governors, and some others. Their appointments bear the privy seal. In the third rank, *sōnin,* are to be found secretaries of bureaus and chiefs of sections. Their appointments also bear the privy seal. *Chokunin* and *sōnin* are collectively called "higher officials" (*kōtōkan*). The fourth grade, or *hannin,* are men appointed by superior officers in the civil service and includes all the lower ranking government officials.

There is a special examination committee concerned with civil service examinations and scrutiny of the general qualifications of applicants. Promotions depend largely on seniority and the recommendation of superiors. There is no very secure legal tenure of office for civil servants, but as a rule individuals are dismissed only for cause or because of retrenchment in some bureau. Aliens are not eligible to any of the four classified grades of the service.

Civil servants may be transferred from one post to another every few years—partly by way of giving broad experience, partly by way of promotion or demotion, and partly as a means of keeping their loyalties to the central government unsullied by local affiliation. This last consideration is especially important in regard to the police.

Administrative Units

Until 1943 Japan was divided administratively into forty-four prefectures (*ken*) and three urban areas (Tokyo, Osaka, and Kyoto) called *fu*. The prefectures are mostly made up of combinations of old feudal fiefs (*han*), the Meiji government having initiated an amalgamation of administrative units which is still going on. Formerly the prefectures were divided into counties or *gun*, but in 1926 these were abolished so that the next administrative unit below the *ken* is the city, town, or village. In 1943 the various prefectures were organized into nine administrative and economic regions, later (1945) reduced to eight. This regional development since the war is more than simply a war measure; it fits in with the post-Tokuwaga trend of centralized administrative and economic units which have gone hand in hand with developments in transportation, communication, and industrialization in general.

Changes in the number or boundaries of prefectures may be made by the Diet, of cities by the Home Minister, and of towns and villages by prefectural governors with the approval of the Home Minister. The Department of Home Affairs exercises general supervision over local government—regional, prefectural, municipal, and rural.

Each prefecture has its own prefectural assembly made up of at least thirty members elected by popular vote (males over twenty-five) for a four-year term of office. Members do not receive salaries. This assembly is called once each fall for a month by the prefectural governor who is appointed by the prime minister on the recommendation of the Minister of Home Affairs in Tokyo. The assembly may deliberate and vote upon legislation introduced by the governor in regard to prefectural laws, taxes, and the budget and, like the Diet, serves the function of bringing up for criticism various points of administrative policy.

A standing committee or council of ten members is elected by the assembly which meets on the call of the governor and which often acts in its stead. Its members are one half from urban and one half from rural constituencies. The governor serves as chairman of this council. On the whole, the assembly has even fewer legislative powers than the Diet. It can be dissolved at any time by imperial sanction and it exercises no direct control over the governor or his staff.

The chief departments of prefectural administration are General Affairs, Public Works, and Police, with often a fourth department, Engineering. Prefectural officials are members of the national civil service and department heads are appointed by the Home Minister sometimes without even consulting the governor. Lower officials are appointed by the governor.

As in Tokugawa days, the national government maintains close supervision over the provinces. Once a year there is a meeting in Tokyo of all the prefectural governors called by the Home Minister to discuss administrative problems and to acquaint them with new developments in national policy. The prefectural heads of police are also generally called to annual conferences.

The organization of prefectures into eight economic blocs in 1943–45 was instituted in connection with a move to decentralize industry and population on the one hand and to centralize economic administration on the other. Each of the blocs has an administrative head who is usually the governor of one of the constituent prefectures. These eight blocs or administrative regions

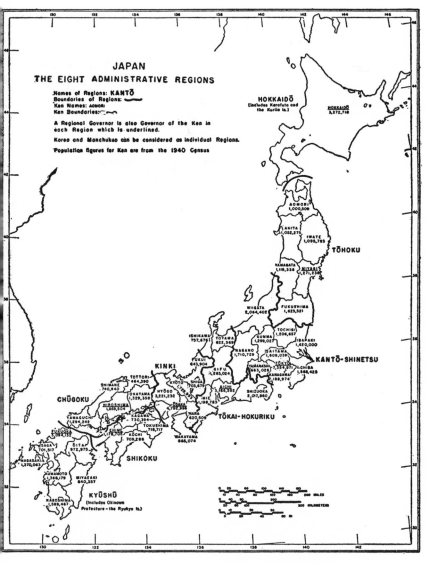

JAPAN
THE EIGHT ADMINISTRATIVE REGIONS

Names of Regions: KANTŌ
Boundaries of Regions:
Ken Names: AOMORI
Ken Boundaries:

A Regional Governor is also Governor of the Ken in each Region which is underlined.

Korea and Manchukuo can be considered as individual Regions.

Population figures for Ken are from the 1940 Census

HOKKAIDŌ
(includes Karafuto and the Kurile Is.)

HOKKAIDŌ
3,272,718

AOMORI
1,000,509

AKITA
1,052,275

IWATE
1,095,793

TŌHOKU

YAMAGATA
1,119,338

MIYAGI
1,271,238

NIIGATA
2,064,402

FUKUSHIMA
1,625,521

ISHIKAWA
757,676

TOYAMA
822,569

GUMMA
1,299,027

TOCHIGI
1,206,657

IBARAKI
1,620,000

NAGANO
1,710,729

SAITAMA
1,608,039

FUKUI
643,904

GIFU
1,265,024

YAMANASHI
663,026

TŌKYŌ
7,334,971

CHIBA
1,588,425

KANTŌ-SHINETSU

KINKI

SHIZUOKA
2,017,860

KANAGAWA
2,188,974

TOTTORI
484,390

KYŌTO
1,729,679

SHIGA
703,679

AICHI
3,166,592

SHIMANE
740,940

OKAYAMA
1,329,358

HYŌGO
3,221,232

MIE
1,198,783

OSAKA
4,792,966

NARA
620,509

TŌKAI-HOKURIKU

CHŪGOKU

HIROSHIMA
1,869,504

KAGAWA
730,394

TOKUSHIMA
718,717

YAMAGUCHI
1,294,242

EHIME
1,178,705

KŌCHI
709,286

WAKAYAMA
865,074

FUKUOKA
701,517

ŌITA
972,975

SHIKOKU

SAGA
701,517

NAGASAKI
1,370,063

KUMAMOTO
1,368,179

MIYAZAKI
840,357

KAGOSHIMA
1,589,467

KYŪSHŪ
(Includes Okinawa Prefecture—the Ryukyu Is.)

FIG. 5.—The Eight Administrative Regions.

79

are Kwantō-Shinetsu, Kinki, Chūgoku, Tōkai-Hokuriku, Shikoku, Tōhoku, Hokkaidō (including Karafuto), and Kyūshū. (See map, Figure 5.) The regional heads meet from time to time with national government officials, such meetings probably replacing in importance the older annual meetings of prefectural governors in Tokyo.

Cities (*shi*) are urban communities of at least thirty thousand inhabitants, and have their own municipal government. As of 1942 Japan had 95 such cities. The six "premier" cities of Japan—Tokyo, Osaka, Nagoya, Kyoto, Kobe, and Yokohama— enjoy somewhat broader powers of municipal government than do smaller ones. In 1944 the city and *fu* of Tokyo was reorganized into a new and special administrative region of its own called *To*.

Cities have mayors elected for four-year terms by a city assembly which is composed of at least thirty elected members. By a wartime law the prefectural governor nominates the mayor—but in actual practice he is probably still chosen by the council, the governor having veto power by not nominating the council's choice if he disapproves of its man. The deputies of the mayor and the treasurer are also elected to four-year terms by the assembly while lesser municipal officials are appointed. There is no merit system or civil service organization for city or town governments corresponding to the national civil service. City assemblymen sit for four-year terms and their number varies from thirty up, depending on the size of the city. Meetings are opened and closed by the mayor and much of the business is done through committees. There is also a council composed of ten or fifteen assemblymen elected by the assembly who meet with the mayor and direct policy making.

Municipalities may own and control gas, electric, and power plants, and sewer systems. They manage their own public health programs and administer their own primary schools. They may make municipal regulations, contract loans, and levy taxes. All these functions are carried on under the general supervision of the prefectural and national governments. No municipality has control of its own police.

The city is divided for administrative purposes into wards or *ku*. In the larger cities there is a local *ku* administrative structure, but in most cities *ku* officials serve to carry out administrative functions for the city office such as collecting taxes.

The Minister of Home Affairs may dissolve the city assembly and the prefectural governor can disallow any action of the city government and appoint a temporary mayor. Despite these handicaps, municipal government with its relatively strong popularly elected assembly is more of a self-governing unit than is the prefecture.

Japanese city government is in some ways similar to the recently developed city-manager system in the United States—a body of voters elects an assembly or council, the council appoints a mayor or manager with administrative training and experience (not necessarily an old resident of the city) and he in turn appoints and supervises departmental heads concerned with the operations aspects of city management.

Two features in the Japanese system which differ sharply from American practice (but not from that of older European countries) are the police and the schools, both of which are part of national organizations with basic policy set in Tokyo. The expenses of local police work and school operations are borne for the most part by local taxes and there is close coordination between the work of local organizations and the city office. While centralized control of these two important aspects of community management detracts from local autonomy it does provide minimum standards of operation in contrast to a purely localized system where it would be possible for the children of one city or region to be well educated and those of another to be almost illiterate, and where it would be possible for criminals to play one administrative district off against another thus escaping capture and conviction.

The Township Organization

All Japan is divided into administrative areas: metropolitan regions or cities (*shi*), small towns (*machi*), and villages (*mura*). The small country towns and villages include within their boundaries a number of local groups or hamlets separated by varying areas of paddy rice land and upland or forest areas. There are no unincorporated communities.

DIAGRAM OF ADMINISTRATIVE UNITS

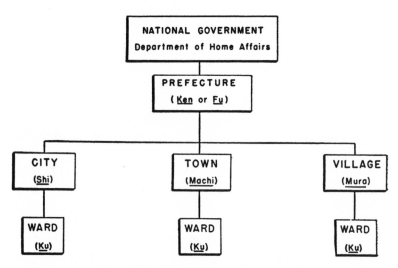

FIG. 6.—Diagram of Administrative Units.

A characteristic spatial arrangement is for one or two commercial centers of a few thousand people to be surrounded by a number of villages which supply the town with food and charcoal and take from it manufactured goods which in turn come to the town from some manufacturing center. The typical country town has a main street lined with all manner of shops, a few inns, and a number of *geisha* houses whose girls may come from neighboring village hamlets. All this is in contrast to the ordinary rural hamlet consisting largely or wholly of farmhouses. Each town has a telegraph and post office, usually a railroad station, a bus sta-

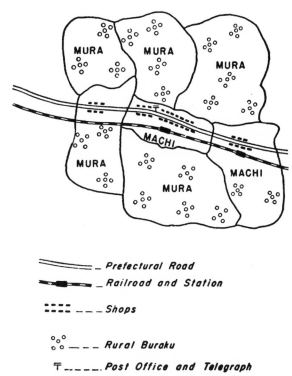

══════ ⸗ *Prefectural Road*

━━━ ⸗ *Railroad and Station*

∷∷ ⸗ ⸗ ⸗ *Shops*

°₀° ⸗ ⸗ ⸗ *Rural Buraku*

〒 ⸗ ⸗ ⸗ ⸗ *Post Office and Telegraph*

FIG. 7.—Diagrammatic Arrangement of *Mura* and *Machi*.

tion, and one or more higher schools such as a girls' high school or an agricultural college. The town thus forms the trade, communications, transport, and educational center of its rural districts as well as a center for district fairs and festivals.

The degree of urbanization of town or village does not appear in its gross population statistics because of the fact that a township includes as a rule a number of scattered hamlets. A community of several thousand may be simply a collection of rural communities under one village administration or it may include a typical urban center and possess the urban characteristics of a *machi*. A *machi*, which by law must have a population of at least five thousand, may include within its boundaries a number of scattered rural hamlets. There are in all about seventeen hundred *machi* in Japan.

Formerly there were about seventy thousand *mura* or villages in Japan but today there are less than ten thousand, largely as a result of the amalgamation of two or more small rural *mura* into single administrative units. This is in line with the general centralizing tendency which amalgamated the old provinces into a smaller number of prefectures and later dispensed with the *gun* or county as a separate administrative unit. When two *mura* have been joined into one, the old constituent *mura* are termed *ōaza*.

Each *mura* or *ōaza* consists of a number of hamlets (*buraku*) or communities of fifteen or so houses, each with its own name, a series of numbered administrative wards (*ku*) which consist of one or more hamlets, and a large number of named geographical subdivisions (*aza*).

Township Government

The central administration of the *mura* is carried on in the township office. Here work the headman and various local officials, and here are held the meetings of the village councilors. All local records are kept in a special fireproof structure in or near the village office. Any visiting official or anyone intending to do business first pays his respects at the village office and visits with the headman.

The head of the township receives his office in the same manner as the city mayor. As a rule he comes from one of the old landowning farm families of the *mura* and commands the respect of the villagers. On his part he takes his duties seriously and identifies his interests with those of the *mura,* and he serves as the representative of the village in relation to the prefectural and national governments. He is responsible for the general well-being of his community and is not above trying to settle disputes between man and wife, or giving a stern paternal lecture to some rambunctious young man in the interests of village peace and harmony. The headman receives for his services an income of a few hundred *yen,* more an honorarium than a salary, so that in order to serve a man must have a fair income of his own, usually from a farm looked after by his wife, children, and servants.

There is also an assistant headman who serves in place of the headman when he is away from the village and who is often the head of some other village organization such as the agricultural association. The assistant headman is also elected by the village councilors and his salary is even less than that of the headman so that he must also depend on a private income, usually from farming.

The village councilors are usually of old respected landowning families and are elected by men twenty and over for periods of four years without salary. In addition to electing the headman and assistant headman, the councilors have a voice in all important matters of village government such as the budget. The headman would not think of acting without consulting them. The nature of village government thus follows the general pattern of government by group agreement.

The village office is staffed by a number of men appointed by the headman and concerned with the administration of local affairs. Their functions include finance and taxes, sanitation and public health, education, property records, and family records. In addition to these local officials there are two officials appointed by prefectural branches of the national government: the policemen and the agricultural adviser. The prewar white-collar salaries of these officials were from forty to fifty *yen* a month. In each *ku*, or ward, there is a local man designated by the village headman as *kuchō*, i.e., head of the *ku* with an honorarium of eight or nine *yen* a year.

The treasury of the village office is concerned with the income and outgo of village funds. It does not determine local financial or tax policy, however, since this is a matter for the village council and the headman to determine in consultation.

The functions of the Sanitation and Public Health Bureau include supervision of the annual smallpox vaccination of children aged one and ten, semiannual housecleaning, and preconscription physical examinations. There is a public health doctor appointed on a part-time basis to carry out such public health measures.

Education is largely in the hands of the local schoolmaster and prefectural branch of the Department of Education, but the village office is responsible for support of the local school. School affairs so far as the village office is concerned may be simply a matter of finance and close liaison between the headman, the schoolmaster, and a local school committee.

Property records are important since the legality of all real-estate transactions depends on the records in the village office. The property records also serve as a basis for taxation.

Family records or *koseki* are among the most important documents in the administrative office. The *koseki* is a legal family record kept in one's native town or village and on it are entered such important events as births, adoptions, marriages, divorces, and deaths in the family, as well as any offenses against the law for which one is arrested. If the crime is committed in another part of Japan the police forward a record to the culprit's home village for entering in the *koseki*. (Often worse than the punishment itself is the fact that one's misdeed becomes a stain on the family record.) Important family events such as marriages and adoptions are entered by the persons concerned who affix their seals to the record in the presence of the records clerk. A child becomes legitimate only upon being recorded in the family's *koseki*, and even a child born out of wedlock may be legitimatized through being entered into the *koseki* as a child of the mother's father or uncle.

The *koseki* is thus an important legal document, but it does not tell everything. Marriages or adoptions which are dissolved before the contracting parties put an entry in the record do not, of course, appear in the *koseki*. This final legal step in marriage or adoption may follow by months or even years the actual event so that if the relationship proves unsuccessful to begin with it goes unrecorded. The later family events of sons or daughters adopted or married out of a family do not appear in that family's *koseki* since their names are blotted out and entered into that of the family into which they are married or adopted. It is not possible to learn the total population of a village or town through its *koseki* since a man may live in a new place for ten or twenty years before finally deciding to have his *koseki* transferred; until this is done he is still technically a resident of the village where his *koseki* is kept. This situation is partly remedied by means of a temporary record for new arrivals in a community.

The agricultural adviser, somewhat like the agricultural extension agent in the United States, is an appointee of the prefectural government in conjunction with the local township and the national Department of Agriculture. His function is to assist farmers in improving agricultural techniques and production. Together with local officials he also encourages the formation of government-sponsored agricultural cooperatives for the benefit of farmers in selling agricultural products, purchasing farm implements, and obtaining credit.

In contrast to the members of the village office staff already mentioned, the agricultural adviser is not a native of the village and so has a special problem in diplomacy: trying to introduce new methods and improve old ones in such a way that the local inhabitants will accept them. He must also be able to get along with the local headman for, while he is appointed by the Department of Agriculture, his appointment is subject to the approval of the local village government.

The policeman is also an outsider, appointed by the prefectural police department. His duties are to take care of minor offenses, make regular reports to his superiors on local conditions, e.g., deaths, disturbances of the peace, public lectures. Since the carrying out of public health measures is also within his jurisdiction, he accompanies the sanitation official on his housecleaning inspections. He also functions to maintain law and order and to aid in administering relief in the event of fire, flood, or earthquake. Under normal conditions rural policemen do not have much to do, since villagers take care of their own problems of law and order, leaving the policeman to be largely a records keeper.

There is also in the village one other group of non-local officials, the schoolteachers appointed through the prefectural bureau of education.

The cost of rural administration is relatively low since none of the elective officials receive a living wage and the salary of the average clerk is modest. In Suye Mura, a rural village of 1,663 people in Kumamoto prefecture, a village budget of 17,071 *yen* in 1933 was as follows:

Expenses

Village office expenses	Y 4,747
Village school expenses (including salaries, young people's school, etc.)	8,574
Contributions to village women's and reservists' associations	495
Land improvement, afforestration, etc.	1,105
Lectures to improve agriculture, making home products, etc.	182
Payment of village debts and taxes on village-owned property, etc.	744
Sanitation and health	155
Expenses for meetings	190
Reserve	230
Other expenses	649

Y17,071

Income

Village household taxes	Y 9,043
Rents from village property	2,823
Money from prefectural and national governments for public health, young people's school, etc.	770
Money from national government as commission for collecting taxes	363
Money from national government for primaŕy school	2,896
Balance from previous year	400
Miscellaneous income	776

Y17,071

The Hamlet

The local government administers the affairs of several hundred households which are in turn grouped together in neighborhood communities or hamlets.

The *buraku* or hamlet is a local social or geographical unit of ten to twenty households and is not part of the formal administrative organization. The affairs of the hamlet as a whole are looked after by a man agreed upon by the older household heads. Since the duties of the hamlet head go unrewarded and may involve considerable trouble on his part, it is regarded as a duty to be shared in turn by each of the more responsible men of the hamlet; hence the office rotates from household to household every year or so. The functions of the hamlet head include looking after any hamlet property, supervising hamlet aid given to families in the event of a death or a fire, deciding the proper days for cooperative work in agriculture, housebuilding or road repair, and announcing, by ringing the fire bell or beating two blocks together in a certain rhythm, the local holidays and rest days.

Each hamlet has its own graveyard, its own fire bell, and its own socio-religious center in a hamlet god house (*dō*). This god house is a small wooden structure housing as a rule some Buddhist image whose festival day is celebrated annually by the people of the hamlet. The god house is also a place where children play by day and a wandering beggar or itinerant may sleep by night. The local bulletin board is likely to be on one of its outside walls and the local fire bell to be erected near by. The *dō* thus functions as a rather humble social and religious center, serving in an informal way as a unifying force for the hamlet. The collective hamlets of a village or town are unified through a common administrative office, a school, and a Shinto shrine.

The only formal administrative structure below the township is the ward or *kū*, which may consist of one or more hamlets each with a local *kuchō* designated by the headman or mayor. *Kuchō* are responsible for tax collections, and other official matters within their own ward. The administrative wards are numbered units in contrast to the hamlets, each of which has its own name.

COMMUNICATION

Within a hamlet the principal mode of communication is by word of mouth. Matters of general concern are carried from house to house by the hamlet head or announced by special rhythms on the fire bell or by clapping together two small wooden blocks audible on still mornings throughout a whole *buraku*. Matters of general village interest are communicated by the headman to the *kuchō* or the *buraku* heads who in turn relay the news. Notices on the bulletin board, and public lectures at the schoolhouse or elsewhere are other means of communication to the village as a whole. In general greater dependence is placed on the spoken word than on the written for effective communication.

There is also provision for communication upward through *kuchō* and village councilor to the village government, and from town and village headmen to the prefectural and national government. This provision for communication of local conditions and attitudes upward tends to avoid some of the weaknesses that might develop in too centralized a government organization without provision for grievances to move upward as well as orders and policies to move downward.

For communication between people of different townships there is the post office and telegraph. The telegram is usually used in the event of a death to inform relatives, while letters are adequate for most other personal communication. A postman from the town post office visits near-by villages daily to deliver and pick up letters. He often relays informally local news and gossip in conversation with the people to whom he delivers mail.

At most levels of government, there is a combination of locally elected and government-appointed officials, so that despite the paternalistic aspects of Japanese government there is also provision for the people's representation. Things of national importance are decided unequivocally in Tokyo, but many things of local importance are left to the local government. In a town or village, for instance, the mayor or headman and the councilors are locally elected and look after the general administration and welfare of the community. They also serve as representatives of their community vis-a-vis outsiders, both governmental and commercial. But the school, while locally supported, is staffed by teachers trained and appointed by the Department of Education. The village agricultural adviser is appointed by the Department of Agriculture and Commerce, and local police are appointed by the Department of Home Affairs. The Shinto priest may be a local man but he holds his official priestly position by appointment from the Bureau of Shrines.

Thus it can be seen that most local affairs are locally administered and the government of the village and town is largely in the hands of the mature, respected local landowners. The prefectural and national governments participate directly in local government in matters of national importance such as public health, law and order, and education. In the event of differences of opinion at the local level, local officials may protest higher up so that the government-appointed agricultural advisers, police, and teachers are to some extent prevented from becoming too authoritarian; at the same time, the government, by carefully controlling local affairs of national concern, keeps the provinces from becoming too provincial at the expense of national unity and prosperity.

COOPERATIVE GROUPS

Cooperation of family, of neighborhood, and of groups in general is a marked characteristic of Japanese society and fits in with the stress laid in Japanese culture on group rather than individual welfare. Cooperation in the accomplishment of agricultural tasks, housebuilding, civic improvements, work involved in weddings and funerals and religious festivals is traditional in Japan and is still the rule in rural areas, making possible the accomplishment of many things with very little outlay of money. The numerous forms of cooperation also provide the villager with a kind of social security whereby he knows that when he needs assistance he will receive it. In urban areas the cooperation takes a more financial form but is very real nonetheless. Instead of being local neighborhood cooperation it takes the form of occupational or guild cooperation.

The traditional cooperative groups in rural areas tend to be on a neighborhood and hamlet basis in contrast to kin groups, which tend to function in ceremonial and more purely formal affairs such as weddings and funerals.

In towns and cities where the old neighborhood solidarity has gradually died away, membership in some commercial guild or professional association has become more important, especially in matters of mutual aid and assistance. Of recent years, however, the government has turned to the neighborhood group to handle such wartime matters as the distribution of rationed goods and the carrying out of civilian defense measures. This procedure is on the surface similar to the block organizations established in the United States after 1941 but there is a much firmer base for such an organization in Japan since it fits right in with traditional cooperative forms of Japanese culture. Today every person in a Japanese city is a member of a neighborhood group (*tonarigumi*) the head of which is in charge of rice distribution and rationing for his group.

When in financial need a farmer or townsman may go to a bank or the agricultural association or he may withdraw savings from a postal savings account, but the commonest way for him to raise money is by means of an old Asiatic cooperative credit club. These mutual financial-aid societies are called variously *kō, tanomoshi,* and *mujin.*

Together with a group of friends an association is formed to lend a man, say, two hundred *yen.* If there are twenty members of the group in addition to the original borrower, each contributes ten *yen* to the total to be loaned. At the first meeting a record is made and the *kō* will be legally registered by the chairman. The receiver of the money signs a note acknowledging his debt.

At the next meeting a lottery is held and the winner receives ten *yen* from nineteen men and twelve *yen* from the original borrower, i.e., 202 *yen.* The extra two *yen* represents interest. At the next meeting, six or eight months later, the same thing occurs again, but this time two men pay twelve *yen* so that the winner receives 204 *yen.* The same procedure is followed till ten or fifteen years later when, at the final meeting, the "winner" receives 220 *yen.* Thus a capital fund of 200 *yen* is revolved among the group without anyone paying in at one time more than ten *yen* (or ten *yen* plus two *yen* interest after receiving 200 *yen*). One cannot draw lots after having received the lump sum.

The lottery *kō* is the simplest form of *kō,* but a more common one is the bidding *kō* whereby an added element of chance adds interest to the meetings. The bidding *kō* commences in the same manner as the lottery *kō* but, after the original borrower receives his money, each person (except the original borrower) puts in a written bid as to what he will accept from those who have not yet won—say, eight *yen*—and then at the next meeting he receives, say, ten *yen* from the original debtor and 160 (8 × 20) *yen* from the rest. Toward the end of the *kō* bids may be very low since most of the people will have to pay ten *yen* anyway and a man who wants cash can afford to bid only two or three *yen*. In general it pays not to win a bidding *kō* till toward the end because then one pays in only six or eight *yen* a meeting while in the end he receives ten *yen* from each of the other men. Since richer men can better afford to hold out to the end, they tend to become the informal bankers in small communities.

A variation on the *kō* is a sort of installment buying plan for umbrellas, shoes, and the like. An umbrella dealer, for instance, organizes a one- or two-*yen* lottery *kō* among a dozen families. They—usually the housewives—meet monthly, each one giving, say, one *yen*. Each winner of the *kō* buys umbrellas with the proceeds. Thus a family may lay in a supply of three or four umbrellas and pay for them at the rate of a *ven* a month for ten months.

In rural areas the motive of economic cooperation is a strong factor in *kō* organizations and serves to take care of sudden financial embarrassment without resort to banks or brokers. In towns *kō* or *mujin* become more commercialized, and their organizers more interested in speculation than in mutual aid. Consequently there may be litigation, and Japanese law has provided rules for commercial credit associations of this type.

LAW AND ORDER

On the home front Japan is one of the most orderly of nations. While much of her modern legal system is derived from French and German law, social and legal controls of the individual in Japan were well developed in Tokugawa days so that borrowed legal codes have been fitted into, and implemented in accord with, Japan's traditional concepts of justice and social control. In general the Japanese legal system is one of code law in contrast to the Anglo-American common-law system.

The judicial power of the state is carried out by four main categories of courts of law in the name of the Emperor: (1) a supreme court located in Tokyo; (2) seven courts of appeal, one each in Tokyo, Osaka, Nagoya, Hiroshima, Nagasaki, Miyagi, and Sapporo; (3) fifty-two district courts, at least one in each prefecture; and (4) several local courts in each prefecture. All of these courts are unified into a single judicial system and all are controlled by the Department of Justice. In addition to these regular courts there are certain special ones such as military and naval courts and colonial courts. There is also an Administrative Court in Tokyo to deal with actions regarding individual rights infringed by an illegal administrative ruling and to settle cases between administrative units such as city and prefecture.

Legal qualifications and life tenure of judges are provided for in the constitution, but promotion depends on the recommendation of the Minister of Justice. While judges are free of executive or administrative interference with judgments, it is only upon the initiative of the public procurator's office that a court of law can take up a criminal case. Since the public procurator's office is responsible to the Ministry of Justice, it is possible for important government officials to escape trial if the ministry so desires.

The supreme court does not pass on the constitutionality of laws. If a law meets the requirements of passage by the Diet, sanction by the Emperor, and promulgation in due form, it is final and no court may question its constitutionality. Imperial ordinances after Diet approval also become law. In this way, incidentally, the law of the land is constantly evolving and the constitution indirectly changed even though never technically amended.

The law is a separate profession from that of procurators and judges, and there are relatively few lawyers as compared to the

United States. As in Tokugawa times most civil cases are decided by arbitration rather than in court. Civil cases and family conflicts which would be settled by lawsuit in the United States are often settled out of court through go-betweens and family councils.

Trial by jury is not characteristic of Japanese law and though a special jury system came into existence in the 1920's it has never been very effective. Main reliance is placed upon the judge, who may question witnesses and whose final judgment may be contrary to the verdict of a jury. Indeed many Japanese regard as inferior a court system whereby a defense lawyer and a prosecutor engage in a battle of wits to influence a jury instead of objectively trying to reach the truth.

Japanese police are under the jurisdiction of the Department of Home Affairs and there is a branch of the police organization in each prefectural office. The prefectural offices supervise prefectural police matters except in the capital city of Tokyo, where the superintendent general of police is directly under the Department of Home Affairs. Cities, towns, and villages within prefectures have no direct control over the police stationed within them.

There are two main bodies of civilian police, the ordinary police and the special police. A special branch known as the Water Police exercises control over all vessels which touch at Japanese ports. There is approximately one ordinary policeman for every thousand people.

The primary function of the civil police is the maintenance of law and order. It is necessary to make this obvious statement because of lurid stories of the Japanese policeman as a man imbued wholly with diabolical impulses. In rural areas police frequently have little to do except keep certain records, but in towns and cities the usual urban need for police is present—robbery, assault and battery, gambling, city traffic.

A policeman may judge minor offenses on his own responsibility and administer up to twenty days' detention and up to a twenty *yen* fine. More serious matters must be referred to the courts. The police may arrest and hold anyone for questioning for ten days without charge and this period may be renewed indefinitely at their convenience. Habeas corpus does not exist in Japan.

A policeman obtains his job as a result of civil service examinations, and while the ordinary officer may have but a middle school education or less, higher police officials are usually university graduates. The salary of ordinary policemen is forty to seventy *yen* a month—about the same as that of schoolteachers. On retirement after twenty-five years' service small pensions are granted.

Police depend on the dignity of their position and their ability at *jūdō* more than on firearms in carrying out their duties. They are usually armed only with a short sword which is more a badge of authority than a lethal weapon.

On the whole the ordinary Japanese policeman is conscientious in carrying out his duties even at the risk of life and limb. An aid to this integrity is the policy of transferring a man every few years or so in order to prevent him from becoming involved in or identified with local pressure groups. The special powers of an officer make him sometimes overbearing, though it is doubtful if the amount of third-degree activities is much greater among Japanese civil police than among some American city forces. The gendarmes or military police in Japanese overseas areas form a separate organization; they have done much to give Japanese an evil name in areas of their occupation.

In addition to the regular duties associated with arrests for crimes and control of traffic, police have other functions:

(1) Supervision of publications. All printed matter must be approved by the police and they may petition the Department of Home Affairs to suppress any publication regarded as detrimental to public welfare and morals.

(2) All public meetings, especially of a political nature, must

be reported in advance and are usually attended by a policeman who may halt proceedings at his discretion. This even includes speeches by candidates for public office.

(3) Supervision of the activities of religious sects.

(4) Jurisdiction over the fire department. Police are also active in the event of emergency such as accident or flood.

(5) Public hygiene. The police participate with the local sanitary inspectors in the inspections of house cleaning, smallpox vaccinations, and the maintenance of quarantine.

(6) Personal records. Local police stations keep an up-to-date record of all persons resident within their jurisdiction and all hotels and brothels are required to report to the police the names of guests who spend the night. These and other reports are used as aids in apprehending both criminal and political offenders.

(7) Licensing of public vehicles, of café waitresses, and of prostitutes is still another function of the police office.

The various controls over the population exercised by the police have increased of recent years, with police functions broadening to include price control and other war measures.

The functions of the special police are not always clearly differentiated from those of the regular police, but in general they are concerned with subversive activities, spies, and seditious publications. Keeping tab on foreigners is also the responsibility of the special police. They, together with regular police, attend political meetings. In general their functions (and attitudes toward foreigners) are similar to those of the Federal Bureau of Investigation in this country.

Firemen's organizations, often of a voluntary nature in rural areas, supplement the police in the maintenance of law and order, not only in the event of fire and flood but also in the apprehending of lawbreakers. The young men's associations (*Seinendan*) are also important as police auxiliaries in some areas.

Written laws are the product of legislators and it is the duty of the police to enforce them, but most behavior in Japan, as elsewhere, is not determined by obedience to specific written codes of law but is culturally determined. Law and order are maintained largely through the sanctions of tradition and public opinion rather than through formal police organization. An individual follows local custom and behaves in the ways approved by his society because of inculcation at home and at school and by imitating his peers. The penalty for breaking rules in rural areas is not the police but conscience and the opinion of neighbors. Especially is there a fear of ridicule, one of the strongest sanctions in Japanese society. In cities, where social solidarity and family unity are weaker, so that the sanction of gossip and ridicule is less effective, and where there are numerous groups with conflicting interests, the role of the police in maintaining law and order is, of course, greater.

THE MILITARY IN GOVERNMENT

Military men play an important role in Japanese government and have done so for many generations. The Tokugawa government was essentially a rule by military men but their overthrow in the nineteenth century did not mean the end of military influence in government. Japan found herself weak and threatened with the colonial fate of the East Indies and the Philippines so that it is not surprising that the new government put strong emphasis on building a strong military machine which inevitably placed great power in the hands of military leaders.

These military leaders are concerned not only with running the army and navy but also take an important part in the government of the country. This is done largely through their special position in the Cabinet and among the Emperor's advisers. The army, which is not above home-front propaganda in its own interests, lays great stress on the position of the army as an extension of the Emperor's authority, thus making it definitely unpatriotic to criticize any military policy or action.

In Meiji days men of Chōshū (Yamaguchi), such as Yamagata,

dominated army policy; men of Satsuma (Kagoshima), such as Tōgō, navy affairs; but today generals and admirals come from almost any province. The policy-making groups in contemporary military government are the Supreme Command (*tōsui*) composed of the Emperor together with the Board of Field Marshals and Fleet Admirals, the Supreme War Council, and the Imperial Headquarters.

The Supreme War Council (*Gunji Sangi In*) is made up of the Board of Field Marshals and Fleet Admirals, the chiefs of the Army and Navy General Staffs, the Inspector General of Military Training, the Ministers of War and of Navy, and distinguished military men appointed by the Emperor. On the advice of this council not only are all military decisions of the Emperor made but many affecting the civil government as well. It is convened only upon command of the Emperor, usually at the suggestion of an army or navy minister or chief of the Army or Navy General Staff who hesitates to assume responsibility for some important decision. There is no vote taken but decisions are made in the traditional manner of discussion and compromise resulting in a unanimous decision. Policies thus decided are then delegated to the agency of the army or navy responsible for implementing them.

The Board of Field Marshals and Fleet Admirals (*Gensui Fu*) is concerned with such matters as awards and decorations and has little influence in policy. The Emperor appoints men to the board in recognition of distinguished service, but during peacetime its membership may consist largely of imperial princes who owe their position to birth rather than to ability or experience.

The Imperial Headquarters (*Senji Dai Hon-ei*) is an emergency organization which meets usually in time of war at the command of the Emperor. Its membership includes the Emperor, chiefs of the Army and Navy General Staffs, and the ministers of War and Navy and such other men as the Emperor may appoint, e.g., the Inspector General of Military Education and the Inspector General of Aviation. On occasion its members meet with Cabinet ministers to work out national policy. Imperial Headquarters puts the Supreme Command on a wartime basis and serves to coordinate military, naval, and civil activities. Its decisions have great prestige because of its direct relationship with the Emperor, a relationship which tends to silence opposition or internal dissension in time of war.

Military control of national affairs is also exercised through the special power of the army and navy Cabinet members to (1) advise the Emperor directly, (2) make or break Cabinets through appointing or withdrawing army and navy ministers. All matters of army and navy organization are in the hands of the Army and Navy General Staffs and the civil officials of government have no direct control over them. Finally, the military may on occasion act independently of the civil government, as in the opening of the Manchurian Affair.

Strictly military affairs are under the direction of four men, the Chief of the General Staff, the Inspector General of Military Training, the Inspector General of Aviation, and the Minister of War. Each is independent of the other and responsible only to the Emperor. The Chief of the General Staff is concerned with the broad phases of military strategy and planning and in wartime his responsibility is great indeed. The General Staff corresponds roughly to the War Department in the United States, but in keeping with Japanese army tradition it is housed in unpretentious old wooden buildings in Tokyo. (By contrast, the much less important Diet is now housed in a magnificent modern structure.) Navy matters are largely the responsibility of two men: the Chief of the Naval Staff and the Minister of the Navy.

Because of the important role of the army and navy ministers in the Cabinet, the Foreign Office is much less significant in determining foreign policy than is, say, the American Department of State. It is rather an administrative channel for the execution of policies made by the Cabinet. Furthermore, officers of the army and navy on delegated authority of the Emperor have by tradition a right to determine action in the field without reference to Tokyo should need arise. This explains the embarrassing position in which the Foreign Office found itself in 1931 when it promised that army forces would not advance in Manchuria. The general in the field thought otherwise.

These top military agencies, like the top civil agencies such as Privy Council and Cabinet, are not completely separate entities. There is overlapping in personnel, and most of the men in them know one another and as a rule prefer to act only after consultation with others. As was remarked of the Tokugawa government, the functions of these various officials are not always clearly defined and high offices are often duplicated or their functions carried out not by individuals but by councils.

In contrast to the hereditary military class of Tokugawa times the modern army is based on universal conscription. Thus the military leaders have in addition to their key roles in the Cabinet and as advisers to the Emperor a close tie with and influence over the young men of the nation. Since workers' and farmers' sons constitute a majority in its ranks, the army leaders are closely allied in interest with these groups and are able to capitalize on the attitudes of worker and farmer against big business interests to gain support for their national socialist program.

During peacetime there is an annual conscription examination for all young men attaining the age of twenty and on the basis of it one man in every three or four is conscripted. The *samurai* tradition gives the soldier high prestige in Japanese life and children are taught in school to admire the soldier. Therefore, it is considered an honor to be allowed to serve in the army, but there are still some peasants who are glad enough when their sons are not among those taken from the farm for a year or two. Military conscription provides the leaders of the military government with an excellent opportunity for training and inculcating the youth of the nation.

There is a special imperial rescript to soldiers and sailors which specifies the virtues of a military man as loyalty propriety, valor, faithfulness, and righteousness and simplicity. This rescript was issued by the Emperor Meiji, but in spirit it is little different from older feudal codes. In keeping with this imperial rescript a basic aspect of the army training is *seishin kyōiku* or spiritual training, which is chiefly an inculcation of the traditional Japanese male virtues: self-discipline, the overcoming of odds, and pride in race and nation. Special emphasis is placed on loyalty to the Emperor and the idea that to die for him is the highest honor.

The general organization of the conscript' army as created in the 1870's is patterned in part on the German system because of Germany's success in defeating France in 1871. Ordinarily conscripts do not advance beyond noncommissioned ranks. Officers, once initial examinations are passed, advance according to seniority and ability without further written tests on the basis of their ability to inspire loyalty in their men, to carry out orders, or even to act on their own initiative contrary to orders when the situation demands it. Finally, a man's loyalty to the Emperor must be unquestioned.

During the early Meiji period practically all army and navy officers were of *samurai* background, but in the course of time more and more men of common background have attended military academies and received commissions so that by 1941 it was estimated that less than fifty per cent of the officer group was of *samurai* descent. A few peers and imperial princes are also in the army as officers, and the commander in chief is, of course, the Emperor.

While the army stresses strict discipline and complete faith in State Shinto, there is also a characteristic element of democracy in it. Although officers rarely rise from the ranks, coming instead from special officer-training schools, they participate in sports with the men and after army maneuvers there is a period of general discussion and criticism. Young officers are free to put forth and try out suggestions for improvements.

On returning home from training, men become members of

the Reservists' Association. This is a national organization with branches in each prefecture and township. Through these reservists' organizations with branches in every town and village, the military exert considerable latent control even in peacetime. Army reservists also help maintain law and order in times of crisis such as flood or fire. The army maintains its own police and intelligence system which in overseas territories is often the principal police organization.

The navy is smaller and takes fewer conscripts than the army so that it is less closely associated with the farmer and more friendly with the noble and, indirectly, the capitalist classes. As in the army, the keynote of training is self-discipline, frugality, and the achieving of ends against all odds. At the same time opportunity is given younger men of ability to present ideas and try out plans. There has been a traditional rivalry between the army and navy in Japan, but of recent years it has not been serious enough to affect fundamental military planning or operation. Both the army and navy have more mobility and adaptability to new conditions than might be expected from a superficial survey of Japan's traditional emphasis on respect for elders and military discipline. Because of the political power and social prestige attached to high military rank in Japan, many of the best brains of the country have followed a military career.

THE RELIGIOUS GOVERNMENT

The Emperor is not only the head of a civil and a military government but of a religious one as well. The Mikado, the Gateway of Heaven, serves as the high priest of the nation, the representative of his people before heaven. The State Shinto of which the Emperor is chief priest serves as a strong force for national solidarity through its emphasis on respect for the throne and the imperial line stemming from the divine Sun Goddess, Amaterasu ō mikami.

In Japanese, as in all societies, religion serves as an important form of social control. Buddhism reinforces family solidarity with its emphasis on respect for the ancestors and tends to keep the masses satisfied by providing a hereafter to work toward. State Shinto enhances national solidarity through an emphasis on loyalty to a divinely descended Emperor and also serves, through local

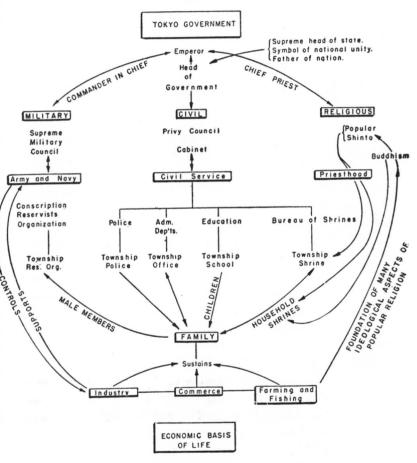

Fig. 8.—Forms of Social Control in Japan.

shrines, to strengthen the social solidarity of local communities and to unite all into a single familial nation whose patriarch is the Emperor. Shinto rituals are the only ones officially observed by the army and navy. Shinto serves not only as a sanction for loyalty but also for bravery in the deification, at the national Yasukuni Shrine in Tokyo, of the souls of warriors who die in battle.

The organization of this religious government is centralized in much the same way as the rest of the Japanese state. (The organization of State Shinto is outlined in Chapter VIII on Religion.)

POLICY MAKERS AND THE PEOPLE'S CHECK THEREON

The Emperor's advisers, the Privy Council, the Supreme Military Council, and the Cabinet, form jointly the top policy-making groups of the Japanese government. These men, by virtue of their position, are all of high social status, but they are of several different social backgrounds. Some come from the nobility such as Prince Konoye, and many are of old *samurai* families. During the 1920's a number of industrial representatives played an important role but the old prejudice against merchants has made big businessmen less important in determining the details of national policy than might be expected. (This does not imply that much of Japan's foreign policy has not been determined by economic developments both at home and abroad.) Behind the shield of the Emperor, representatives of the various groups carry on their struggles for power. The Privy Council may be pitted against the Cabinet, and an army clique against the Emperor's civil advisers, who in turn may be representing some powerful economic group. Since 1936 the military have greatly increased their representation and strength in the top policy-making group and they gained almost complete control of civil as well as military affairs in 1941 when Tōjō became prime minister. It is worth noting, however, that in various governmental reorganizations since Pearl Harbor consideration has had to be given to representatives of the major economic interests and heed has had to be paid to the technical advice of various civilians in regard to emergency economic and political controls.

The national government is a government by groups who assume collective responsibility for important decisions. Thus the Privy Council, the Cabinet, and the Supreme Military Council advise the Emperor, and the policies are enunciated in his name without public debate on the issues involved.

There is care taken, however, to come to unanimous agreement within groups before issuing recommendations as, for example, the custom of the Cabinet's coming to some compromise agreement on a problem rather than settling it by a vote, and the organization of the Privy Council in such a way that incoming members have the approval of old incumbents. This fits another Japanese tradition that the embarrassing spectacle of dignified men squabbling in public should be avoided at all costs. Count Ōkuma's absence from the Privy Council discussions of the constitution to avoid altercation with Prince Itō is a good example of this custom. Other examples of these patterns of policy making are the group responsibility aspect of the Imperial Conference decisions and the custom whereby the Cabinet reaches important decisions without allowing public debate in the Diet.

While the government is primarily a government from above and all important decisions are the primary responsibility of groups in Tokyo, the people and social classes not directly represented have a number of sanctions at their disposal to check policies which diverge too far from their special interests. First of all there is the influence which can be exercised through the vote and the elected prefectural and national assemblies. This sanction is by no means to be disregarded despite the weak political position of the assemblies.

Public opinion in general can also carry weight through newspaper criticisms and through interpolations in the Diet. During wartime such expressions of criticism of government policy are strictly limited, but their importance in peacetime has often been underestimated, especially by foreign observers.

Finally, in carrying out new policies, the government has long since learned the wisdom of working with and through the social groups concerned whether it be the big business *zaibatsu*, the farmers' organizations, or even a brothel keepers' association.

If, as a result of the lack of direct representation in policy making, certain groups interested in social change feel slighted, they may join a society which believes in direct action. Then a representative of such a society may assassinate the man connected with an unpopular policy. Such an act does not necessarily indicate hatred for the man shot, but is rather an expression of disapproval of some act or policy of his group or class, and the man who actually carries out the assassination usually gives himself up voluntarily to the authorities. Prime ministers, privy councilors, and even high military officials have all been subject to such sanctions from time to time. This sanction tends to be resorted to by conservative and reactionary groups in protest against liberal or internationalist policies.

The "new structure" or Imperial Rule Assistance Association, organized as a means of consolidating national unity and replacing the party system, provides not only an Executive Council to "convey the will and orders of those who govern to those who are governed," but also a Central Cooperative Council with branches in every prefecture, town, and village to "convey the will and orders of those who are governed to those who govern." Just how clear the channels are for the people's will and ideas to move upward since the war began is not certain, but the significant aspect of the new structure is that the governors thought it necessary to make specific provision for taking into account social developments and attitudes among the governed.

Thus, while the Japanese government is strongly centralized and paternalistic from the point of view of an American, it is sensitive to the needs of the people to a greater extent than any other government in Asia with the possible exception of the Philippines. Other Asiatic countries were, before the war, either under the domination of overseas governments or run by a very small governing clique as in China and Thailand. The extensive interrelations between central government and local community can be parelleled only in the United States or some European countries. The existence of a national Diet elected by the people, limited though its powers may be, is not to be found elsewhere in Asia excepting, again, the semicolonial Philippines. Even during the present war members of this Diet continue to raise interpolations concerning government policy, and the government feels it expedient to adjust its administration to accommodate technicians, farmers, and industrialists as well as military men. Since the Japanese have managed to govern themselves for a good many hundreds of years, the present government forms can be understood as the end result of a long indigenous development coupled with national responses to external political and economic forces.

GOVERNMENT AND SOCIAL SOLIDARITY

The government here outlined is but one broad aspect of the social entity known as the Japanese nation. Other broad aspects include, for instance, the economic organization and the religious organization. All such institutions as the church, the school, and the government, commerce, and industry are interrelated and interacting aspects of a total society. As a national entity Japan proper is, perhaps, more compact and centralized than England and infinitely more so than China or the United States. It is less compact as a social unit than a small Melanesian tribe or one of its own constituent units such as the family or the hamlet. The closest parallels are to be found in Germany or prewar France with their strong centralization of government, economic organization, and the educational system in the capital.

To understand the structure and functioning of this national entity, it is worth noting that it possesses certain characteristics which are found in *all* societies. One of these is a tendency toward social integration and social solidarity. In a modern nation this is in part maintained through concepts of patriotism and national symbols of unity such as a flag, a constitution, a history. Any threat to national unity is resisted. In Japan, the Emperor is the prime symbol of national unity solidly backed up by the consciousness of a long national history. Critics of the symbols of solidarity such as the Emperor, or the long national history, or mystic terms of national philosophy such as *kōdō,* the Imperial Way, are the subject both of general social and specific legal sanction. "Thought control" is one response of the nation to threats of national disunity. The basic function of the national political structure is to preserve social stability and national security.

All aspects of a society's culture—its customs at marriage and death, its attitudes of approval or disapproval of personal conduct, its concepts of good and bad—serve some function in maintaining the total social organization. If any one is seriously affected, all the rest will also be affected. For this reason, all societies, the Japanese included, resist change in their basic structures and their peoples are ethnocentric. Social solidarity demands some degree of chauvinism in the majority of a nation's members, a chauvinism which in recent Japan has sometimes taken extreme forms.

NATIONAL SOCIETIES

An aspect of the national social structure in part affiliated with and in part separate from the governmental organization is a series of national societies or associations. Characteristically these

associations have a national headquarters in Tokyo with some
high government official or prince as honorary head. The national
structure of each society includes prefectural, city, town, and village units. Within the local units sponsors are usually school-
masters and village headmen or town mayors. Five such national
associations are the Reservists' Association, Young Men's Association, the Firemen's Association, the Women's Patriotic Association, and the Cooperative Association. The new Imperial Rule
Assistance Association is organized along lines similar to these
older societies and has recently absorbed some of them within its
larger over-all structure.

Reservists' Association (*Zaigō Gunjinkai*)

All men who have been to the barracks or served in the army
are automatically members of the Reservists' Association on their
return home. Local matters of a military nature such as the return
of a soldier from the barracks or the annual memorial service for
dead soldiers call for participation by the association. There is in
each local district an annual examination of reservists (*tenko*)
at which time a military officer from the nearest divisional headquarters comes to inspect the men, who don uniforms and engage in military exercises for the occasion. The visiting officer
improves the occasion by speeches not only to the reservists but
also—in words of one syllable—to the local Women's Patriotic
Society. Through this organization the army maintains close ties
with the people and is able, on such occasions as *tenko,* to incul-
cate the politically unconscious with proper ideas of nationalism
and the Japanese spirit.

Women's Patriotic Society (*Aikoku Fujinkai*)

This association is in many ways the distaff side of the Reservists' Association. All Japanese women belong normally to one or
another branch, though in past years relatively few were really
active and most of the organization and leadership were carried

out by male schoolteachers and other government officials. Each local branch has its own uniforms and the members function as helpers on various official occasions when food is to be served, such as the annual Reservists' Inspection. They also prepare comfort kits and thousand-stitch belts for men overseas. Since the war the local units of the Women's Patriotic Society have been enlisted into civilian defense activities, learning how to extinguish incendiaries and how to look after the wounded. There is little doubt that the role of women in civic affairs has grown as a result of the expanding function of this society in recent years.

Young Men's Association (*Seinendan*)

On graduating from grammar school, boys become eligible for membership in the Young Men's Association. In rural areas it usually carries on its activities at school with practice drill under the leadership of one of the reservists and some vocational and physical training under the direction of one of the teachers. On big school occasions, members dress in khaki and may put on some program. In cities, members of the Young Men's Association assist in civilian defense activities. While not every young man in a village or town belongs to this society, a majority do, and it functions as an informal adjunct to the school system on the one hand and the army on the other. Young men normally remain members until about the age of twenty when those eligible are conscripted.

The *Shojokai* or Young Women's Society is a comparable association for girls, the young ladies at their meetings learning cooking, sewing, and some physiology. They also turn out at school graduation exercises and on other big occasions dressed in gray smocks. Membership in Young Women's Societies is smaller and less active than that of the *Seinendan*. Young ladies fade out of the organization as the time for marriage approaches.

Firemen's Association (*Shōbō Tai*)

In smaller towns and villages, fire fighting is still done on a volunteer basis. Today one man from each household between the ages of twenty-five and forty belongs to a local firemen's association which goes into action in the event of fire or flood. When on duty all wear special caps and coats. As already noted, the firemen also serve as auxiliary police.

Every January there are special firemen meets with contests in handling equipment, and speeches by local and government officials which serve to maintain morale and national spirit. As with the other societies, the Firemen's Association cuts across all social class and occupational lines, thus giving strength to the national structure at the expense of class or occupational group loyalties.

National Cooperative Association (*Sangyō Kumiai*)

The National Cooperative Association is organized along lines similar to the other national societies but also carries on important economic functions. The cooperative "movement" in Japan, as this national organization is sometimes called, was set up in Japan as a paternalistic measure and was first introduced by the government about 1900 on the model of German cooperatives.

Like the other national associations, headquarters are in Tokyo, and there is a branch in every prefecture which has under its jurisdiction the local units in town and village. Four types of cooperative are provided for: Credit (*Shinyō Kumiai*), Marketing (*Hanbai*), Purchasing (*Kōbai Kumiai*), and Enterprises (*Ryo Kumiai*). Individual shares in local cooperatives cannot exceed fifty *yen* and no one member is allowed to own more than ten such shares. These cooperative organizations are exempt from taxation on income.

In 1938 there were 15,328 cooperative societies with a paid-up capital of 279 million *yen,* the majority of them agricultural.

(Urban cooperatives are limited to credit associations.) Local cooperative associations as a factor in rural cooperation and credit have been growing of recent years as local hamlet solidarities have been gradually giving way to the wider ones of the *mura*.

The credit associations provide for the borrowing of money at relatively low rates of interest. Anyone may deposit money in a credit association but only members may borrow—the amount depending on the number of shares the borrower holds and the approval of the directors of the local association. The marketing association provides a cooperative organization for the marketing of rice and other grains and is of great aid to the farmer, who formerly had to depend principally on brokers; the purchasing association provides channels for buying rubber work shoes, soap, medicines, and other articles at a saving; the enterprises association provides facilities for constructing cooperative grain mills and footgear factories. This last association has not been appreciated by Japanese businessmen.

The national cooperative issues an inexpensive monthly journal, *Ie no Hikari,* which has a wide circulation in rural areas—providing stories, housekeeping and farming advice, and some news.

Government agricultural advisers cooperate with local branches of farmers' cooperatives, which thus serve as a means of encouraging progressive farming techniques and so improving the economic position of the nation.

The national cooperative association is a nice example of the dovetailing of government controls with local interests and needs Cooperation in one form or another is a characteristic of rural areas—indeed almost a necessity to farmers with their small incomes. The local branches of the national cooperative association bring together, under a single government-sponsored but locally run organization, cooperative credit and marketing facilities, and at the hamlet level the association provides convenient ways for the exchange of labor at rice transplanting. Thus, by judicious government planning, the Japanese farmer has had certain economic needs provided for before local sore spots and independent farmers' organizations could become a serious threat to the national equilibrium.

Patriotic Societies

In addition to the national associations there are a number of reactionary patriotic societies which play a role in government. In sharp contrast to the neat and orderly arrangement of the government-sponsored or -approved associations such as those of the firemen and the young men, the patriotic societies are as likely as not to be against the government and are not afraid to say so. Frequently their organization is secret and the extent of membership difficult to determine. On the whole they are perhaps smaller and less influential than some romantic writers or their own chauvinistic leaders would have one believe, but nonetheless, with their fire-eating proclamations appealing to popular prejudice and their willingness to indulge in assassination, they have on occasion undoubtedly influenced the actions of individual government officials.

While some of the members, especially the leaders, of such societies are probably sincere patriots, many of the followers are the spiritual descendants of the *rōnin* or masterless *samurai* who were always causing trouble to the Tokugawa with their fights and vendettas. Others are simple thugs or *sōshi*.

The societies and their memberships are constantly changing and they have none of the ideal stability so desired by the Japanese government. In general they are anticapitalist and antiforeign, stressing the vague virtues of national Japanese polity (*Kokutai*), the Imperial Way (*Kōdō*), and the Japanese Spirit (*Nihon seishin*).

One of the oldest and best known of these patriotic societies is the *Kokuryū Kai,* commonly translated as Black Dragon Society although the name actually means Amur River Society. It was founded in 1901 to make propaganda for a war with Russia and to advocate a Japanese advance to the Amur River. The Chinese name for the river is Heilungchiang or Black Dragon River. The founder of the society was Ryōhei Uchida, a follower of Toyama, not Toyama himself as is sometimes said. Of recent years the society has sponsored the Pan-Asia movement and has conceived the mission of liberating the dark races from white oppression.

A newer patriotic society is the *Jimmu Kai*, named for the first ruler of Japan. It was founded by an intellectual, Dr. Shūmei Ōkawa, and sponsors the *hakkō ichiu* (eight corners—one roof) doctrine. Jimmu is said to have stated that it was Japan's mission to bring the eight corners of the world under one roof, and modern patriots have adopted the phrase and used it as a slogan and sanction for Japan's divine mission to bring Japanese peace and order to the whole world. The society also stresses emancipation of the non-white races. Like other patriotic societies it has attacked the plutocrats and politicians and advocated improvement of the farmers' lot by various national socialistic measures. (Not infrequently men who were Marxists in the 1920's became members of patriotic societies in the 1930's.)

Men like Araki in the army have stimulated young officers along similar lines, with the sobering climax of the February 26 incident in 1936 at which time a group of young officers assassinated a number of high government and military officials and attempted to bring about a complete change in government. They even defied an imperial order to disband. The revolt itself failed, but some of its objectives were attained. Since then the army has given more attention to problems of army discipline.

Such social developments are in part traditional in Japanese society, following the principles of sudden direct action by a group which feels itself slighted, and they are in part the result of stresses in Japanese society because of industrialization at home and Japan's international relations as a consequence of this industrial coming of age. The secret societies are stronger in urban areas than in the truly rural regions and their leadership slogans have a strong appeal to various middle-class "forgotten men" who find it easy to put the blame for their difficulties on big business and the machinations of foreign nations.

Chapter IV

Social Class System

THE traditional social classes of Japan consisted of the warrior, the farmer, the artisan, and the merchant in that order, with pariahs still lower and the Imperial Family.above all. After the Meiji restoration this class system, which had legal as well as traditional sanctions, was abolished so far as the law was concerned. The facts that farmers could now dress in silk and that *samurai* were not to carry swords did not, of course, abolish the old class distinctions overnight and there are today many of the old class attitudes still very much alive. The official attitude of the government, in the interest of national unity, does not admit the existence of social classes beyond that of noble (*kazoku*) and commoner (*heimin*), but despite this emphasis on the racial and social homogeneity of the Emperor's subjects, there are numerous distinctions in social status, some ethnic, some economic, and some based on inherited rank.

The contemporary class hierarchy may be roughly divided into seven main categories:

(1) The topmost or upper group is that of the Imperial Family, those who "Dwell above the Clouds." This group includes, in addition to the Emperor and Empress, princes and princesses directly related to the Emperor, as children or brothers and sisters. The ancestry of the Imperial Family is traced back to the founding deities on the authority of State Shinto's sacred records, the

Kojiki and the *Nihongi*. No member of this hereditary class is supposed to deal directly in either business or politics and while princes and princesses may serve as heads of various civic organizations, or hold military titles, they serve rather as prestige-giving figureheads than as active managers. Prince Chichibu, reported to possess some independence of spirit and a desire to be more than an Emperor's younger brother, is said to be in official disfavor and his movements under restraint.

(2) The nobility or upper class is also a hereditary group, the upper members of which trace their ancestry back to the Age of the Gods. The Emperor's consort is a woman from a family in this class, the present Empress Nagako being the eldest daughter of Prince Kuni. Younger sons of the imperial family gradually fall into the nobility class. The nobility also includes princes, marquis, and barons who received titles in lieu of their feudal rank. Various *de facto* rulers of the Meiji Era were also given titles such as Genrō Prince Saionji and the army leader Prince Yamagata. A few of the older and stronger financial magnates also have titles, e.g., the several barons Mitsui.

As ministers of the Imperial Household, members of the Privy Council and the House of Peers, this upper-class nobility sometimes exerts considerable influence in Japanese government. The more influential members of this hereditary class are sometimes referred to collectively as the *monbatsu* in contrast to the military or *gumbatsu* clique.

(3) The big business families comprise a class which its not, strictly speaking, hereditary although most of the big names go back to Tokugawa times. It includes both the older commercial and financial controlling families and the new industrialists. There is also a collective term for the more influential members of this group—the *zaibatsu*. The *zaibatsu* includes some of the richest families in Japan—Mitsui, Iwasaki (Mitsubishi interests), Sumitomo, Okura, and Yasuda. Behind the scenes these families have influenced not only the political parties but also certain army

cliques. In periods of international cooperation men in the Foreign Service from *zaibatsu* families often held positions of influence. Since these families are economic rivals they often oppose one another's political influence, as was done in the days of political parties. Newer industrialists such as Aikawa in Manchuria favored the army's expansionist policy at a time when the Iwasaki and Mitsui opposed such moves on economic grounds. Possibly as a heritage from Tokugawa times, there is a popular distrust of the big financial interests and they are often targets of attack as, for instance, when Mitsui was charged with making a profit from dollar holdings when Japan went off the gold standard, or when the same group was accused of selling to China the barbed wire which held up the Japanese advance at Shanghai and so cost the lives of Japanese soldiers. To allay such criticism and the envy of other groups, including the nobility, the *zaibatsu* have established philanthropies, endowed research projects, and made generous gifts of equipment to the military forces. The young officers' revolt of 1936 was in part a reaction against highly placed pressure groups, both *zaibatsu* and *monbatsu*.

While it usually takes some special influence to rise to the upper financial brackets, one interesting exception is the Japanese custom of adoption used by business leaders as a means of bringing able new blood into the management. Frequently, if a businessman's own son is not adept at financial matters, he may adopt a bright and conscientious young man who is working in his organization or appoint such a man as general manager of the family corporation.

(4) The upper middle class, or the more well-to-do of the middle-class group, consists largely of businessmen and industrialists, many of them engaged in foreign trade and manufacturing for a foreign market. Others are found in the upper middle sections of the civil service. Families in this class have often acquired their wealth recently (becoming *narikin* or *nouveau riche*) and indulge in conspicuous display such as golf and automobiles—the

latter still a real luxury in Japan. In its financial enterprise aspect this group has probably been hard hit by the present war with its increased governmental control of all phases of life.

The lower middle class includes small retail merchant families and white-collar wage workers who make up a large proportion of the urban middle-class population. From the same family one son may carry on the family business while a second son becomes a white-collar worker, a civil servant or a technician. The professional men—doctors, dentists, judges, lawyers, and teachers—often begin life in lower middle-class families. As an urban class interested in bettering itself there is a fair amount of upward mobility in this group and many of the upper middle-class families come from it. A certain close attention to the value of a *yen* and at the same time a desire to appear sophisticated in both Japanese and Western culture makes the typical lower middle-merchant-class person both a hard worker and a nervous man. The lower, together with the upper middle class and the bureaucrats, possesses a matter-of-fact attitude on getting along in this world and some at least bow at a Shinto shrine more because it is expedient to do so than because of any deep belief in its sanctity.

A new and rising group is that of technical industrial workers —some drawn from the lower middle class and some from the upper-lower urban classes. Their social status to begin with is rather low and they get their hands dirty in their work, but their wages are relatively good, adding up to an income higher than that of many a white-collar worker. This group is rising in status as the national need for technicians with specialized industrial knowledge increases.

(5) The farmers, who produce the food the people of all classes eat, are regarded by members of the above four classes as fine simple folk, honest and hard working, but hardly to be classed as equals economically, intellectually, or socially. There is also in urban Japan the characteristic city dweller's attitude of superiority

to the rustic—and the preceding four classes are largely urbanites. Like the rural populations of parts of Europe, they form a peasantry, i.e., an old stable population with well-integrated social and religious patterns of social life but little active interest in or direct influence on national politics.

Members of the military classes, however, many of whom originated in rural areas and most of whom feel an identity of interest between the farmer and the army, have considerable respect for the peasant. Partly for this reason the army has always agitated for the farmers' interest in matters of taxation and government welfare and relief measures. Within a given rural area a small merchant or shopkeeper may have a lower social status than that of one of the old landowning farmers of the district. This traditional attitude whereby the farmer has a better status than the merchant is in part reflected by important army leaders —the modern *samurai*—who favor the farmers' interests as against that of the financiers (even though financial favors may be accepted from the latter).

On the whole the government maintains the same general attitude toward the farmer that the Tokugawa did—that of a father toward his children—keeping them reasonably healthy and peaceful and encouraging in them the virtues of industry and frugality. The government has also continued and increased its early interest in improving agricultural production. The first aim—health and peacefulness—is accomplished by providing government relief in the event of earthquakes, fire, flood, or drought; by providing government-trained teachers who stress the virtues of peace and cooperation; by encouraging the formation of farmers' buying, selling, and credit cooperatives; and finally by leaving local matters up to locally elected officials. Increased production is attained by having government-trained agricultural extension agents aid the farmers with advice on improved agricultural techniques. The farmer is of primary economic importance and both the government and the army realize this fact even though the peasant has but little direct political influence.

(6) The urban workers are the day laborers, factory workers, miners, and others who carry on the hard manual labor necessary for the life of an urban civilization. Their social status is low and they do not even possess the farmers' compensation of a traditional reputation for virtue.

There is very little independent organization among the worker groups, which is another contrast with the farmers who have within their own villages economic cooperatives for buying and for selling. While the government favors such cooperatives (even though merchants object), it frowns upon similar organization among workers as being dangerous to the state. Labor unions have been formed as well as workers' political parties, often under the leadership of earnest young men of college education, but as a result of the government program of unity in the late 1930's, all such independent labor unions were disbanded, giving way to a government-sponsored Patriotic Industrial Association. The ability of this new association to put forth workers' grievances very strongly is dubious.

(7) Submerged minorities include the *suiheisha* or *eta* class, officially abolished by the Meiji government, when all were declared *heimin* or commoners; nonetheless, it is still in existence and there remains today a very strong prejudice against people of *eta* origin. This makes it almost impossible for such people to marry into other classes or to rise in the social or political hierarchy—a man of *eta* origin cannot even rise in the army or navy since the men under him would not give him the proper respect. About half the million-odd *eta* are engaged in farming while others are tanners, shoemakers, and butchers. Girls sometimes become prostitutes and it is said that some of them find life in a licensed quarter preferable to life in an *eta* community.

The term *eta* is one of derogation as are some of its synonyms such as *shinheimin* (new common people), *chorinbo* or the holding up of four fingers (symbolizing a four-footed animal). The people themselves have organized for their social betterment into a *Suiheisha Undō* (equalization or water-level organization), and the term *suiheisha* is a more polite term for members of this group and is used by educated people today who deplore the old attitudes of prejudice. The government also discourages discrimination and it is possible for a man of *eta* origin to gain satisfaction from the courts if he can prove he has been subjected to social discrimination.

There are over a million Koreans in Japan, many of them laborers brought in by the industrialists because they will work for less. They sometimes become scapegoats in time of crisis such as the Tokyo earthquake of 1923, when many were killed on the basis of an alarmist rumor that they were revolting and looting.

Every town and village has its own class hierachy with its own upper-, middle-, and lower-class groups. In general, length of residence in an area, economic standing, and social status are correlated. In a small rural village the old native landowning families have greater prestige and influence in local affairs than newcomers, who are usually either very poor or else came in as shopkeepers or brokers. Families descended from the old warrior classes have high local prestige even though today they may be very poor financially. People of the paddy lands outrank people of the hills.

The association of nativity and social rank is also found in the national hierarchy—it is easier for a man of one of the old provinces such as Satsuma or Chōshū to reach high national rank than for a man from the newer, less historic provinces in the north or in Hokkaidō. People from Okinawa Ken (the Ryūkyūs), while legally treated as citizens, do not stand a chance of reaching positions of influence because of a general prejudice against Okinawans as being not quite Japanese. This prejudice is even stronger in regard to people from Korea or Formosa.

THE POSITION OF WOMEN

As wives and daughters of the men in the major class group-ings the women of Japan are also members of these various groups. At the same time the social position of women as such deserves a word of comment. From the point of view of American society, the social position of women is low: politically, they have very little voice, since they can neither vote nor be elected to government office; they are seldom educated beyond the high school level since there is little place in Japanese society for a woman highly educated in the social, biological, or physical sciences; and finally, while a divorce by mutual consent may be obtained as simply as a marriage registration, if there is disagree-ment, the husband may divorce his wife at will while she can divorce him only for serious cause and with considerable legal difficulty.

In the upper- and middle-class groups the social life of women is greatly restricted while men have varied social lives as a result of their daily business contacts. The whole emphasis of the culture is to make a woman dutiful, patient, and good-natured. Among the upper classes with servants, women usually •acquire some ladies' accomplishments such as playing on the musical *koto* or performing the tea ceremony.

Among the farmers and poorer classes, women are more nearly the social equals of men––partly as a result of the economic inter-dependence of the sexes, partly perhaps because the old Japanese and Confucian traditions of woman's inferior role are less firmly intrenched. Lower-class women are much freer in speech and gesture than middle- or upper-class women, and married women are free to drink and smoke together with their menfolk.

This general picture of a woman's lot in Japanese society would strike an upper-middle-class American woman as restricted in the extreme. On the other hand, a Japanese woman has certain social advantages. Her social role is clearly defined so that she need not struggle between keeping up a career and a home at the same time; she may count on the company and friendship of other women all of similar social standing and background; it is she who shapes her child's early life most completely; and she virtually controls the domestic aspects of the family finances. If her husband has a wandering eye and takes up with a *geisha*, she can be reasonably sure that such action will not lead to a breakup of the home and that in the long run his family obligations will outweigh his personal whims. In the event of misfortune she has a family, usually that of her husband, which automatically looks after her needs. In other words, while the Japanese middle-class woman lacks certain political and social "rights," she has a large share of social and psychological security.

The *geisha* or dancing girls of Japan are women who have been trained in playing the *samisen,* singing, and clever repartee. Their function is to serve drinks, dance, and provide entertaining company at a banquet in the tradition of the court ladies of old Japan. To be a *geisha*, a girl must undergo an apprenticeship training period and then pass an examination, after which she is licensed by the police. A *geisha* is not required to sleep with her patrons but as a rule becomes the more or less faithful mistress of some man, often a rich patron. In small towns, however, *geisha* are little different from ordinary prostitutes.

Geisha play an important role in urban Japanese society. While a married woman is expected to be a dutiful and patient wife who carries out her cooking, washing, sweeping, and mending in the spirit of conjugal love, she is not expected to engage in banter with her husband or to exhibit sex appeal. The glamour a wife lacks is to be found in the *geisha* dressed in gaily colored *kimono*, telling risqué jokes as she pours the *sake,* and in general providing a stimulating social atmosphere. Because of the greater freedom of the peasant woman, the farmer does not feel the same need for such recreation—and even if he did he lacks the money to buy it.

Of distinctly lower status than the *geisha* is the *jorō* or prostitute who lives in a licensed quarter under police supervision and is under contract to a brothel keeper to serve in her profession for two or three years. These girls come mostly from poor families of low social status. Farmers of respectable position in villages do not "sell" their daughters. Technically the girl's own consent is required before a contract may be entered into, but actually parental authority is sufficient to obtain such consent and there is no public opinion to back up any objections the girl may have to the arrangement.

The present social position of women has not always been true of Japan; there have been Empresses in the past who led armies, and court ladies who were accomplished writers. Of recent years there are again indications of change. Feminist leaders such as Baroness Ishimoto have done much to "awaken" women to their own importance, and to the value of birth control as a step toward emancipation. Women's organizations, such as the Women's Patriotic Society, while scarcely of spontaneous origin, probably will eventually do much to take women's interests outside the home. Wartime labor needs have provided opportunities for women to enter many occupations once reserved to men. All these developments may lead to rather fundamental changes in Japanese social organization so far as the social role of women is concerned.

SOCIAL MOBILITY

The social hierarchy of the nation is basically a division of society into economic and occupational classes. The groups at the very top (Imperial Family and nobility) and at the very bottom (*Suiheisha* and Koreans) are more in the nature of castes, being largely hereditary so that it is difficult for one not born into the top group to enter it and for one born into the bottom group to get out of it. The custom of adoption, however, provides a special channel whereby individuals may rise in social rank—even into the nobility. Similarly girls may climb the ladder through marriage even into the Imperial Family. A sister of Prince Tokugawa, for instance, is the wife of the Emperor's younger brother, Nobuhito. Such changes of status by marriage or adoption are rarely of more than one rung in the ladder in one generation. An exception to this rule was the marriage of Setsuko, a daughter of Tsuneo Matsudaira of an upper-middle-class family, to Prince Chichibu, younger brother of the Emperor. Despite advice to the contrary the Prince insisted on marrying Miss Matsudaira; hence the situation was saved by her being adopted into another branch of the Matsudaira family which is of the nobility. In this way the marriage was the traditional one of an imperial prince with a daughter of the nobility. The fact that this stratagem, while legitimate, was stretching a point is reflected in the critical attitude many people took toward Prince Chichibu's bride, remarking that she should not have let the prince marry her.

It is with the in-between groups that social mobility is greatest, and in times of great social change such as the Meiji Era many men like Itō and Yamagata rose from low *samarai* rank to membership in the nobility. Not a few of the present big business families come from lower class origins only a few generations back. It is necessary to stress the existence of this social mobility in Japanese society because of the general impression that, due to the centralized political organization and general emphasis on social class, it is impossible for a man of ability to rise. One of Japan's great strengths lies in the indirect opportunities the society provides for men of ability to reach positions of power—through adoption or marriage, through civil service and military organizations, and through scholarship and professional attainment. The very looseness of some of the top governmental groups makes it possible for men of varied origins to attain influential positions.

Chapter V

Education

MUCH of the present strength of modern Japan as a nation is due to the remarkable growth in her system of public education. There is no nation in Asia which even approaches the record of Japan in school attendance and literacy. Japan also has an efficient public health program and it is probably generally true that there is a correlation between industrialization, literacy, and public health. It is certainly true that the Meiji government, in reorganizing the nation to fit the modern industrial world, placed a high priority on public education.

PRESCHOOL TRAINING

Since the education of the Japanese child begins before he goes to school, it is necessary to outline preschool educational influences before describing the formal school system. The Japanese mother gives birth to her child alone, and without crying out, in accordance with the tradition that childbirth is a time of uncleanness and shame for the mother. Of recent years Japanese publicists have made much of the "Japanese spirit" of their mothers whereby they do not cry out at childbirth as do their weaker Occidental sisters.

In most towns and cities today a midwife is on hand at a birth and she usually comes again a few days later to give the first bath and attend a small naming ceremony held by the parents with a few close relatives and near neighbors. At this time the infant, dressed in dull blue garments if a boy, bright red if a girl, is passed from guest to guest as part of the ceremony. Thus he receives a name and is introduced to society.

For a year or so the infant is the favored one in the family. At any time he may drink milk from his mother's breast and whatever he cries for will be given him. He learns many things by imitation and by habit, thus acquiring his vocabulary from family and neighbors and his food habits from his daily diet. At the same time he is taught early to control himself, being held up unceremoniously outside the doorway to urinate and he soon learns that to soil the floor mats (*tatami*) is wrong. It becomes almost a reflex action for a child to stop eating or touching anything the moment his mother cries "Dirty!" This early training in cleanliness is associated with the almost ritualistic habits of cleanliness in Japanese society—the daily bath, the leaving of shoes outside the house, the purification rituals of Shinto. Compared with middle-class Western children, however, a Japanese child is less rigidly inhibited as to times of eating and sleeping, and as he grows up in the neighborhood he does not suffer from as many conflicting examples as to proper behavior for his age and sex.

When the mother bears another child the first one suffers his first hard knocks in adjusting to society. The mother now devotes her attention to the newcomer and the older child is turned over to an older sibling or nursemaid who carries him on her back as she goes about her own affairs. The child now learns that the world is not completely centered on him—though a first-rate temper tantrum may still bring results. Before long he becomes acquainted with other children and becomes part of a two- or three-year-old age group. Gradually he learns to get along with his contemporaries.

A strong emotional tie of affection usually develops between a child and his mother which persists throughout life. The mother feeds and bathes the child daily and sleeps next to him at night. It is interesting to note that the officer assigned to look after and help new conscripts in the army is sometimes called the mother of a new soldier.

During the years before primary school there are different educational influences on boys and on girls. Boys, especially first sons, learn that they may obtain almost anything from their mothers and sisters if they make enough noise, while girls soon learn that they must give in to the desires of their brothers. This special attention to boys probably accounts in part for the pride of the adult male and his easy susceptibility to real or supposed insult. Boys are taught to be leaders, girls to be followers. Girls trained in obedience grow up to be remarkably patient women, making ideal Japanese wives and mothers. A strong sense of duty is instilled in both sexes, making it possible for both men and women to undergo great privation, even to the point of death, in order to fulfill an obligation of honor. Such behavior may be on behalf of a relative, a friend, or an employer—even a foreigner—as well as for Emperor or nation.

One sanction employed in child training is repression by ridicule. Corporal punishment is rare. Children are more afraid of ridicule than of bodily injury and the adult Japanese is always careful to behave so as to avoid it. To be ridiculed is to lose dignity—i.e., to lose face. A special positive sanction for young girls is that they must learn this or do that in order to make a good wife. A girl's mother is careful to teach her daughter those things which will help her to get along with her future mother-in-law.

INTRODUCTION TO SCHOOL

When a full six years of age, children dressed in school uniforms go with their parents to the local Shinto shrine, where the priest performs a ritual, gives a brief talk on the purity of the Japanese spirit and loyalty to the Emperor, and hands to each child a first book of ethics published by the Department of Education. After this service they go to the primary school. This first visit to the shrine may not mean much to the child at the time but it is significant of the close association between State Shinto and the public school system.

At school, children have their social horizons widened, meeting for the first time other children from outside their own neighborhood and kinship circle. The constant association of children, rich and poor, for six years makes for local unity and tends to prevent class lines from becoming dangerously wide. The ties of men who have been classmates in school are frequently very close; this is especially true of classmates in higher schools and colleges. To have been the classmate of a prominent financier or military man is a distinct aid to success in business or in the army.

Boys on one side of the room, girls on the other, stand and bow to the teacher at the beginning of a class and he bows in return. Each school morning for ten minutes before classes begin there are setting-up exercises in the schoolyard under the leadership of the teachers and to the direction and tune of a national radio broadcast so that from 7:50 to 8:00 the entire youth of the nation goes through the same daily dozen to the shrill directions of the same government radio station.

THE NATIONAL SCHOOL SYSTEM

As with other aspects of government in Japan, the educational system is centralized, with the Ministry of Education setting the educational policy for the nation's schools and for the training of teachers. Each prefecture has its own branch of the Department of Education and each township and municipality its own bureau of education which is partly an administrative extension of the Tokyo department.

The educational system includes primary schools to provide six years of compulsory education for all children, a number of high schools, and a smaller number of universities and teachers' colleges. This whole organization has been built up since 1872, when the basic law on education was issued incorporating many methods learned from a study of European and American school systems. Before that time, primary education was restricted to temple schools of uneven quality, and higher education to the children of the *samurai* class and those of a few wealthy merchants who had the opportunity and desire to attend the school of some private teacher in one of the big cities. One possible reason for the scarcity of educational facilities for the ordinary commoner was the old Confucian doctrine that "the peasant should be made to follow but should not be made to know." It is significant that the practical and secular plan of education set forth in the law of 1872 was supplemented in 1890 by the philosophical Imperial Rescript on Education. As in other fields, the wholesale adoption of Western forms in the early Meiji period was followed by a reaction leading to a renewed emphasis on traditional moral principles in government and in education.

Elementary Schools (*Kokumingakkō*, formerly *Shogakkō*)

Every urban district and rural township in Japan has its own elementary school with a required six-year course. The local district, with some assistance from the national government, supports the schools and pays the teachers. As of 1938 there were 25,906 such schools with 11,793,000 pupils and 268,700 teachers. Most local communities support their schools wholeheartedly, and the finest building in a village or town is likely to be its school— a reflection of Japanese pride in education and love of children.

The aim of the elementary school curriculum is to teach children to read and write about two thousand characters, and learn some elementary geography, arithmetic, history, and a little general science. The curriculum also includes generous doses of athletics, ethics, and singing.

Special attention is paid to character training, which is regarded as an essential of all Japanese education. Children are taught the virtues of bravery and self-sacrifice through stories of both Japanese and foreign heroes such as Saigō Takamori, Oda Nobunaga, Florence Nightingale, and Abraham Lincoln. There are no luxuries at school—textbooks are small paper-bound volumes, the wooden desks are small, and the pupils themselves are expected to clean up the schoolroom and schoolyard. Thus they learn the virtues of frugality and hard work. They are also expected to put up with various discomforts, such as cold in winter, and any complaints are answered by telling them to think of the hardships of Japanese soldiers overseas. Respect for superiors is instilled by teaching the children to obey their teachers as they would their fathers.

A special feature of Japanese elementary school education is the taking of children on periodic tours to famous shrines and historic spots. In this way children widen their mental horizons and teachers may teach history, ethics, and geography by interesting and concrete example. The government railways provide special rates for such tours.

Practically all children in the elementary schools are promoted every year, the emphasis in teaching being as much on the ethics of human relations as on the accumulation of knowledge. Teachers feel that if some child were left behind his class he would feel very much upset, and that the resulting psychological effect and family chagrin would not be compensated for by any good the child might receive from repeating the school grade. Similarly, at school athletic contests all entrants, not only the first three, receive prizes, so that no one feels unduly slighted. While students are shown the virtues of initiative, inventiveness, and leadership, they are also admonished to be cooperative and work for the common good rather than for individual reward.

Another influence toward equality and uniformity among school children is the school uniform, which minimizes differences in appearance between rich and poor. While social class is important in Japanese society, there is in the school an emphasis on the fact that by perseverance and hard work anyone, regardless of class, may rise to greatness.

There is a special fireproof structure in most schoolyards in which is kept the Emperor's portrait. Anyone entering or leaving the school grounds must bow toward this building as a sign of loyalty to and respect for the Emperor. Thus the schoolhouse as well as the local Shinto shrine serves as a center for inculcating by precept and ritual a national patriotism in regard to the Emperor, his sacred land, and his nation.

Higher Schools

Young people's schools (*Seinengakkō*) are schools organized in conjunction with the young men's and young women's associations. They serve to provide in afternoon or evening classes some instruction for elementary school graduates who do not go on to middle school. The curriculum is largely one of military drill, with some vocational training for the boys, and sewing and home economics for the girls. It is possible for a young man to reduce his normal period of military service by attendance at the military drill classes of the *Seinengakkō*.

The middle school (*Chūgakkō*) is a five-year secondary school for boys—mostly boys from towns and cities. It corresponds roughly to high school in the United States except that fewer students attend.

Agricultural and technical schools provide vocational education and are on the same academic level as the middle schools. The sons of well-to-do farmers who intend to make a career of farming attend the agricultural school nearest to their native village while sons of small-town businessmen attend the nearest commercial school. Of recent years much emphasis has been laid on specialized vocational training, especially in the urban areas, and in 1938 there were 1,355 technical schools with 478,000 students.

There are thirty-two special schools (*Kōtōgakkō*) preparatory to the university on somewhat the same level as American junior colleges. They have a three-year course and admit graduates of middle schools. There are also 179 professional colleges (*semmon gakkō*) on this same academic level—higher agricultural, commercial, technical, and normal schools.

It has been reported by the Tokyo radio that the amount of education required to enter the university has recently been reduced by two years. Whether these two years were cut from the *Chūgakkō* or *Kōtōgakkō* or both was not announced. Despite occasional protests from patriotic laymen, English still appears to be a required subject for students in middle and higher schools.

Universities (*Daigaku*)

University education is carried on in both public and private institutions—some forty-five in all. The eight Imperial Universities of Japan (including one in Formosa and one in Korea) are the most important of the national universities. Keiō University, founded by Fukuzawa, and Waseda, founded by Ōkuma, are among the better-known private institutions. Only a small number of students, mostly men, ever reach the university, and in 1938 the enrollment in all universities was just under 73,000.

A degree from one of the Imperial Universities is almost a necessity for a governmental career, and a degree from certain universities such as the Imperial University of Tokyo is almost a sure passport into the civil service. Graduates from private universities such as Keiō and Waseda are more likely to become businessmen, writers, or newspapermen. Mitsui draws many of its bright young men from Keiō and Mitsubishi from Waseda.

There are also special training colleges for army and navy officers similar to West Point and Annapolis.

Education in foreign universities has been an important factor in Japanese education. In the past not only have some career diplomats spent a number of years in a foreign university, but the big industrial firms have often sent their younger men abroad for specialized training in engineering, chemistry, and other technical fields. For many years all promising biologists and medical students went to Germany for graduate training. Of recent years, however, the number of students sent abroad has declined; in fact the trend has been in part reversed, the Japanese government encouraging students of China and Southeast Asiatic countries to come to Japanese universities for study.

Girls' Schools

Except for elementary schools, which are coeducational, all the schools mentioned above are for men. There are, however, a fairly large number (996) of girls' high schools (*jogakkō*) attended by the daughters of wealthier farmers and most middle-class town and city girls. Here girls are given some higher education and much finishing in the form of sewing, flower arrangement and etiquette. In 1942, courses in English and French were being replaced by courses in home economics. Altogether about 454,000 girls were attending one *jogakkō* or another in 1938.

Educational opportunities for women in Japan are few as compared with those for men, and higher education of women has not been generally encouraged. There is some government and private provision for higher education, however, notably Miss Tsuda's School and the Peeresses' School, but these are pretty well restricted to the daughters of the noble and the rich. There are also two women's higher normal schools for teacher training. Under certain conditions girls may sit in on courses at the Imperial Universities. There are also a number of mission schools and colleges for women regardless of social rank.

Peers' School

A special educational institution outside the Department of Education is the Peers' School of Tokyo administered by the Imperial Household for children of the titled classes. There are three grades of instruction—elementary, middle, and higher courses. The number of students is less than a thousand and its role in shaping national leaders is not great.

The Peeresses' School, already mentioned, is for daughters of the titled classes and is also in Tokyo. It has an enrollment of a few hundred. Recently both the Peers' and the Peeresses' Schools have been opened to selected children of nontitled families.

Normal Schools

There are over a hundred teacher-training schools in Japan, and each prefecture is required to maintain at least one normal school for the training of elementary school teachers. In addition to the prefectural normal schools there are four national higher normal schools to train teachers of middle, university, and girls' high schools—two for boys (Tokyo and Hiroshima) and two for girls (Tokyo and Nara).

In 1937, there were 19,744 men students at the prefectural normal schools as against 10,512 women students and 1,787 men and 871 women in the higher normal schools. Schoolteaching is largely a man's profession in Japan as it is in Germany.

The Japanese schoolteacher usually takes his responsibilities seriously and develops a personal fatherly interest in his pupils— taking the class on special trips to visit famous places, calling on the parents of problem children, helping the slow-witted and encouraging the quick. In addition to his duties as a dispenser of knowledge he is also a representative of the government in the town or village to which he has been assigned and in such matters as national history and foreign relations he may be counted on to instill the proper patriotic attitudes. The loyalty of teachers to the Emperor has been demonstrated by more than one teacher who has lost his life in attempting to save the Imperial portrait from the flames of a burning school building.

The sharp drop in school enrollment after the elementary school level is due in part to the fact that examinations must be passed before middle and technical schools are entered and in part to the fact that free education is not provided beyond the elementary school level. In 1938, 11,793,000 pupils were attending elementary schools, but only 1,296,000, two thirds of whom were boys, were in middle schools or technical schools of comparable grade, and only 73,000 were in universities. This drop in attendance is mainly due to policy on the part of the Department of Education rather than to any lack of desire on the part of prospective students. In 1937, for instance, while 100 per cent of the applicants for primary schools and young people's schools (*Seinengakkō*) were accepted, only 60 per cent of applicants for middle schools and girls' high schools could get by the entrance examinations, and only 45 per cent of the applicants for universities, 32 per cent for normal schools, and 16 per cent for higher technical schools were accepted. The mortality in technical school applicants was doubtless partly caused by a shortage of facilities, a shortage the government has been taking steps to overcome in recent years.

Even with this great mortality among applicants for higher education there were before the war more college graduates in the cities than there were jobs for them to fill. The taxis of Tokyo which swarmed the streets in the 1930's each contained two young men—driver and helper, both of whom were often men of education. Yesterday's liability is doubtless today's asset since these men are probably useful to the nation in the field of mechanized warfare.

RECENT TRENDS

A criticism leveled against the school system in Japan before the war was that too many young men received a college education, especially in some of the private colleges of lower academic standing, and then could not find sufficient white-collar jobs. This unemployment of the highly educated became enough of a problem for various ministers of education to worry about, and a number of proposals were made to remedy it. Some of these proposals have been to (1) lengthen to eight years the period of compulsory elementary education; (2) reduce the number of higher schools and provide in them more vocational training to fit the graduates for adult life—thus students would come to regard the middle school more as a completion of education than simply a step toward the university; (3) reduce the number of years of schooling necessary to enter the university; and (4) reduce the number of private universities, especially those of lower standards.

Just before the war began the Diet passed a law lengthening to eight years the period of compulsory education, but up to 1945 this had not been put into effect. A number of revisions in middle school curricula have actually been made, however, and there has been an increase in vocational training. Recently the preparatory schooling necessary for university entrance was reduced by two years. It is more than likely that in the future the number of private universities will be reduced, and that students will be encouraged to attend their local government or Imperial Universities in order to avoid too great an enrollment in Tokyo.

The war has had a number of effects on the educational system. Increased attention to military training in the school curriculum is one of these; the growth in kindergartens, which were found only in the larger cities before the war, is another. With the drafting of women into war jobs, the national school system has paid more attention to the general field of "preschool" education. The war need for skilled and professional workers has led to a number of recent moves to increase opportunities for women in higher education, but a recent war measure suspending most higher education in the interests of war production may have offset this advance.

LITERACY AND JAPANESE WRITING

Japan's impressive array of schools has produced a high degree of literacy in its population—over 95 per cent—a remarkable achievement for so young a school system. Literacy, however, is a very difficult term to define. In countries using alphabets, a person who can read and handle twenty-six letters can usually read a newspaper; but two men, both able to read a newspaper, may differ widely in their degree of literacy. In Japan, the situation in regard to literacy is even more complex. There are two sets of forty-eight syllable symbols in current use, but once having mastered these two syllabaries, a child is still unable to read much more than a primary school reader or a telegram. To read a newspaper he must learn about two thousand characters or ideograms. On leaving elementary school a bright student may know two thousand characters, but the chances are that he will not, and if exposed to no further schooling for a few years the average country child, especially if a girl, may lose much of this limited knowledge. For this reason most newspapers and popular magazines run syllable symbols (*kana*) in small type beside the more difficult characters as an aid to pronunciation and understanding.

There have been sporadic but rather unsuccessful attempts to persuade the government to adopt Roman letters, at least in elementary schools, but there seems to be no prospect of this radical simplification in the near future. The whole weight of literary tradition is against such a simplification just as English literateurs hold up their hands in horror at the prospect of such minor simplifications in English usage as "thru the nite." It is not impossible that some elements in the government prefer the traditional system for the very reason that it does limit literacy and makes it more difficult for dangerous thoughts to be spread rapidly among the masses. There are reports, however, that the government found it necessary to compile a simplified series of characters for the teaching of Japanese in the regions of Southeast Asia which Japan invaded in 1942.

EDUCATION AND NATIONALISM

In the field of moral education the basic aim of Japanese educators is to produce a population at once literate and peaceable, a population with all the knowledge necessary to get along in the modern world, but not of such a nature as to question the ways of Japanese culture. Dangerous thoughts lead to dangerous acts.

The educational system is preponderantly a government-supported one and is well fitted to the purpose of dispensing knowledge in just the proper quantity and quality. The basic code for all Japanese educators is embodied in the rescript of the Emperor Meiji on education issued in 1890:

> Our Imperial Ancestors have founded Our Empire on a basis broad and everlasting and have deeply and firmly implanted virtue; Our subjects ever united in loyalty and filial piety have from generation to generation illustrated the beauty thereof. This is the glory of the fundamental character of Our Empire, and herein also lies the source of Our education. Ye, Our subjects, be filial to your parents, affectionate to your brothers and sisters; as husbands and wives be harmonious; as friends true; bear yourselves in modesty and moderation; extend your benevolence to all; pursue learning and cultivate arts; and thereby develop intellectual faculties and perfect moral powers; furthermore advance public good and promote common interests; always respect the Constitution and observe the laws; should emergency arise, offer yourselves courageously to the State; and thus guard and maintain the prosperity of Our Imperial Throne coeval with heaven and earth. So shall ye not only be Our good and faithful subjects, but render illustrious the best traditions of your forefathers.
>
> The Way here set forth is indeed the teaching bequeathed by Our Imperial Ancestors, to be observed alike by their Descendants and the subjects, infallible for all ages and true in all places. It is Our wish to lay it to heart in all reverence, in common with you, Our subjects, that we may all thus attain to the same virtue.

The strong emphasis on moral values as well as intellectual attainments embodied in this rescript is carried out in all Japanese education. Courses in ethics and morals are given in every year of a child's education from first grade to the last year of college. In an old nation whose patterns of social relations are well set, there is also a characteristic emphasis on proper relations—it is more important to cultivate "harmonious relations" than a selfish "personality."

When an official visits a school and gives a talk to the local inhabitants about economic reconstruction or taxation or any other subject, the talk is always linked with patriotism, with love of Japan and reverence for the Emperor. During the ten years before 1942, public speakers indicated a continuous crisis in the nation's affairs owing to suspicious foreigners, vicious Russia, unfaithful and insincere China. At the same time the people are endlessly told: "We are a peculiar people—descended from the gods and of superior flesh. Our Emperor comes down in one unbroken line for 2600 years. While other nations kill [Russia] or depose [Germany] their kings, we revere ours as our father."

Schoolteachers, as civil servants trained in government normal schools, owe their primary loyalty to the central government rather than to any particular region to which they may be appointed for a few years. As such they are well fitted to instill the nationalism which is so important a phase of Japanese education today. They tend to accept without question all educational directives issued by the Department of Education in Tokyo.

The emphasis of teacher and curriculum on ethics and character building should not becloud the essential fact that the Japanese school system is doing an efficient job of teaching the children of the nation to read and write, to learn something of world history and the rudiments of the natural sciences. As compared with all other areas of Asia and most of Europe, the average Japanese twelve-year-old is well educated. Furthermore, every effort is made by teachers and friends to see that a promising scholar gets a chance at higher education even though he comes from a poor family.

In the realm of higher education, also, the Imperial Universities maintain high scholastic standards. The inquiring mind is encouraged along lines of mechanical inventions, medicines, and bacteriology, and even into archeology and comparative religion. Inquiries into the origins of the present Japanese social order which might cause criticism of the Japanese form of government are definitely repressed as are similar researches in many other countries. Even fairly conservative speculations concerning political science and the role of the Emperor in the Japanese state may cause a professor of history or political science to lose his job if he comes to unorthodox conclusions. While original research in the social sciences has thus been hampered by government restrictions, that in the physical and biological sciences has not. Such research sponsored by Japanese universities and research institutes has been of a high standard, higher than many an Occidental is willing to admit.

Chapter VI

Mass Communications

ANOTHER aspect of the national social structure in addition to government, social classes, and the educational system is the large-scale system of mass communication which has grown up in modern Japan. The extensive facilities of radio, newspaper, and motion picture serve as important media for imparting information, providing recreation, and influencing the attitudes of the masses in regard to national policy and polity.

RADIO

Of these media the newest is radio. All broadcasting is under government control through the Japanese Broadcasting Corporation, which in turn is under the supervision of the Department of Transportation and Communications. This organization maintains two high-powered transmitters in Tokyo and Osaka and a number of smaller ones in other parts of the empire. About one person in fifteen had a radio before the war as against one in two or three in the United States and one in thousands in other parts of Asia. Most of the Japanese radio owners are city dwellers. There might be more domestic listeners if it were not for a monthly government fee of one *yen* required to operate a receiving set. Practically all sets are restricted to domestic broadcasts for to own a short-wave set requires a special license not easy to obtain.

This was true even before 1941 and may be regarded as part of the government's general policy of national thought control.

Domestic programs are free from advertising and a good deal of radio time is spent on educational features such as lectures and radio exercises, while entertainment programs and music take up less than a fifth of the broadcast time. All the usual Western radio features are present, however: stock market quotations, radio dramas, children's hours, women's programs, and both Western and Japanese styles of music, drama, and story. The difference is that in a women's program, for instance, the aim of a soap opera is not to sell soap but to promote national unity.

Although the home front cannot have short-wave radio sets, the Japanese government maintains extensive short-wave programs for overseas audiences. There are special programs beamed toward the United States, Manchuria, Southeast Asia, Australia. Over twenty languages and almost as many "propaganda lines" are employed, depending on the audience to be reached. When Japan acquired Malaysia these short-wave programs served as a valuable media for the dissemination of news and the promotion of political and cultural solidarity within the area.

NEWSPAPERS

As media of communication the newspapers and magazines are probably more important than the radio—more people read them and they contain more information. The total newspaper circulation before the war was about six million copies a day or one paper to eleven or twelve people. As in England, there are in Japan a few large newspapers with nation-wide circulation through branch printing establishments. The large newspapers of Tokyo and Osaka, several with circulations well over a million, divide the country roughly into two areas—the Osaka papers supplying the southern half of Japan and the Tokyo papers the northern half. The influence of these papers on the prefectures is increasing because of improved transportation and communication facilities and a broad news-gathering network. Most papers issue both morning and evening editions, and the cost is less than five *sen* for a four-to-eight-page paper. There were in all about two thousand daily papers being issued before the war.

The management of the newspapers is in private hands, there being nine large newspaper companies. About half their financial support comes through advertising while the other half comes from the selling of the papers themselves.

Such an important influence on public opinion as the press could scarcely escape some form of government control. Press censorship is within the jurisdiction of the Department of Home Affairs and is usually exercised through the police. The police are authorized to inspect the proofs of all newspapers and may suppress not only special items but may seize whole issues. There is strict censorship of all articles and publications "prejudicial to public order or good morals." This means that censors pay special attention to anything Leftist and to anything that smacks of lese majesty such as too direct criticism of the army or navy, or comments on the constitution. No military matters not included in army releases may be mentioned nor may criminal trials be reported before settlement. There are also special bans issued on the publication of certain information from time to time. Anything that smells of "dangerous thoughts," i.e., ideas likely to upset the present sociopolitical *status quo,* is also subject to censorship.

It is necessary for the management of any paper dealing with current politics to deposit with the authorities a security ranging from 750 to 2,000 *yen*, according to frequency of publication, to cover possible fines. Almost all popular newspapers have dummy editors who may be imprisoned in place of the real editor in the event the paper in some way transgresses the law.

Still another means of government control is through the semi-official news agency *Dōmei* which has a complete monopoly of foreign news and is the largest single purveyor of domestic news and photographs. The Cabinet Information Board, created in 1940, serves as the clearinghouse for all official news somewhat as does the Office of War Information in the United States, although army and navy officials still sometimes make independent statements.

Despite all these restrictions the press has considerable influence on public opinion and on government. Newspapers can sway mass opinion, especially in urban areas, and editors may whip up mass attitudes of hostility toward or friendship for certain countries in accord with national policy. Since the libel laws are less strict than in most countries, newspapers may mercilessly criticize individual political figures on a personal basis and through this device cast doubt on their policies. Even during the war newspapers have not hesitated in criticizing government policy, especially on the home front.

In addition to the regular Japanese press there have been a number of newspapers published in foreign languages, the four best known being the *Japan Advertiser*, the *Japan Times*, the *Japan Chronicle*, and the English edition of the *Nichi Nichi*. Until recently the *Advertiser* was an independent newspaper under American management and the *Japan Chronicle* under English, but they were forced to sell out to Japanese interests shortly before the war. The *Advertiser* was combined with the Japanese-managed *Times* and is still being issued as an English-language newspaper.

These English-language newspapers, especially the *Japan Chronicle*, which began its career under the protection of extraterritorial rights, have played their part in shaping Japanese attitudes. Because of the critical, self-righteous line toward the Japanese government taken by the *Chronicle* concerning faults known to exist but discreetly avoided in public prints, Japanese officials came to the conclusion that the foreign press and foreigners generally were habitually critical of things Japanese.

MAGAZINES

There are a number of popular magazines with circulations of over a million in Japan. Of smaller format than American magazines, they are more like a book in size and shape, often with five or six hundred pages in a single prewar issue. The appeal of these big circulation magazines is largely to women, and they contain stories and romances, pictures of Japanese motion-picture stars, articles on housekeeping and child care, popular articles on new developments in science, and foreign affairs. These magazines serve to broaden somewhat the mental horizon of the Japanese housewife and through the articles and advertisements they undoubtedly do much to arouse an interest in and desire for modern manufactured goods. The most popular of these serial magazines are *Fujin Club, King,* and *Shufunotomo.* For the intellectuals there are a number of "serious" magazines comparable to *Harper's* and *The Atlantic Monthly.* The most popular rural magazine is *Ie no Hikari,* a publication of the National Cooperative Association. Since 1941, most of these magazines have been considerably reduced in size and some have been eliminated altogether.

There is also a large volume of children's literature issued under the general supervision of the Department of Education including comic books and magazines all carefully graded for various age groups.

MOTION PICTURES

In the 1930's Japan was producing more motion pictures a year than Hollywood. Since 1937, when 2,500 different films were produced in a single year, there has been considerable retrenchment. Production is largely in the hands of two large combines, Shōchiku with 85 per cent of the field and Tōhō with 14 per cent.

Most of the films produced in Japan are for domestic consumption, though of recent years a number of special films of high technical and dramatic quality for overseas showing in East Asia and Malaysia have been made.

In 1938 an average of almost five visits annually per person to the motion pictures was reported as against six for Germany and thirty-one for the United States. There are no adequate figures for Asia, but attendance at motion-picture theaters is undoubtedly much greater in Japan than in any other area in East Asia or Malaysia. In general, motion-picture attendance is greater in cities than in rural areas and there are very few theaters in small towns and villages, films being shown from time to time in any convenient building or even out of doors.

The legitimate drama is an important mode of recreation in Japan and until 1933 attendance at plays was greater than that at motion pictures. Even in the motion-picture theaters a special "talker" or *benshi* used to help out at each showing, explaining the action of the film much as was done in old Japanese drama, but with the advent of talking pictures the *benshi* is being gradually displaced. Like Japanese drama, Japanese feature films are long, usually running over two hours.

In content, Japanese screen and drama often depict heroes and heroines who overcome personal desire for duty—duty in the form of loyalty to family, class, or country. At the same time, there is a characteristic Japanese appreciation of natural beauty reflected in the films. They often convey very well an atmosphere of nostalgia and homely domestic scenes—especially when the hero or heroine is in a foreign land. Japanese motion pictures often have unhappy endings and are liberal in their sentimental appeal, and so provide the spectator with an emotional catharsis. For the less sophisticated trade there are innumerable *samurai* thrillers comparable in blood and thunder to American Westerns.

The Department of Home Affairs exercises control of the

films just as it does over newspapers and magazines. In 1939 a motion-picture law was passed which placed not only negative censorship control in the hands of the government but also positive control over production and distribution of films in order to coordinate them with general government policy for domestic education and thought control. All scenarios must now be submitted to the Department of Home Affairs for approval before filming; all branches of the industry must have special permits to operate; and each program must have in addition to the entertainment feature an approved education film. All films to be shown to children under fourteen must have the approval of the Department of Education.

Despite the great domestic production, foreign films, especially American, were popular in Japan before the war and constituted about 20 per cent of the showings in urban areas. They were usually presented with original sound track and Japanese subtitles. These films were subject to double censorship—first by the customs office and then by the Department of Home Affairs. Such films as "King Henry the Eighth" are banned because of disrespect to royalty, and most love scenes in American films are heavily censored because kissing and embracing in public is considered indecent in Japanese culture.

American films have had considerable influence on Japanese ideas. They gave the general impression, in line with Japanese official propaganda, that Americans are luxurious, frivolous, and immoral, lacking in ethical values and a sense of duty. At the same time they created admiration for American material wealth and technology. Japanese students often picked up English words and American slang from the films as well as a taste for American jazz. These influences from motion pictures and other sources have resulted in the entrance into the Japanese language of a fairly large number of English terms and in the development of a Japanese jazz which possesses a character and appeal of its own.

LECTURES

The first public lecture as an educational device is said to have been made by the great innovator of the Meiji Era, Fukuzawa Yūkichi. Whether or not that is true there is no doubt that the lecture is today a much-used device for communicating information in both urban and rural Japan.

When regional or prefectural governors meet in Tokyo prominent government officials such as the prime minister address them; prefectural and national meetings of societies such as the Women's Patriotic Association, the Reservists' Association, or the Young People's Association are given numerous lectures by government officials. In many of the factories the employers provide lectures for their employees. In towns and villages throughout the country when some new policy is to be adopted the headman, the schoolmaster, and visiting government officials may all give lectures to the people at the schoolhouse or in some civic auditorium. In rural areas, especially, more reliance is placed on such oral communication than on the printed word. Lectures at the ground level also permit of questions and explanations to assist in clarifying the issues involved, serving as a valuable point of contact between the governors and the governed.

Lectures by government officials serve not only as a means of communication but also of indoctrination. On almost any occasion a lecturer may take it upon himself to discuss and praise Japanese foreign policy, history, and national spirit and to compare it with that of other nations. The lecture system thus serves as still another medium for strengthening national unity.

Public lectures being an important means of communication and indoctrination, they are also subject to government control. Every public talk, even of a political candidate, is subject to censorship by the police at least one of whom is always present.

Chapter VII

Family and Household

THE FAMILY

IN JAPAN, as in all countries, the basic social unit is the family. Where Japanese society differs from American is in the fact that the Japanese family group is usually larger and the network of rights and duties between the members is more clearly defined. The European family system as found in prewar France resembled that of Japan in many ways.

The Japanese family consists of the family head and his wife, the eldest son of this couple and his wife and children and any unmarried children of the head. Thus the "normal" Japanese family living in one household includes two elementary family units.

In addition to this basic or "immediate" family there is the extended family group consisting of the brothers and sisters of all male members of the house, and children of the family head who may have married or been adopted out. This extended kin group assembles on the occasion of weddings and funerals and may form a mutual-aid group in the event that one or another member needs assistance either in labor or in money.

Family ties are reinforced by emphasis on ancestral worship, i.e., maintenance of ancestral tablets, and Buddhist memorial services for deceased family members. Until the Meiji restoration only families of the *samurai* and noble classes used family names.

Farmers and workers legally and officially had only personal names and for identification were referred to by their occupation or place of abode. Every family today has its own name and its own crest, which is reproduced on the formal *kimono* worn by family members, and in wealthy families may be found on its lacquer ware and chests for clothing.

The family name is a very important thing in Japan, something to be kept always shining. In feudal times one of the worst punishments was for a *samurai* to have his house, i.e., his family name, extinguished, and today the fear of a bad record being placed in one's official record (*koseki*) is a serious matter even in poor families and those which have acquired names since Tokugawa times. It is a disgrace not only to one's own character but to the good name of the family, deceased, living, and yet to be born.

Rich and noble families have their own family codes governing the behavior of members, and all important decisions such as financial investments, foreign travel, and in some families even marriage and divorce are subject to the approval of a family council consisting of the older family heads of the chief and branch families, sometimes also including the widows of deceased family heads. Thus in the upper classes there is a family government by consultation and group decision.

The roles of the various family members are well defined. The male head of the house is the final authority within his family. His family rank is recognized by his being the first to be served at mealtime, the first to use the family bath, but not the first to arise in the morning. He is the sole owner of most of the family property and income and he dispenses money to the various members of his family as they may need it. The house head represents his family in dealings with outsiders and with the local and national government. While he has the various rights just outlined, he also has heavy responsibilities and must look to the prosperity of the house and welfare of its members.

The wife is mistress in her own house, being in charge of the servants, the household budget, and the family shopping. She is the one to look after the children's needs, and such family matters as preschool education and marriage arrangements. All domestic work is done by the wife of the head assisted by her daughters and maidservants. If the eldest son of the head is married, the daughter-in-law is expected to take over much of this work. Since the daughter-in-law is dominated by the older woman, friction may develop which in turn may lead to a divorce, especially in the early stages of a marriage. The wife does not get out of the home so much as her husband and in middle-class urban areas her social life is largely limited to family affairs and women's groups.

The eldest son, as heir to the headship, is usually trained in the occupation of his father, taught respect for the family ancestors, and inculcated with a sense of responsibility to fit him for succession to his father's estate and position. Younger sons must not only obey and respect their father but also their elder brother as prospective head of the family. On the other hand, their responsibilities are fewer and they have a freer choice of profession.

Daughters, lowest in the family hierarchy, learn the domestic arts from their mother and acquire attitudes of respect for their parents and brothers. In general, age rank is important, older family members having greater rights than younger ones and in turn having obligations to look after the welfare of younger brothers and sisters.

A family head and his wife when they reach the age of sixty may wish to resign as active members of the family and go into retirement. This procedure and state of retirement is known as *inkyo*. The retired persons may dwell in a separate room or even a separate small house free from the duties and responsibilities of running a family and household, participating only in family festivals, weddings, and funerals.

Social status in a community is dependent on family status. In an upper-class family the eldest son maintains the status of his father, but a younger brother who establishes a branch family has as a rule a somewhat lower social standing. A daughter's status depends ultimately on that of the man she marries and this in turn may affect that of the family into which she was born.

ADOPTION

The importance of the family name is reflected in the widespread custom of adoption. Through adoption the maintenance of the ancestral tablets is assured, as well as the continuity of the family itself.

If a couple have no son they solve the problem by adopting one, frequently a younger son of the family head's brother. If a couple have a daughter but no son, a son may be adopted to marry the daughter. Occasionally in the event of no children, but as a means of maintaining the family line, a daughter, often a niece, is adopted and then a son to marry her. Still another form of adoption is one whereby a man with no sons may adopt as a son his own younger brother who is fifteen or twenty years his junior. In business families, if the own son of the head of the firm does not take to commerce, a son may be adopted from among the more promising men in the firm.

The primary function of adoption is to insure heirs, but an associated function is to insure the prosperity and good name of the family; hence the prospective son is carefully chosen, frequently from among the children of one's relatives. Attention is paid to his character, his health, and his general aptitude. Since adopted sons have all the rights and privileges of a real son, adoption by a prosperous business superior or uncle provides a means of rising in the social scale.

Adoptions to be legalized must be recorded in the *koseki*. They may be dissolved if they prove unsatisfactory, a procedure which also requires a legal change in the *koseki* unless, as sometimes happens, the adoption has not yet been recorded.

The custom of adoption in Japanese society makes possible the maintenance of the family independent of the procreative powers of the parents. While family lines may die out from a biological point of view, adoption insures the perpetuity and stability of the family lines as institutions.

The basic family pattern here outlined is found in every town and village; furthermore, it is equally important among the upper classes and in other aspects of Japanese society. Big business houses are conducted on the basis of the head as a father to his employee; in the army older soldiers play the role of elder brothers to newcomers. The nation itself is conceived of as one great family with the Emperor as the head and benevolent father. During the push southward Japanese government spokesmen used the line that Japanese are the elder brothers responsible for the welfare of their younger brothers in Southeast Asia and Malaysia. These younger brothers, of course, owe the Japanese respect and gratitude in return.

The family also attempts to maintain its solidarity and there are in Japan, as in most countries, social and religious sanctions to maintain its integrity. The strong social and economic interdependence of the family members in Japan helps to give solidarity to the family and, through this, stability to the nation. Just as all three forms of social control are united in the Emperor on the national level, so they are again united in the individual family. The master of the household is the civil head and responsible for the good behavior of his family, as a reservist he serves to link his family to the army, and his religion serves to unite the family and the nation in common bond of respect for ancestors— he must not behave in any way to bring disrespect to them or to the family name.

HOME AND HOUSEHOLD

In an earlier day, and even today in rural areas, the important unit of a community was not the individual or even the small family but the household consisting of the immediate family, perhaps an old grandparent or two, and the family servants living together in the home almost as part of the family.

The house in which this household dwells is far more than a simple shelter. Often it has great age and character and always it is under the beneficent protection both of the ancestral spirits whose tablets are kept in some sacred alcove and of various kitchen and household deities to whom flowers or rice and tea are daily offered.

In its physical aspects the Japanese home varies greatly from the simple thatch-roofed house of a farmer to the elegant tile-roofed town and city dwellings with expensive interior woodwork and sliding screens decorated by talented artists. There are a number of basic traits of all Japanese domestic architecture—the houses are of plain unpainted wood with unimposing exteriors, usually of one story, sometimes of two, with a restful horizontal line predominating both inside and out.

The rooms of the house are measured according to the number of three-by-six-foot straw mats or *tatami* they contain. In the parlor or *zashiki* where guests are received, there is a special alcove or *tokonoma* in which is hung a scroll painting (*kakemono*) often set off by a simple-looking but carefully constructed flower arrangement proper to the season or the special occasion. In the *tokonoma* is often hung a picture scroll of the Emperor and of some Shinto or Buddhist deity.

The *tokonoma* is in the "upper" part of the room, the place where honored guests are seated. By observing which guests are seated by the *tokonoma* and which below, one can estimate their relative social rank. In small communities the mayor or headman and the schoolmaster hold high rank as do visiting dignitaries. Older male members of well-to-do local native families also rank high. It is good form to decline the host's first offer of a place by the *tokonoma.*

Sleeping rooms, smaller than the *zashiki,* contain no beds and when night comes, quilts are brought out of a closet and laid on the quiet resilient mats to form mattress and covers. In the kitchen, part of which is often dirt floored, may be found stoves, pots, and jars of various sizes containing supplies of pickled radish, soy bean paste (*miso*), and a kitchen sink of stone or metal-covered wood. In rural areas the stoves are usually brick, heated by wood or charcoal, in the towns oil stoves are coming into use, and in cities oil and gas stoves had tended to replace charcoal ones before the war. The stove is placed at the side of the kitchen away from the rest of the house, probably as an old safety measure. A poster saying beware of fire, given out by the firemen's association, may be pasted somewhere on the wall.

In rural districts, rooms are heated by a fire pit (*irori*) and portable charcoal heaters (*hibachi*). In cities, *hibachi,* oil, gas or electric stoves are used. A very popular heater in both rural and urban areas is the *kotatsu,* a lattice-like wooden structure placed over the *irori* and covered with a heavy blanket or quilt. People of all ages like to sit around this heater with their folded knees under the quilted covering. The fire pit and *hibachi* is the center of sociability, the source of heat for the ever-present tea kettle, and the place to relight interminably one's diminutive pipe.

The various rooms are separated by sliding screens which may be removed on special occasions, such as a wedding banquet, to double or triple the expanse of a room.

In rural areas there are separate outhouses for toilet and bath but in urban areas these are part of the main structure. Modern plumbing is generally lacking so far as the toilet is concerned, human excreta being used as fertilizer. In most cities this "night-soil" is collected regularly and sold to the farmers. Once when the Tokugawa were thinking of making a government monopoly of this business a local Patrick Henry proposed that, as a protest, the people cease production.

The Japanese bath (*furo*) has its own etiquette, often but poorly understood by foreign visitors. The usual time for the bath is in the early evening either before or after dinner. Before stepping into the deep and very hot water one is expected to wash and rinse oneself—the aim of the deep hot water being not to clean but to warm and relax one. After the guest has bathed, the head of the house may follow, then the wife and children and finally, late in the evening, the servants. In hotels and public baths, several people may occupy a large bath at once, talking and relaxing together in pleasant sociability.

At night wooden shutters are pulled to, to keep out both robbers and night air, and at an ungodly hour of the morning the wife or maidservant noisily opens them again.

Physical privacy is not obtainable in the ordinary Japanese dwelling and there is an accepted household etiquette to provide for privacy by proxy—one simply does not observe people under certain circumstances such as when they are undressed or otherwise not presentable. The closeness of home life, whereby small children are rarely left alone, may have something to do with the adult Japanese tendency to do things together and in groups.

MARRIAGE

Marriage in Japan, as in France, is primarily a family matter and marriages are made on earth to insure the future perpetuation of the family in its proper social class. The primary function of marriage is to provide for heirs to carry on the family name. Equally important is the establishment of an economically interdependent household unit whereby certain occupations are performed by the husband, others by the wife. The lone individual is at both a social and an economic disadvantage in such a society.

In accord with this situation whereby the social and economic functions of marriage so far outweigh matters of mere personal fancy, the individual does not take the initiative but rather awaits his family's decision as to a proper spouse.

Since the joining of two families in marriage involves many delicate issues of family background and financial status, great reliance is placed on a go-between or *nakōdo*. When, let us say, a young man's family feels that the time for marriage has arrived, the matter will be discussed with some family friend who may act as go-between. This man and his wife may suggest a number of suitable young ladies of proper social status, and finally, on the suggestion of the boy's parents, they will undertake marriage negotiations with one of these. The initial call of the go-between on the girl's parents will be of the most tentative nature, the subject of a possible marriage being suggested in passing. A good deal will depend on the initial reaction of the girl's family, and if they are opposed to the match, the whole affair may be dropped then and there with no loss of face to anyone concerned.

If all goes well, the go-between will continue his good offices and the girl's family may also find a friend to serve as their representative in the negotiations. In addition to working out the plans of the wedding itself, the go-betweens have the ticklish job of negotiating a suitable dowry, of investigating family backgrounds to discover whether or not there are any family skeletons such as leprosy, insanity, or tuberculosis, and whether there are any particularly evil crimes recorded in the family's *koseki*. All of this is work that by Japanese etiquette the families themselves could not do directly since it could all too easily lead to embarrassing face-to-face situations. The go-between, being a member of neither family, can smooth over any difficult situations that may arise.

The families concerned have definite obligations to the go-between. The bride- and groom-to-be must conduct themselves with propriety; if they were to act in any improper way before the marriage arrangements were completed the go-between would lose face by having his efforts nullified. Any direct contacts between two families during this period would also undermine the position of the go-between.

The wedding itself is strictly a family affair to which are invited many relatives of both the bride and the groom. The wedding ceremony proper usually takes place at the groom's home and consists of a ceremonial drink exchange of rice wine (*sansankudo*) between the bride and groom. The go-betweens and their wives are present at this ceremony, which corresponds in ceremonial sanctity to a church service in European countries. The ceremony is followed by a sumptuous banquet at the end of which the bride serves tea to the parting guests—a symbol that she is now the housewife in her husband's home.

In cities some families now have the wedding ceremony in a Shinto shrine according to Shinto rites but this is a post-Meiji development, weddings being traditionally a purely family arrangement. Another urban development is that of holding the wedding banquet in a hotel.

Legal registry of the marriage takes place sometime following the wedding and in rural areas there may be a lapse of many months or even a breakup of the marriage before such registry takes place. Usually the recording is done sometime before the birth of the first child to insure its legitimacy.

Shortly after the wedding the bride and groom call on the go-between with a gift, partly in return for his good offices and partly in return for his wedding gift. The duties of the marriage go-between do not cease at marriage. In the event of any difficulties between bride and groom he steps in as peacemaker, and, like a relative, he is invited to family affairs such as the naming of the first child or the funeral ceremony after a death.

The new wife now faces a difficult period of adjustment for which her early training in patience stands her in good stead. She must learn the many little customs of her husband's family, she must adopt his family's Buddhist sect, she must please her mother-in-law with her good housekeeping, and finally she must show herself to be a good mother. After the birth of a child, especially a boy, the new wife's status improves considerably, and the bonds of the marriage itself are greatly strengthened.

At marriage a girl symbolically leaves her family of birth, in some regions even being dressed in white *kimono,* and her name is blotted out of the *koseki* of her parents and entered into that of her husband. Despite all of this, however, a girl usually maintains close ties with her parents, going home the first New Year's after her marriage to visit them. If her husband or his family mistreats her, she may in extreme cases return home. If her parents are of as good or better social standing than those of her husband, the fact that an insult to the girl is also an indirect insult to her family serves to protect her interests.

In the event of a marriage by adoption the whole procedure is reversed—negotiations are initiated by the girl's family, the marriage takes place in her home and the husband takes her name and is blotted out of the *koseki* of his parents. The personal problems of an adopted husband are greater than those of a bride since he has not had the same training in patience.

A young woman who has a clandestine affair, even though she becomes pregnant, is not because of this fact likely to marry the man of her desire. He may be of the wrong social class and, furthermore, it would be difficult to find a man to sponsor such a match by acting as go-between since his role has been flouted by the couple in question. The usual fate of the unmarried mother is to marry somewhat below the social class of her birth and for her child to be adopted either by her husband or by some other family. Sometimes a couple may elope, with the result that both families are likely to disown them and so make life for the newlyweds most difficult—or the lovers may commit *shinjū*—double suicide.

DEATH

Death, with its wound to the well-being of the kin group, is an occasion for the whole family to forgather. Telegrams are sent to relatives far and near and all who are within range come to the home of the deceased as mourners. The Buddhist priest is called to conduct a funeral ceremony in which all the relatives, even including small children, participate by dipping powdered incense before the coffin.

The funeral ceremony is followed by a farewell meal at which the priest, as the visiting specialist, occupies the place of honor. The spirit of the deceased is not soon forgotten, for there is a series of seven ceremonies during the first forty-nine days after death during which strict mourning is observed, family members eating no fish and visiting no place of amusement. There is also a series of memorial services held at intervals during the next fifty to one hundred years. Thus the family pays its respects to its progenitors and possesses unity through the generations.

Chapter VIII

Religion

THE religion of a community of people may be defined as its body of sacred belief and practice. In most societies things of great social value to the community and the nation acquire religious values—food, birth and death, the changing seasons, war, and finally the nation itself as represented by a flag or an emperor. The religious system of a people may also include certain elements of ritual and belief acquired from other communities or nations, e.g., Buddhist beliefs and practices in Japan.

Religion in Japan is all-pervasive and no other modern nation has a greater dependence on sacred ritual and belief not only at the household and community level but also on a national scale. An American president may call on God's protection in a speech, and Congress is opened with prayer, but in Japan government-supported priests perform rituals on behalf of the nation regularly throughout the year. And the founder of the nation is more than a hero; he is a deity.

Most of the religion of Japan is covered by two familiar terms —Shinto and Buddhism. These terms are somewhat misleading since they imply on the one hand a clear-cut distinction between two religious systems which does not exist in the lives of many Japanese, and on the other include under a single term—Shinto —a number of distinct aspects of religious belief and practice.

SHINTO

Japanese Origin Myth

The earliest recorded use of the term *Shintō,* The Way of the Gods, is in an eighth-century document, the *Nihongi*, where it is employed to distinguish native Japanese religious practices from those of the newly introduced Buddhism. In its broadest sense Shinto may be interpreted to mean all native sacred beliefs and practices both old and new in contrast to introduced religions such as Buddhism and Christianity. Modern Shinto includes the characteristic sacred rituals and beliefs by which the Japanese celebrate, interpret, and support the chief values of their national life such as the seasons and agriculture, health and prosperity, patriotism and national unity. In actual practice Shinto includes three overlapping bodies of religion—State Shinto, Sect Shinto, and Popular Shinto. It also includes the Japanese myth of origin which must be described before taking up the three aspects of contemporary Shinto.

This mythological story of origin is to be found in the *Kojiki* and *Nihongi*, the two earliest Japanese books extant. It is on the basis of these texts that the Emperors claim descent from the Sun Goddess and Japanese patriots claim themselves and their lands to be divine descendants of the early gods. It was largely to establish the legitimacy of the contemporary reigning family and to secure the social position of the court nobles of the seventh century that the *Kojiki* and the *Nihongi* were compiled.

In the beginning a number of deities were born and "hid their persons," i.e., were never heard from again. Then there came into existence the primeval couple, Izanagi, the Male-Who-Invites and Izanami, the Female-Who-Invites. This pair was given a heavenly jeweled spear and commanded by the Heavenly Deities to "make, consolidate and give birth to this drifting land." So the deities, standing upon the Floating Bridge of

Heaven, pushed down the jeweled spear and stirred the brine below, then drew up the spear and the brine which dripped down from the end of it piled up and became an island.

Then Izanagi and Izanami came down from heaven to earth, erected a hall and a "heavenly august pillar." According to the *Nihongi* (as translated by Aston):

Now the male deity turning by the left, and the female deity by the right, they went round the pillar of the land separately. When they met together on one side, the female deity spoke first and said:—"How delightful! I have met with a lovely youth." The male deity was displeased and said:—"I am a man, and by right should have spoken first. How is it that on the contrary thou, a woman, shouldst have been the first to speak? This was unlucky. Let us go round again." Upon this the two deities went back, and having met anew, this time the male deity spoke first, and said:—"How delightful! I have met a lovely maiden."

Then he inquired of the female deity, saying:—"In thy body is there aught formed?" She answered, and said:—"In my body there is a place which is the source of femineity." The male deity said:—"In my body again there is a place which is the source-place of masculinity. I wish to unite this source-place of my body to the source-place of thy body." Hereupon the male and female first became united as husband and wife. . . .

Here is described the first and original marriage ceremony and here also it is established that in matters between a man and woman the man should take the active initiative role, the woman that of passive acceptance.

From this primeval marriage sprang many offspring both of islands and of deities, many of whose names reflect aspects of nature important to the people, such as Deities of Food, of Trees, and of Winds. Finally, in giving birth to the Fire God, Izanami is burned so that she sickened and lay down. According to the *Koïki* (as translated by Chamberlain):

So then His Augustness the Male-Who-Invites said:—"Oh! Thine Augustness my lovely younger sister! Oh! that I should have exchanged thee for this single child!" And as he crept round her august pillow, and as he crept round her august feet and wept, there was born from his august tears the Deity that dwells at Konomoto near Unewo on Mount Kagu, and whose name is the Crying-Weeping-Female-Deity. So he buried the divinely retired Deity Izanami on Mount Hiba at the boundary of the Land of Idzumo and the Land of Hahaki.

In grief and anger Izanagi now beheads his son the Fire God. Additional deities are born from the blood and body of the decapitated deity.

Thereupon His Augustness the Male-Who-Invites [Izanagi], wishing to meet and see his younger sister Her Augustness the Female-Who-Invites [Izanami], followed after her to the Land of Hades. So when from the palace she raised the door and came out to meet him, His Augustness the Male-Who-Invites spoke, saying:—"Thine Augustness my lovely younger sister! the lands that I and thou made are not yet finished making; so come back!" Then Her Augustness the Female-Who-Invites answered saying:—"Lamentable indeed that thou camest not sooner! I have eaten of the furnace of Hades. Nevertheless, as I reverence the entry here of Thine Augustness my lovely elder brother, I wish to return. Moreover I will discuss it particularly with the Deities of Hades. Look not at me!" Having thus spoken, she went back inside the palace; and as she tarried there very long, he could not wait. So having taken and broken off one of the end-teeth of the multitudinous and close-toothed comb stuck in the august left bunch [of his hair], he lit one light and went in and looked. Maggots were swarming, and [she was] rotting, . . . Hereupon His Augustness the Male-Who-Invites, overawed at the sight, fled back, whereupon his younger sister Her Augustness the Female-Who-Invites said:—"Thou hast put me to shame," and at once sent the Ugly-Female-of-Hades to pursue him. So His Augustness the Male-Who-Invites took his black august head-dress and cast it down, and it instantly turned into grapes. While she picked them up and ate them, he fled on; but as she still pursued him, he took and broke the multitudinous and close-toothed comb in the right bunch [of his hair] and cast it down,'and it instantly turned into bamboo-sprouts. While she pulled them up and ate them, he fled on. Again later [his younger sister] sent the eight Thunder-Deities with a thousand and five hundred warriors of Hades to pursue him. So he, drawing the ten-grasp sabre that was augustly girded on him, fled forward brandishing it in his back hand, and as they still pursued, he took, on reaching the base of the Even Pass of Hades, three peaches that were growing at its base, and waited and smote [his pursuers therewith], so that they all fled back. . . . Last of all Her Augustness the Princess-Who-Invites [Izanami] came out herself in pursuit. So he drew a thousand-draught rock, and with it blocked up the Even Pass of Hades, and placed the rock in the middle; and they stood opposite to one another and exchanged leave-takings; and Her Augustness the Female-Who-Invites said:—"My lovely elder brother thine Augustness! If thou do like this, I will in one day strangle to death a thousand of the folks of thy land." Then His Augustness the Male-Who-Invites replied: "My lovely younger sister, Thine Augustness! If *thou* do this *I* will in one day set up a thousand and five hundred parturition-houses. In this manner each day a thousand people would surely die, and each day a thousand and five hundred people would surely be born. . . ."

Thus mortality came to mankind. The story of the chase is a common folklore plot found in Europe and elsewhere, its inclusion in this cycle simply indicating that the compilers of the mythology have managed to amalgamate into a single narrative a number of incidents which were originally separate stories; perhaps the legends of more than one group of people in prehistoric Japan. The reference to the peach in this passage is interesting in view of the importance of the peach as a symbol of woman, fertility, and strength among the rural folk of contemporary Japan and as reflected in the popular tale of the Peach Boy, Momotaro, who overcomes demons and rewards his foster parents.

After this unhappy visit to the Land of the Dead Izanagi had to wash in a stream to purify himself. A number of deities were born on this occasion, the most important of which were Amaterasu ō mikami, born as he washed his august left eye; Tsukiyomi no kami, born as he washed his august right eye; and Susanowo no Mikoto, born as he washed his august nose. Amatersu is the Sun Goddess, contemporary Japan's most important deity and the divine ancestress of the Emperor; Tsukiyomi is the moon deity and is little heard from in the rest of the story, while Susanowo, a rough god of winds and storms, is often interpreted as the dynamic uncontrollable aspect of human nature.

Amaterasu, the Sun Goddess, was assigned to rule over the Plain of High Heaven, Tsukiyomi over the Dominion of the Night, and Susanowo over the Ocean. But Susanowo, true to his nature as a "Swift Impetuous Male Augustness," was dissatisfied and wished to meet his mother (Izanami) in Hades. Izanagi, angry at this, expelled him from Heaven but before going he visited his sister, Amaterasu. She, being suspicious of his motives, challenged him as to his purpose in coming and he replied that he came only to bid farewell. At this point they held a contest in creating more deities in which Susanowo claimed to be the winner. Then, "impetuous with victory" he broke down the divisions of rice fields, filled up ditches and strewed excrements over the dining hall of Amaterasu's palace. Like a true sister she tried to excuse all these offenses, but he continued his misbehavior, finally breaking a hole in the top of Amaterasu's weaving hall and dropping in a heavenly piebald horse which he had "flayed with a backward flaying." The weaving women were so frightened by this that they greviously injured themselves with their shuttles.

Shocked and angry, the Sun Goddess hid herself in a cave and the world became dark.

Hereupon the voices of the myriad Deities were like unto the flies in the fifth moon as they swarm and a myriad portents of woe arose. Therefore did the eight hundred myriad Deities assemble in a divine assembly in the bed of the Tranquil River of Heaven, and bid the Deity Thought-Includer, . . . think of a plan.

He then made arrangements for a special ceremony, calling for the making of an eight-foot string of curved jewels, a special mirror, the use of a stag's shoulder blade, and the sacred *sakaki* tree. Offerings were made and liturgies recited. Then as a climax a dance was performed by—

Her Augustness Heavenly-Alarming-Female hanging [round her] the heavenly clubmoss from the Heavenly Mount Kagu as a sash, and making the heavenly spindle-tree her head-dress, and binding the leaves of the bamboo-grass of the Heavenly Mount Kagu in a posy for her hands, laying a sounding-board before the door of the Heavenly Rock-Dwelling, and stamping till she made it resound and doing as if possessed by a Deity, and pulling out the nipples of her breasts, pushing down her skirt-string down to her genitals. Then the Plain of High Heaven shook, and the eight hundred myriad Deities laughed together. Hereupon the Heaven-Shining-Great-August-Deity was amazed, and, slightly opening the door of the Heavenly Rock-Dwelling, spoke thus from the inside: "Methought that owing to my retirement the Plain of Heaven would be dark, and likewise the Central Land of Reed Plains would all be dark: how then is it that the Heavenly-Alarming-Female makes merry, and that likewise the eight hundred myriad Deities all laugh?" Then the Heavenly-Alarming-Female spoke, saying:—"We rejoice and are glad because there is a Deity more illustrious than Thine Augustness." While she was thus speaking, His Augustness Heavenly-Beckoning-Ancestor-Lord and His Augustness Grand-Jewel pushed forward the mirror and respectfully showed it to the Heaven-Shining-Great-August-Deity, whereupon, more and more astonished, she gradually came forth from the door and gazed upon it, whereupon the

Heavenly-Hand-Strength-Male-Deity, who was standing hidden, took her august hand and drew her out, and then His Augustness Grand-Jewel drew the bottom-tied rope along her august back, and spoke saying:—"Thou must not go back further in than this!" So when the Heaven-Shining-Great-August-Deity had come forth, both the Plain of High Heaven and the Central Land of Reed Plains of course again became light.

This interesting incident, well known to all Japanese, gives a description of an early Shinto ceremony and also accounts for the origin of the sacred mirror and jewels which are now preserved as part of the sacred imperial possessions. The burlesque performance of the Heavenly-Alarming-Female is not too different from the dances at convivial banquets in parts of rural Japan even today.

Susanowo was punished for his sins but, nothing daunted, he continued his impetuous life and adventures. Finding a community where an eight-headed dragon yearly devoured a maiden, he undertook to kill the dragon. This he managed to do by feeding wine to all eight heads and then as they dozed in a drunken stupor, he cut them off. In the tail of the dragon he discovered a sword which, together with the mirror and jewels of the cave incident, form the three imperial treasures. He married a beautiful girl in connection with the dragon adventure and had, of course, more offspring. One of his descendants was Deity Master of the Great Land, who created other parts of Japan.

There are then recounted numerous other romances, adventures, and the begetting of various other earthly deities. The deities dwelling by the Tranquil River of Heaven are not satisfied with the conduct of these earthly deities and after a number of attempts to correct their ways, they finally persuade (with some force) the Deity Master of the Great Land to abdicate in favor of another deity approved (after considerable discussion) by the Deities of High Heaven. The new ruling deity, Ninigi no Mikoto, a grandchild of Amaterasu, the Sun Goddess, then descends to earth to take over the rule thereof. He is given to take down to earth with him the sacred jewels, mirror, and sword with the specific injunction to reverence the sacred mirror as if it were Amaterasu herself.

Ninigi marries a beautiful princess. Her father sends along her less beautiful sister also but Ninigi sends her back. The father, shamed and hurt, says:

"My reason for respectfully presenting both my daughters together was that, by sending Princess-Long-as-the-Rocks, the august offspring of the Heavenly Deity, though the snow fall and the wind blow, might live eternally immovable like unto the enduring rocks, and again that by sending Princess-Blossoming-Brilliantly-Like-the-Flowers-of-the-Trees, [they] might live flourishingly like unto the flowering of the blossoms of the trees: to insure this, I offered them. But owing to thy thus sending back Princess-Long-as-the-Rocks, and keeping only Princess-Blossoming-Brilliantly-Like-the-Flowers-of-the-Trees, the august offspring of the Heavenly Deity shall be but as frail as the flowers of the trees." So it is for this reason that down to the present day the august lives of Their Augustnesses the Heavenly Sovereigns are not long.

Ninigi's wife has two sons, Fire-Shine and Fire-Subside, who have a quarrel over fishhooks. Fire-Subside marries a Sea Princess and lives for some time at the bottom of the ocean. Later, becoming homesick, he desires to return home and his wife comes back with him. When she is about to give birth to a child she retires to a birth house, asking her husband not to look in on her, but, like the husband of Izanami, Fire-Subside does peep in and is horrified to see a crocodile writhing about. His wife, shamed to be seen thus, leaves her child, returns to her ocean home and closes the boundary so that ever since people of the sea have been separated from people of the land.

But even though she left her husband she could not fully restrain her longing heart and sent back to him a song. Her hus-

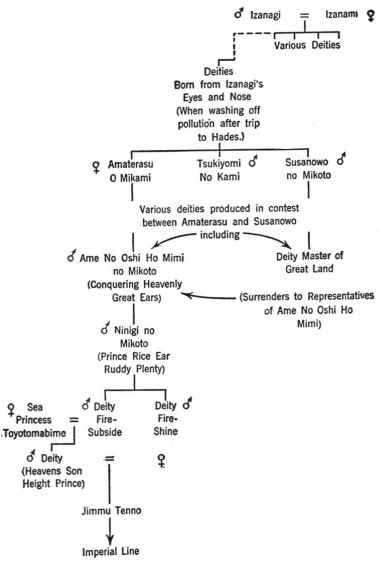

FIG. 9.—Summary Genealogy of Japanese Deities.

173

band replied with another song: "As for my younger sister, whom I took to sleep [with me] on the island where light the wild-duck, the birds of the offing, I shall not forget her till the end of my life."

The child born to the Sea Deity's daughter and His Augustness Fire-Subside, the son of Ninigi, who was grandson of Amaterasu, now marries and has children, the youngest of whom is His Augustness Divine Yamato Ihare Prince. This man, on his death, was given the name Jimmu, and is the first "historical" ruler of Japan.

Thus ends the Age of the Gods. The next book takes up the beginnings of history with Jimmu's conquests in Kyūshū (Tsukushi) and Southern Honshū (Yamato).

A Western reader, when first confronted with such a strange mythological story of origin, may regard its numerous deities and supernatural events as childish and naïve. But this story of origin, like most origin mythology of the world, serves to explain such fundamental matters as how heaven and earth came to be, the origin of man and the origin of death, i.e., it serves to explain the world as it is.

The names of the deities and some of their activities reflect the cultural values of the early Japanese: to break down the divisions between rice fields was a serious offense, hardly pardonable even in a god; childbirth was a private affair not to be witnessed even by one's husband, and contact with death was a pollution after which one must purify oneself. The ocean, the wind, the fertility of crops and of men all receive attention. The origins of most modern Shinto deities as well as of much Shinto ritual are traced by Shinto theologists to deities mentioned in the *Kojiki* and *Nihongi*. The Japanese story also accounts for the origins of the imperial line and the court nobility.

The Occidental reader in interpreting this story may gain perspective by bearing in mind that the European mythology of origin has its share of supernatural events: an August deity creating the world and man in six days, the first woman made from the rib of the first man, Lot's wife turning into a pillar of salt and his daughters making him drunk in order to commit incest with him to carry on the family line, the August Deities displeased with the activities of the Earthly Beings and causing a forty-day rainstorm, Jonah swallowed and regurgitated by a whale. Such "rational" interpretations of the Bible as the one that the story of creation in six days really represents six epochs find their parallels in similar interpretations of the *Kojiki* by Shinto theologians—for instance, that the story of Susanowo killing the eight-headed dragon really represents a conquest of eight tribes.

On the whole, Japanese mythology is comparable to that of the Greeks, the Plain of High Heaven resembling Mt. Olympus, and the afterworld to which people go after death being similar to the Greek Hades. And like the Greeks, the various aspects of nature, such as the sea, the wind, and the forest, have their special deities.

Modern Shinto theology is considerably more sophisticated than the *Kojiki* but depends upon it for its foundation. Ordinary people do not read these early books but they know the stories from them which are incorporated into public school textbooks. Attitudes taken toward the mythology itself vary considerably depending upon social and educational background. On the whole, there has been an increasing dogmatism concerning beliefs in the mythology as historical since the Meiji period, partly as a result of the revival of "Pure Shinto" and partly because the government at this time made a conscious effort to set up the divinely descended Emperor as the symbol of national strength and unity.

In general, then, it may be said that the Shinto myth of origin serves three main functions in contemporary Japan: to explain the nature of the world and of man, to enhance imperial prestige and through this central imperial line to give unity to the nation.

State Shinto

State Shinto is a relatively new phenomenon in Japanese history, having begun with the restoration of the Emperor and the revival of "Pure Shinto" in the nineteenth century. Just as the leaders of the nation looked about for new governmental and economic forms with which to replace the feudalism of the period of seclusion, they also groped for new religious policies. The Restoration had come into existence on the crest of an anti-Tokugawa, antiforeign, and anti-Buddhist wave. The Tokugawa were deposed, but the antiforeign movement had to be repressed for the welfare of the nation as a result of such incidents as the bombardment of Shimonoseki and the imposition of extraterritorial rights. Buddhism, being the favored religion of the Tokugawa, was in official disfavor so that the anti-Buddhist wave was not stopped so quickly, and for a period after the restoration earnest Shintoists in their zeal to separate Shinto from Buddhist influences burned temples, persecuted priests, and destroyed much sacred Buddhist art. Only after priceless heirlooms of the nation had been lost and the religious security of the common people had been badly upset did the new government realize that it was weakening the nation internally at a time when it needed all its strength to face the drastic changes coming from without.

As a result of trips abroad by Japanese leaders, and a number of rather unsuccessful governmental measures at home, a solution of the religious problem was finally reached. Private religious belief was declared free and this freedom guaranteed in the constitution of 1889. This meant not only the protection of Buddhism but also of any other religion including Christianity. At the same time, as a means of strengthening national unity and as an aspect of political control, all Japanese subjects were required to participate in shrine worship, and the story of the age of the gods and the Emperor's divine ancestry was to be taught in the schools. To keep within the letter of the new constitution this State Shinto was specifically defined as being *not* a religion and its priests were forbidden to proselyte.

Affairs of State Shinto—"not a religion"—were placed in charge of a Bureau of Shrines in the Home Office and all "religious" matters—Buddhism, Christianity, Sect Shinto—were placed within the jurisdiction of a Bureau of Religion in the Department of Education.

State Shinto was an outgrowth of the movement which led to the anti-Buddhist excesses immediately following the restoration. The aim of this movement, led by Shinto scholars, was to revive loyalty to the Emperor as against the *shōgun* and feudal lord. It also departed from the traditional Confucian ideals then in vogue, charging that Confucianism exaggerated filial piety at the expense of national loyalty. Shinto leaders, such as Motoori (1730–1801) and Hirata (1776–1843), stressed the importance of the Japanese tradition of respect for the Emperor and claimed that this had kept the country immune from the revolutions and changes of dynasty which often disorganized other countries, especially China. They stressed the importance of the *Kojiki* and *Nihongi* rather than the Buddhist sutras as sources of authority and placed great emphasis on the Sun Goddess (Amaterasu ō mikami) as founder of the state and ancestress of the Imperial Line. According to the doctrines of the new Shinto leaders, Japanese are, by virtue of their descent from the *kami*, braver, more virtuous, and more intelligent than other races of mankind and their divinely descended Emperor is destined to extend his sway over the entire earth. This nationalistic religious movement was doubtless in part a reaction to the serious economic dislocations occurring in feudal Japan resulting in a search for security in new absolutes. The further dislocating effects of the advent of Western powers on Japan's shores only increased the need for some such steadying doctrine.

In choosing Shinto, previously unorganized and neglected, as the state creed, the government chose something which fitted in well with the spirit of the restoration movement. Shinto possessed other advantages as a state religion: ancient sacred books, a broad base in folklore and popular belief, and finally, an emphasis on the superior position of the Imperial Family descended from Amaterasu. Shinto was the logical choice for an ideology to be fostered as a national unifying force.

In order to carry out its policy of propagating the new State Shinto, the government naturally turned to the schools. Since the constitution guaranteed religious freedom, religion could not be taught in state-supported schools, but since the official cult was legally declared not to be a religion, its teaching could be part of the curriculum on the same basis as civics or history. Furthermore, its rituals of patriotism in the form of bowing at shrines, and respect for the Emperor, could be required even of private schools —a requirement which caused constant conflict with Christian mission schools.

One of the first steps taken to organize the scattered Shinto shrines of the country on a national basis was to abolish the hereditary status of the Shinto priesthood in 1871. Priests were now put under the control of national, prefectural, and local governments for appointment and support. (Sect Shinto and Buddhist priests must depend on the contributions of their followers for their income.) The shrines of the nation were organized and graded into twelve groups. At the head stands the Ise Dai Jingū, the Grand Imperial Shrine of Ise in Mie Prefecture. It forms in itself the top class. The other eleven grades range from government shrines (*kampeisha*) with four subclasses, and national shrines (*kokuheisha*) with three subclasses, down through those of prefecture (*kensha*), district (*gōsha*), and village (*sonsha*). There is also a large group of some sixty thousand ungraded shrines (*mukakusha*) and beyond these are tens of thousands of small shrines not officially recognized. The government and national shrines are state supported, while the prefectural and local shrines are maintained by the local governments. While all the larger shrines have priests, many of the unranked and most of the unrecognized shrines have no priests and are looked after by local believers. Priests of the national shrines are appointed by the government under civil service regulations, those of the local shrines through local appointment subject to the approval of the Bureau of Shrines in the Home Office.

In line with the centralization of administration and reduction in the number of villages there has also been a reduction in the number of local village and district shrines. According to figures of the Bureau of Shrines (as given in Holtom's *National Faith of Japan*) there were 196,357 shrines in 1900 while in 1936 there were only 110,967.

Rituals and ceremonies to be performed in shrines have been set forth by the government with minute directions for all occasions. The Shinto priests or "ritualists" of the national hierarchy operate in a legally defined framework of grades and duties. Thus the Shinto organization parallels that of the political with the central government and Emperor at the top of a broad pyramidal structure made up of prefectural, district, town, and village units.

Shinto edifices are termed *jinja, jinsha,* or *miya* in contrast to Buddhist edifices which are called *tera. Jinja* is an official term, *miya* or *omiya* an older, more popular usage. The term *jinja* means "dwelling place" and *miya* "honorable house," thus the shrine is the dwelling place in which the deity (or deities) worshiped in the local shrine is supposed to live, or to be present when summoned according to Shinto ritual. These deities are termed *kami* in contrast to Buddhist deities who are termed *butsu.* Just as the Buddhist *tera* is a place where one may communicate with the *butsu,* so the Shinto *miya* is a place where one may communicate with the *kami.*

Shinto shrines and sacred places range from little wayside holy places, such as sacred rocks or trees, to the Grand Imperial Shrine of Ise. At the entrance of most Shinto shrines there is a gateway or *torii.* These *torii* are usually of plain unpainted wood, but some

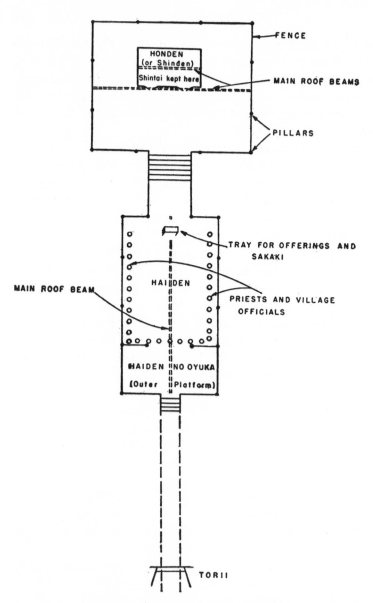

FENCE

HONDEN
(or Shinden)

Shintai kept here

MAIN ROOF BEAMS

PILLARS

TRAY FOR OFFERINGS AND
SAKAKI

MAIN ROOF BEAM

HAIDEN

PRIESTS AND VILLAGE
OFFICIALS

HAIDEN NO OYUKA
(Outer Platform)

TORII

FIGURE 10.—Plan of Shinto Shrine.

modern shrines have *torii* of stone or bronze and those before the popular deity Inari are painted red.

The shrine itself is usually of plain unpainted wood, elevated above the ground on pillars. The Great Shrine at Ise and most small village shrines have thatched roofs and projecting rafters, the whole effect being similar to that of certain Malaysian house types.

There are two main parts of the shrine—the outer less sacred *haiden* and the inner more sacred *honden*. Most rituals take place in the outer *haiden* with priests and officials participating. Ordinary worshipers simply clap their hands and bow before the entrance of the *haiden*. (See Figure 10.)

The inner sanctuary or *honden* is the holy of holies where only priests may enter. Here is kept the *shintai* or god body. This may be simply a stone or a mirror of little intrinsic value but great sacredness as the object in which the enshrined deity takes up residence. Most modern shrines as well as that at Ise have mirrors as *shintai*; other shrines may have such things as phallic emblems, sacred texts, ancient swords, spearheads, or jewels. No layman is supposed to touch or even look on these sacred objects and to do so is, according to popular belief, to risk being smitten blind or struck dead. As a rule there are no images in Shinto shrines.

On the occasion of some ceremony or festival the priest first prepares the shrine, perhaps a day or so ahead of time, by sweeping out the floor, cleaning the grounds, hanging up a sacred straw rope or *shimenawa* across the *torii* and preparing other ceremonial articles. At larger shrines ceremonial articles including a sword, a mirror, and a stone necklace—the three treasures—are exhibited. (The original three treasures, claimed to have come down from mythological times, are an essential part of the enthronement ceremonies and their possession is a prerequisite to imperial legitimacy.) Banners in the five auspicious colors (white, yellow, red, blue, and purple) may also be set up. Before any proceedings begin the priest purifies the shrine by waving a paper and hemp pompon called *nusa,* sometimes also scattering salt and bits of finely cut *nusa.*

Priests and local officials take their places in the *haiden* or outer part of the shrine, the priest purifies them all as they bow by waving the *nusa* over them thrice, the doors of the inner shrine are opened by the priest, and a prayer or *norito* is recited. Sometimes the priest utters a weird high-pitched cry which serves to "call down" the deities. Offerings of rice wine, fish and vegetables are now presented on a ceremonial tray. Another prayer is read, this time concerned with the matter in hand—a prayer for good crops, thanks for good harvest or the announcement of some special event.

Individuals in order of rank now perform a ritual before the altar. Each man presents a *tamagushi,* a small branch of the sacred tree (*sakaki*) with strips of white paper on it—after which he bows low and returns to his place. The presenting of the *tamagushi* is an indication of a pure and sincere soul. At the end of the *norito* and presenting of *tamagushi* the priest may "send back" the deities with the same call which was used to draw their presence. The doors of the inner shrine are now closed and on big occasions sacred dances (*kagura*) may be performed by priests to the accompaniment of flutes and drums.

The sacred rice wine (*omiki*), and even the food offerings, may be consumed by the participants after the chief ceremony is finished. The priest then removes his ceremonial robes, cleans up the shrine, and departs.

The numerous official ceremonies, all of which follow the general pattern just outlined, are attended by local officials, the schoolmaster, and one or two men of the community who serve officially as the people's shrine representatives (*ujiko sōdai*). The ceremonies are performed on behalf of, but are not participated in by, the community.

An exception to this series of formal official Shinto rituals is the local popular festival in honor of the gods of a particular shrine, which is participated in not only by the officials in the manner already described, but also by hundreds or even thousands of people, each of whom bows in turn outside the shrine and then goes on to enjoy the festivities of the day by participating in or watching wrestling matches and purchasing knicknacks from vendors who have set up their stalls for the occasion. On such important local festival days the deities may be carried through the streets and in the evening there are likely to be special sacred dances performed in the *haiden*. Such an annual local festival is an aspect of Popular Shinto in contrast to the more formalized and newer State Shinto. These popular festivals occur on different dates in different districts, but a good many of them occur in the fall after the rice harvest.

The official ceremonial days are legal holidays and are marked by ceremonies at all official shrines from the local village shrine (*sonsha*) to the Great Ise Shrine. Except for hanging out the national flag before their houses, farmers and fishermen usually go about their business as usual on these days, the holiday being observed officially by schools and administrative offices. Legal holidays are reckoned by the Gregorian calendar (new calendar —*shinreki*) in contrast to local holidays, including New Year's, which are still reckoned according to the old lunar calendar (*kyūreki*) in rural regions. These legal holidays, twelve in number, are divided into two classes—fete days and grand festival days as follows:

I. Fete Days (*Shuku-jitsu*)
    (1) Jan. 1, New Year's Holiday (*Shin-nen*). Early morning worship in the four direction (*Shihōhai*) at the shrines of the Imperial Court and elsewhere.
    (2) Jan. 5, New Year's Holiday (*Shin-nen*). New Year's Banquet (*Shin-nen Enkai*) at the Imperial Court.
    (3) Feb. 11, the Anniversary of the Accession to the Throne of Emperor Jimmu (*Kigen Setsu*), more recently called

Kenkokusai, i.e., Emperor Foundation Day). Special services at the three shrines of the Imperial Court.

(4) April 29, The Emperor's Birthday (*Tenchō Setsu*). Services conducted by the Emperor at the three shrines of the Imperial Court.

(5) Nov. 3, The Festival of Emperor Meiji (*Meiji Setsu*). Devoted to the commemoration of the great achievements of the Meiji Emperor and of the Meiji Era. Special services at the Meiji Shrine and in all schools.

II. Grand (Religious) Festival Days (*Daisai-Jitsu*)

(1) Jan. 3, Festival of Sacrifice to the Origin (*Genshi Sai*). Shinto ceremonies of thanksgiving to the ancestors conducted by the Emperor at the three shrines of the Imperial Court. Similar ceremonies at the important shrines of the country.

(2) March 21 (approximately), The Festival of the Vernal Equinox (*Shunki Kōrei Sai,* lit., Spring Season Imperial Spirit Festival). The Emperor worships the spirits of the Imperial Ancestors at the Kōrei Den (Imperial Spirit Sanctuary) of the Imperial Palace.

(3) April 3, The Anniversary of the Death of the Emperor Jimmu (Jimmu Tennō Sai). The Emperor worships the spirit of Emperor Jimmu at the Kōrei Den of the Imperial Palace.

(4) Sept. 21 (approximately), The Festival of the Autumnal Equinox (*Shūki Kōrei Sai,* lit., Autumn Season Imperial Spirit Festival). The Emperor worships the spirits of the Imperial Ancestors at the Kōrei Den.

(5) Oct. 17, The Festival of Presentation of First Fruits (*Kanname Sai*). The first fruits of the new harvest are presented as offerings at the Grand Imperial Shrine of Ise. Similar services at the important shrines of the nation. The Emperor performs distant worship (*yōhai*) toward Ise.

(6) Nov. 23, Autumn Thanksgiving Festival (*Niiname Sai,* The Festival of New Food). The Emperor worships the

deities who have given the harvest and partakes of the new rice crop. Similar ceremonies at all important shrines.

(7) Dec. 25, The Anniversary of the Death of Emperor Taishō, Father of the Reigning Emperor (*Taishō Tennō Sai*). The Emperor worships the spirit of his father at the Kōrei Den.

The ritual prayers or *norito* recited by Shinto priests at these ceremonies are in archaic style and form a part of Japan's oldest literature. Since the restoration they have been standardized by law, certain ones to be used on certain occasions and not to be altered by local priests. The content of the *norito* are concerned with such matters as a desire for abundant crops, thanksgiving for harvest, prayer for a unified and prosperous nation, for a long and glorious Imperial Reign. There are also special prayers for the announcement to the gods of important affairs of state—victory in war, conclusion of peace treaties, new accessions to the throne.

Ordinary worshipers at Shinto shrines simply wash their hands and sometimes rinse their mouths at a near-by stream or at a sacred font in the shrine grounds, approach the *haiden*, throw a copper toward the offering box, clap hands, bow a moment, clap hands again, and retire. Some shrines have a bell which may be rung by pulling a rope hanging from it. Hand clapping and bell ringing serve to announce the beginning and ending of the ritual just as do the calling down and sending back of the gods by the Shinto priest in his more elaborate ritual.

It is possible to worship at a distance. On arising in the morning some people clap hands and bow in the direction of the Emperor's palace. Similarly, one may worship Amaterasu ō mikami or one's district shrine at a distance.

Shinto ritual lays great stress on cleanliness and purity. *Oharai,* or purification ceremonies, are performed at the commencement of all ceremonies, and worshipers must cleanse themselves by washing before entering the shrine. Death and blood are regarded as contaminating influences and it was for this reason that Shinto priests traditionally performed no funeral ceremonies, leaving such matters to the Buddhists. Today members of Shinto sects may be buried by the rites of their sects and there has been developed a special Shinto burial rite, but funerals are still for the most part a concern of Buddhism. Another reflection of the taboo on blood is the rule that a menstruating woman must not visit Shinto shrines, or if she must make a visit, she should avoid passing under the *torii* when entering the shrine grounds. Traditionally Shinto priests did not participate at wedding ceremonies, these being purely family affairs, but since Meiji a wedding ritual has come into existence and city people are often married according to Shinto rites.

The most important shrine in the country is that of Dai Jingū at Ise in Mie Prefecture. This is the great national shrine of Amaterasu ō mikami, the Sun Goddess, and Toyo uke hime-no-kami, the food goddess. Thousands of pilgrims visit it annually and have done so for centuries. Thus it is a living part of Popular Shinto as well as the principal shrine of modern State Shinto.

The shrine itself consists of a number of buildings, built of plain wood and constructed in archaic style. The structure is rebuilt every twenty years, the wood from the old building being cut into small pieces and sold as protective charms.

On important occasions the Emperor, as chief priest of the nation, visits Ise and performs rituals at Dai Jingū. Any important event such as an earthquake, a declaration of war, or a treaty is announced to the Sun Goddess by the Emperor. Government officials frequently make special (and well-publicized) visits to Ise.

Each New Year's orthodox Shinto calendars and special paper talismans called *taima* are distributed to the people of Japan through the local Shinto shrines. The *taima* are put on the Shinto shelf or *kamidana* in each home.

Yasukuni Shrine, one of the most honored shrines in the country, enshrines the souls of dead soldiers and sailors. In Meiji days a shrine was erected in Kyoto for the spirits of those who died for the Imperial cause beginning in 1853. Later this was transferred to Kudan Hill in Tokyo and in 1897 received its present name of Yasukuni Jinjia or Country Protection Shrine. Here the souls of all soldiers and sailors who die overseas in the service of their country are enshrined and a grand festival is held in their honor each year on October 23.

Yasukuni is a good example of the way in which the state has resuscitated or developed special shrines to attain particular objectives in line with national solidarity and devotion to the Emperor. Yasukuni, of course, serves to stress the glory of death in defense of the Emperor.

A third shrine of great national importance is Meiji Jingū, where are enshrined the souls of the Emperor Meiji and his consort. In addition to its veneration because of the great esteem in which the memory of Emperor Meiji is held, the outer garden of the shrine has an athletic ground and is a center of numerous government-sponsored activities for young men.

There are many other shrines of special importance to the nation, but for the mass of the people the important shrine is their local village or town *omiya* wherein are enshrined the patron deities of their community.

State Shinto and National Solidarity

The primary aims of State Shinto are to secure support for the state, create national solidarity, and give strength and stability to the nation in the face of political and social change. Whereas the Tokugawa stressed a feudal and social class *status quo* as a means of maintaining social stability, the modern government stresses the Emperor's central position, and an orthodox history to gain the same ends.

From childhood the Japanese are taught that proper attitudes and usages connected with Shinto shrines are a prerequisite of good citizenship. The whole body of State Shinto is stressed in the school system to provide a basis for "national morality." The constitution in Article I says: "The Empire of Japan shall be reigned over and governed by a line of Emperors unbroken for ages eternal" and in Article III: "The Emperor is sacred and inviolable." Thus one of the central themes of State Shinto is written into the constitution itself. Another important official document stressing similar ideas is the Imperial Rescript on Education.

Such legal postulates make it necessary for the schools to emphasize the historic rather than the mythological nature of the early records concerning Amaterasu and Jimmu Tennō and the early story of the founding of Japan. School textbooks present genealogical tables to show the origin of the present Imperial Line back to and including Izanagi and Izanami, but greatest stress is laid on Amaterasu ō mikami as the original ruler of Japan and ancestress of the Emperor.

Jimmu Tennō's advent in Kyūshū is officially dated as February 11 of 660 B.C., the year 1 of Japanese chronology. (Objective history places this date about six centuries later.) The story of the age of the gods, somewhat bowdlerized, is also given to school children as history. The children are told that in a remote period of Japanese history, some three thousand years ago, the Sun Goddess appeared among men as an actual human being of lofty character and conferred great blessings on the people over whom she ruled. The beginnings of the Japanese state, founded on the principle of divine imperial sovereignty, may be traced back to her express commands. Her worship at Dai Jingū by the Imperial Government serves as an example of the reverence to be paid to Amaterasu.

The implication of this "history" is that the Japanese are one people, united through descent from the *kami* and ruled by a single ruling family for ages eternal. Unlike other countries, Japan does not have revolutions against her divinely descended rulers. The nation is one great family with the Emperor as the head.

Such is the orthodox national patriotic belief. It should be remembered that few intellectuals in Japan are truly orthodox, and such an authority as Sir George Sansom has testified that he has never met a Japanese who believed he was divinely descended. Truly orthodox individuals no doubt exist, but they are pretty largely restricted to the priesthood. The power of State Shinto doctrine lies not in its supernatural aspect but in its elements of historic truth—Japan's long national history, single imperial dynasty, and ethnic unity.

Sect Shinto

A manifestation of the renewed interest in Shinto during the Meiji period was the development of a number of Shinto sects, a movement corresponding to the growth of Buddhist sects some centuries earlier. The government, in its revival of "Pure Shinto," had not counted on this growth of sects and was a little embarrassed by them. The eventual solution has already been mentioned: i.e., that State Shinto was declared to be not a religion and so was subject to government propagation in the schools, while sect religions—Buddhist, Christian, and Shinto—were a matter of individual religious belief (and as such were not to be taught in the schools). Like Buddhism, Sect Shinto is within the jurisdiction of the Bureau of Religions of the Department of Education. The government has also carefully restricted the use of certain terms, such as *jinsha* for shrine, to official Shinto, and has even suppressed certain sects regarded as dealing too freely with sacred ancestors of the Emperor.

Shinto sects were for the most part founded by individual leaders, often on the basis of revelation in dream or vision. Deities selected for special veneration are usually from the orthodox Shinto pantheon and most of the ritual is similar to that of regular Shinto. Shinto sects differ from State Shinto and resemble Buddhist sects in that the followers form a definite and exclusive church—i.e., the members of a particular sect do not participate in activities of another sect either Buddhist or Shinto. The priests (or priestesses) give lectures or sermons at church meetings and the sect membership may engage in social welfare work and overseas mission work. Faith healing is a dominant interest in several of the sects just as it is in some forms of Popular Shinto noted below. In their ornateness the church buildings sometimes have more resemblance to Buddhist temples than to Shinto shrines.

The number of sects now officially recognized is thirteen but there are also numerous subsects. The total number of sect members is over seventeen million (as against forty-two million members of Buddhist denominations). The membership in the thirteen recognized sects as of 1937 (as given by Holtom in his *National Faith of Japan*) is as follows:

1.	Tenri Kyō	4,312,383
2.	Taisha Kyō	3,365,955
3.	Mitake Kyō	2,051,546
4.	Shinri Kyō	1,503,076
5.	Honkyoku	1,268,430
6.	Konkō Kyō	1,092,046
7.	Shinshū Kyō	777,117
8.	Taisei Kyō	727,918
9.	Kurozumi Kyō	563,407
10.	Fusō Kyō	555,111
11.	Shūsei Ha	408,683
12.	Jikkō Kyō	407,839
13.	Misogi Kyō	343,008
	TOTAL	17,376,519

These sects may be classified into five main categories.

(1) Pure Shinto Sects (Honkyoku, Shinri Kyō, and Taisha

Kyō) which stress the traditional Shinto forms of Old Japan. Their priests are conservative and stress loyalty to the Emperor after the manner of Hirata and Motoori. They insist that Shinto is a religion and resent the governmental efforts to deny the religious nature of State Shinto.

(2) Confucian Sects (Shūsei Ha and Taisei Kyō) whose theology has a definite Confucian character. Their leaders stress the stabilizing influences of Confucian doctrine, and point out the Confucian elements in Japanese institutions and in such documents as the Imperial Rescript on Education.

(3) Mountain Sects (Jikkō Kyō, Fusō Kyō, and Mitake Kyō) which have as their center of worship sacred mountains such as Mount Fuji. Mountains are traditional dwelling places of the deities and the objects of pilgrimages in Japan so that these sects are built on concepts deeply imbedded in popular tradition.

(4) Purification Sects (Shinshū Kyō and Misogi Kyō). Ritual cleanliness is a characteristic of all Shinto but becomes a central theme in these two sects, which lay stress on both mental and physical purity.

(5) Faith-Healing Sects (Kurozumi Kyō, Konkō Kyō, and Tenri Kyō). Tenri Kyō and Konkō Kyō are two of the most popular sects in Japan. They are also the two Shinto sects most active in propagating their faith through overseas missions. Tenri Kyō in particular, founded by a woman, has often been compared with Christian Science as to its essential doctrine (the teaching of divine reason), the nature of its appeal (man should attain a full free life abounding in health and happiness), and in its rapid growth.

In general the Shinto sects emphasize sincerity and purification in their followers, though they appeal to many largely through faith healing. All of them are built on concepts old in Japanese culture—ritual purity, healing through faith or incantation, and sacred mountains. Some of the larger sects such as Tenri Kyō also undertake religious education and social welfare activities and find a large following in some of Japan's industrial centers. About a third of their teachers are women, and most of their more active members are women. Through activity in a Shinto sect, as in a Buddhist or Christian sect, Japanese women find a means of self-expression lacking in State Shinto rituals and in traditional Japanese social forms. With the gradual decline of Buddhism as a dynamic religion the Shinto sects form today one of the most active religious forces in Japan.

Popular Shinto

All Japanese are affected by State Shinto, and seventeen to eighteen million are members of Shinto sects, but this does not exhaust the field of Shinto belief and practice. There are a great many local shrines and unofficial Shinto priests connected with local deities and sacred places. In addition many people put faith in sacred paper charms, in popular household deities, and in various other traditional Japanese sacred beliefs and practices. All of these beliefs and practices taken together may be classified as Popular Shinto. Elements of Popular Shinto are also to be found in both State Shinto and Sect Shinto, for both these newer forms have developed from the broad traditional base of Popular Shinto.

The local Shinto shrine which is a unit of the state system is also the central point for a number of popular beliefs and practices. It is popularly supposed that the souls of dead Shinto priests and others dwell within the shrine grounds. The deities form the *uji-gami* or patron deities of the township, and in the annual shrine festival in their honor most of their "children" participate. It is to the local shrine that a mother brings her month-old child for a private ceremony by the priest and it is in the precincts of a shrine that certain black magic may be performed by a jealous woman against her rival. On a national scale, beliefs in regard to Ise Shrine are as much a part of popular belief as of State Shinto.

Regular Shinto priests may be called upon to perform many

special rituals outside the confines of the shrine such as a "purification" of land on which a house is to be built and ceremonies at the completion of a public bridge or building to insure the welfare of the users. These and many other Shinto rites are concerned with appeasing spirits of land, sea, or air who may be upset by some work of man.

Local shrines outside the state system often have special priests of their own, the most popular being shrines of Inari. Indeed the Inari cult, if organized, could easily become a Shinto sect. Inari shrines are characterized by red *torii* and replicas of the fox, the messenger of the deity Inari, sitting outside the shrine. The priest or priestess is usually someone who has had a vision involving a visit from a fox as a messenger of Inari commanding him to build or look after a shrine of Inari. This deity is regarded as a god of prosperity and of good crops, and as such he is very popular both in villages and in towns. Inari is also the patron deity of *geisha* and of prostitutes; hence a small shrine in his honor may be found in every *geisha* house and brothel of the nation, the girls praying to him for good fortune and patronage. Small-town Inari priests are often faith healers with both regular and occasional followers who make gifts to the shrine in return for prayers to the deity offered by the priest. The festival day of Inari is the first day of the horse in the second month, at which time Inari priests hold special ceremonies.

Other popular deities worshiped at local shrines include Tenjin and Hachiman. Tenjin is a deification of the scholar Sugawara Michizane (845–903), who was exiled from the court because of intrigue, but who continued loyal to his Emperor. He is especially a deity of scholars and schoolboys. Hachiman is popularly believed to be a deification of the Emperor Ojin and is today regarded as a deity of war. Hachiman shrines frequently receive special governmental attention and their festivals are encouraged as a means of maintaining admiration for warriors. Here again State Shinto and popular beliefs overlap.

Each region of Japan has its own sacred mountain, Mount Fuji being the most famous, to which people make pilgrimages and on which are erected shrines to the local mountain deities. Many other animistic beliefs exist among the country people. Rivers have river gods, rather dangerous spirits likely to cause drownings in time of flood; curiously shaped trees or rocks inevitably receive some ritual attention.

At nearly every Shinto shrine which has a priest one may obtain for a few *sen* protective charms and paper talismans. A common type is a *fuda* or paper slip bearing on it the name of the shrine which gives the owner general protection. The purchaser may paste one or more on a pillar by his doorway. Others, *mamori,* often consist of small objects wrapped in white paper and stamped with the shrine seal. *Mamori* are often for such specific things as easy child delivery; they may be given by loving mothers and sisters to soldiers going overseas. Charms may also be pasted on barns to protect the health of livestock or put on a stick in the fields to protect the crops. The *taima* issued by the Great Shrine at Ise form an example of such talismans being issued on a national scale. Charms are thus associated both with Popular Shinto and with State Shinto.

Finally, in rural areas, there are beliefs in bewitchment and black magic. Bewitchment usually occurs as a result of jealousy or envy and is generally performed by means of a dog spirit (*inugami*) or cat spirit (*nekogami*). The person bewitched may fall ill, or become possessed and act like a dog, going about on all fours and barking; he may even die. A person believed to be bewitched may be cured by an Inari or other healing priest, who exorcises the evil spirit through the intercession of his patron deity. Persons believed to be witches (*inugami mochi*) are generally older people, often women. Sometimes the evil dog spirit is associated with a particular household, so that witchery passes down from mother to daughter-in-law.

A less-feared form of bewitchment is that of foxes, who are

believed to have supernatural qualities. Foxes cause mischief, may make a man lose his way in the woods, or bewitch him by taking on the form of a beautiful woman. Beliefs in regard to foxes are more in the realm of folklore than actual living experience, but this is not true of willful bewitchment by means of the dog spirit, an event to be seriously reckoned with among the less sophisticated.

In addition to the series of legal holidays celebrated in State Shinto there is a series of seasonal holidays celebrated by and participated in by the people. In rural areas this is still done largely according to the lunar calendar. Such festivals are marked by the making of special foods and often by the observance of a number of special rituals. Most of these festivals are concerned with things of social value to the community, including the celebration of the seasons as such—the coming of the New Year, of spring, and of autumn—which are important to people who live by farming and are dependent on the weather for prosperity.

The most important of the seasonal celebrations are New Year's, Girl Day and Boy Day, Bon, the annual festival of the local shrine, and the Moon Festival. In addition there are many local regional festivals, often on the fifteenth of the lunar month, i.e., at the time of the full moon.

New Year's is the most important festival of the whole year, and in normal times people celebrate it for at least three days. Before the end of the old year all old business, including debts, must be cleared up so that on New Year's Day everything may begin anew. People take ceremonial first baths, eat ceremonial first food, drink ceremonial first wine. The gateway of the house is decorated with pine and bamboo, symbols of longevity, and over the doorway is placed a citrus fruit (*yuzu*), ferns, and rice straw, and occasionally a bright red lobster, traditional New Year decorations. During the holiday period relatives call on one another, and there are many banquets.

Girl Day and Boy Day are primarily family festivals. Girl Day is celebrated on the third of March, especially by families who have had a daughter born to them during the past year; Boy Day, the fifth of May, is celebrated especially by families who have had a son born to them during the past year. The families concerned invite relatives to a small banquet, the relatives in turn send gifts for the occasion—girl dolls for girls and dolls of national heroes for boys—which are placed on display in the *tokonoma* during the celebrations. In addition banners and paper carp are flown on Boy Day. The carp is a symbol of courage and energy because it swims upstream, overcoming great odds to attain its objective.

The Moon Festival is the fifteenth of the eighth month in honor of the moon. Special offerings are made to the moon and special local customs mark the occasion, such as the making of giant straw sandals to be put by some near-by sacred stone and ritual tugs of war between the young people of different hamlets. These moon festival activities of young people are today about as serious as Hallowe'en activities in the United States.

There are also a number of popular Buddhist festivals, such as Bon, as noted later. Both the festival calendar and the daily household religion of most Japanese is neither Shinto nor Buddhist but a combination of both, stressing family ties, community solidarity, changing seasons, aspects of nature of social value, and finally, through state ceremonies, national unity.

Those aspects of Shinto in which the masses of the people actively participate are the Sect and Popular forms, while the governmental "nonreligious" Shinto, consciously used to mold the national attitudes of the people in something new, more the concern of officials and schoolteachers than of farmers and workers, and of men rather than of women.

Farmers, both men and women, place considerable faith in local faith-healing doctors or priests, both Shinto and Buddhist, as well as in the protective powers of the local patron deities (*ujigami*). The college-educated might smile at these practices, yet he would not hesitate to bow before a shrine or before the Emperor's portrait any more than would the average American hesitate to remove his hat when the national flag goes by in a parade.

Shinto, then, includes a wide variety of beliefs and practices— national religio-political dogma, dynamic churches or sects, and a vast body of popular beliefs and practices surrounding local patron deities, deities of agriculture and prosperity, and cere- monies marking changes of season. Ancestor worship also plays a part, but a limited one, in the form of prayers to the imperial ancestors and for the welfare of the Emperor as the father of his people. In particular, the distinction between State Shinto and Sect Shinto should be kept in mind in view of the possibility of a postwar abolition of State Shinto. If this were to occur it would not necessarily mean an abolition of Sect Shinto or Popular Shinto any more than the abolition of State Catholicism at the time of the French Revolution meant an abolition of private churches and popular Christian practices in republican France.

BUDDHISM

History in Japan

In 552 A.D. the ruler of Pakche in Korea, desiring the military assistance of Japan, sent as a special gift to the Emperor of Japan an image of Buddha together with some sacred texts. Court offi- cials were divided as to the advisability of adopting this new religion, so that it was decided that the Soga family, which advo- cated its adoption, should take and worship the image of Buddha as an experiment. No sooner was this done than a pestilence broke out and Soga's political rivals who had opposed Buddhism, arguing from cause to effect, gained the Emperor's permission to burn the temple and dump the image into the Naniwa canal.

Despite this unhappy beginning, Buddhist influences from Korea continued and finally, under the reign of Empress Suiko, of Soga blood, Buddhism found imperial favor. This was largely due to the efforts of the prince regent, Shōtoku Taishi (572–622 A.D.), strong advocate of the new religion. Korean priests were brought to teach the new doctrine, and temples were built. In 616 the oracle of Miwa declared that Buddhist priests were the proper persons to perform funeral rites. In 685 orders were sent out from the court that in every house there should be a Buddhist shrine to which worship was to be paid and offerings of food made. This edict is regarded as the origin of the Butsudan found today in nearly every household of the land.

Buddhism now grew rapidly in influence, but Shinto ritual and belief also remained very much alive both in the court and among the people. Buddhism was accepted in addition to, not instead of, the native religion. Shinto ceremonies of the court continued, rites in honor of the deities of heaven and earth, and the Shinto priesthood remained a force to be reckoned with. The *kami* were regarded as capable of sending pestilence and earthquake if annoyed.

Ultimately a combination of Buddhism and Shinto called Ryōbu Shinto developed under the influence of such Buddhist leaders as Kōbō Daishi (774–835). Shinto deities came to be regarded as simply Buddhas and Bodhisattvas in different form, a convenient theory permitting the worship of both *kami* and *butsu*. This amalgamation of the two religions lasted until the end of Tokugawa times.

Early contributions of Buddhism to Japan were as much in the field of humanism and the arts as in that of religion. Old Shinto sacrifices of men and of horses at funerals were discontinued, and the Buddhist prohibition against taking life encouraged a largely vegetarian diet. The development of pariah castes associated with the killing and tanning of hides was a less happy byproduct of this Buddhist tenet. The introduction of Buddhism greatly stimulated the development of the arts—sculpture, painting, architecture, and literature. Together with other influences, Buddhism also stimulated the study of Chinese philosophy and culture through the sending of men to study Buddhism on the mainland. Native Japanese beliefs in turn influenced Buddhism in Japan, as, for example, the stress on ancestral worship found in Japanese Buddhism.

After the thirteenth century few new religious developments in Japanese Buddhism occurred, but throughout the period of its ascendancy Buddhism played an important educational as well as religious role, and such schools and colleges as existed before Meiji were for the most part founded and maintained by Buddhist priests. It was Buddhist priests who kept alight the lamp of learning during Japan's dark periods of civil war.

During Tokugawa times, after the initial split of the great Shinshū sect into two churches, the *shōgun* patronized Buddhism as a stabilizing force. Partly because of the reaction against Christianity, every household was required to belong to some Buddhist sect. The temples thus came to be the registrars of the nation, each one maintaining records of the births, marriages, and deaths in its member-families. These temple records were the precursors of the modern family record or *koseki* kept in township and municipal offices. Having become an established religion and arm of government, Buddhism gradually lost its vitality so that when the Meiji restoration came it was Shinto, not Buddhism, that served as the stimulating religious force.

Buddhist Sects

In most regions of Japan a majority of the people belong to one Buddhist sect or another, but the degree of faith and participation in the church varies widely from families who are simply parish members to those who are active and devout followers.

The parochial Buddhists are those whose names are registered with the local temple and who are buried according to its

rites but who rarely attend church services. They may make dona-
tions to worthy church causes and their womenfolk go on pilgrimages which are as much recreational picnics as religious activity. The parochial Buddhists are a modern carry-over of the
old Tokugawa rule whereby every family was required to belong
to some temple.

The devout followers, fewer in number than parochial Buddhists, are found especially among members of the Nichiren sect
and, to a lesser extent, Zen and Shinshū. Their temples are well
kept up, and the churches may maintain educational and social
welfare activities.

A third and rather small group might be termed philosophical
Buddhists, scholars interested in the history or philosophy of
Buddhism. A characteristic of all three types of Buddhists is that
they are buried according to the traditional rites of their family
sect.

The early sects of Buddhism introduced in the sixth century
are today either extinct or exist only as relics of the past as, for
instance, Hossō. The rise of Tendai and Shingon in the eighth
and ninth centuries which favored Ryōbu-Shinto marked the
development of Buddhism as a popular religion, but even these
sects are today of relative unimportance. The important present-
day sects are those which developed in the twelfth and thirteenth
centuries as protestant reactions to the older established churches.
While sect rivalry exists, especially in Nichiren, Buddhism stresses
tolerance, and it is often said that enlightenment is like a mountain peak with many pathways to the summit.

The major Buddhist sects in contemporary Japan, in order
of the number of their temples, are Shinshū, Zen, Shingon, Jōdo,
Nichiren, and Tendai.

Shinshū was founded in the thirteenth century by Shinran
Shōnin (1173–1262). This sect today has 19,742 temples and
16,043 priests and is by far the most popular form of Japanese
Buddhism among the masses of the people, both urban and rural.

The chief tenet of Shinshū is salvation by faith in Amida. To say, sincerely, "Namu Amida Butsu," often recited as "Namanda, Namanda, Namanda" by the devout as they bow before an image of Amida, is to be saved by Amida and be assured of a place in the Western Paradise. Personal humility before the holy savior and loving kindness in human relations also form part of Shinshū teaching.

Shinran, the founder of Shinshū, was a radical reformer who discarded ascetic practices such as celibacy and the tabu on meat eating. He brought religion to the people, protesting against the rich older churches of Shingon and Tendai, where all religious matters rested in the hands of priests, who claimed a monopoly of sacred power and through whom the common people had to approach Buddha and the saints. Shinran also denounced the current beliefs about lucky and unlucky days and directions, but most Shinshū followers today still place a good deal of faith in them. During the period of Buddhist ascendancy imperial princes usually became the head priests of great temples or monasteries and Emperors abdicated early in life to become monks. In consideration of this past relationship the court conferred titles of nobility on the three chief abbots of Shinshū when the peerage was instituted in 1884.

Zen was introduced into Japan from China at the end of the twelfth century by Eisai (1140–1215) and Dōgen (1199–1253). This sect is second to Shinshū in popularity. Its chief tenet is quite the opposite of Shinshū, emphasizing salvation by self—one attains enlightenment by self-discipline both mental and physical. Zen also holds that absolute truth is not taught in scripture and is not expressible in words. The doctrine of self-control and self-conquest fitted well the old *samurai* code and contributed to the development of Bushidō. Zen, like Shinshū, was part of the protestant movement in Japanese Buddhism bringing religion back to the people. Today the "conscious" followers of Zen include a number of young officers, schoolteachers, and others, but the mass of its followers are more in the nature of parochial members, i.e., they simply belong to the Zen temple because it is their neighborhood temple and their parents belonged to it before them. Zen has three subsects, Rinzai, Sōtō, and Obaku. Sōtō is the largest of these with 14,257 temples and 12,472 priests. (Rinzai has 5,797 temples, and Obaku 587.)

Shingon was founded early in the ninth century by Kōbō Daishi (774–835). Its headquarters are Mount Kōya in Kii Prefecture. Today there are 11,990 Shingon temples with 8,200 priests. In the Middle Ages this sect was very strong, and played its part in the civil wars, but today Shingon temples in rural regions are often little more than the headquarters of some healing priest. Local hamlet god houses (dō) may enshrine Kōbō Daishi and are then called O-Daishidō.

Jōdo was founded in 1174 by Hōnen. This sect, like its child Shinshū, stresses salvation by faith. It has today 8,245 temples and 6,734 priests.

Nichiren or Hokkeshū was founded in the thirteenth century by Nichiren (1222–1281) and has today 5,031 temples and 4,497 priests. Nichiren, the founder of the sect, was a zealous and intolerant religious leader who denounced the older sects as having lost touch with real Buddhism. In contrast to the gentleness of Shinran, founder of Shinshū, Nichiren was extremely aggressive in his iconoclasm. The older established churches brought pressure to bear on the government and he was exiled and at one time even sentenced to death. According to one story, just as he was to be beheaded lightning struck beside him. Before such an omen the g_vernment retired. Active Nichiren followers today are militant and aggressive and tend to support Japan's nationalistic trends.

Tendai was founded early in the ninth century by Dengyō Daishi with headquarters at Mount Hiei. Today it has 4,437 temples and 2,935 priests. Together with Shingon, Tendai held great temporal power in the Middle Ages, many princes and ex-emperors becoming priests or monks of one or the other of the two sects. Today, in rural areas, Tendai priests tend to be more faith healers than true priests.

Some minor sects of contemporary Japan are Ji, Yūzū, Hossō, and Kegon. Ji was founded in the thirteenth century by Ippen as one of the lesser protestant sects. Today it has 493 temples and 358 priests. Yūzū, another of the protestant sects, was founded in 1117 by Ryōnin. Hossō was one of the original sects introduced in the sixth century but Hossō today has only 42 temples and 20 priests. The most famous of its temples is Hōryūji, near Nara, which is a fine example of early Buddhist architecture. Kegon is another of the original sixth-century sects but today it is also small, with only 35 temples and 26 priests.

Most Buddhist sects have their headquarters in or near Kyoto, where they maintain not only great temples but also theological schools for the training of priests who then go out to become priests or assistant priests in provincial temples.

Buddhist Pantheon

The most important deities in the pantheon of Japanese Buddhism are Amida and Shaka, but there are also many lesser deities including some which are found only in Japanese Buddhism. As in Shinto, so also in Japanese Buddhism, great men may be deified as, for instance, Kōbō Daishi enshrined in local Daishi Dō.

Amida (Amitabha) is the central figure in Shinshū Buddhism, the most popular sect in modern Japan. Friendly to man, Amida is regarded as a savior by Shinshū and Jōdo followers who believe that sincere faith in him will assure one of a place in paradise. Many of the great statues of Buddha in Japan, including the Daibutsu at Nara, are representations of Amida.

Shaka or Oshakasama is Gautama Buddha, the central figure of such Japanese sects as Zen and Nichiren.

Dainichi (Vairocana) or Dainichi-nyorai is the central object of worship in Shingon Buddhism.

Kwannon is the same as the Chinese Kwanyin, a deity generally regarded as a goddess of mercy. She is venerated throughout Japan, especially by women about to become mothers, and is also an object of special attention in most Zen temples.

Jizō (Kshitigarbha) is a male figure often represented as a Buddhist priest or pilgrim. He is a savior of children's souls, a helper of people in trouble and a protector of dangerous places.

Still other figures in the Japanese Buddhist Pantheon are Fudō, Yakushi, Benten, Binzuru, and Kompira. Fudō, portrayed with grimacing face and red flames shooting out from him, is regarded as a deity of fire. Yakushi is a popular deity of healing, and Benten a goddess of good fortune. Binzuru, a deity of healing, and Kompira, god of healing and happiness, appear to be native to Japan and are perhaps a mixture of a Buddhist original and some native deity.

All of these deities find a place in local popular beliefs regardless of sect, and one may find local hamlet god houses with figures of one or another of them as the protecting deities of hamlet and roadside.

Ceremonies and Holidays

Buddhist temples vary from great structures such as Zōjōji in Tokyo or Kiyomizudera in Kyoto to humble little ten-foot-square halls serving to house some neighborhood deity. In contrast to the severe simplicity of Shinto shrines, the architecture is often flamboyant with characteristic flaring roofs, elaborate wood carving, and colorful wall paintings. In place of the humble *shintai* as the sacred object of worship in a Shinto shrine, Buddhist temples house wood or metal images of the deities, often elaborately carved and of imposing magnitude.

Services and rituals in the temple, as in Shinto shrines, are usually carried out by the priest in behalf of the worshipers. However, the congregation may participate by a series of Japanese equivalents of "Amen."

An ordinary worshiper in approaching a Buddhist temple, large or small, first throws toward the altar an offering of a *sen* or so, then, holding in his hands his Buddhist rosary (*juzu*) and assuming an attitude of prayer he bows and murmurs a ritual which varies according to sect, bows again, and then retires or, if there is a service taking place, joins the rest of the congregation.

The predominant role of Buddhism among the masses of the population is at funerals. Where Shinto in its popular forms is concerned with temporal prosperity and the prevention of sickness, Buddhism is concerned with the soul and the afterworld. Until the Meiji Era all funerals were performed by Buddhist priests and the great majority of them still are.

A Japanese funeral is followed by a series of memorial services for the dead, and a man who in life may have had little to do with Buddhist temples will still be buried according to the Buddhist rites of his family sect. The ancestral tablets are kept in the Buddhist alcove and the deceased are spoken of as Buddhas (*hotokesama*) just as Shinto dead are referred to as *kami*. Ancestral tablets bearing Buddhist posthumous names are made by the priest of the family temple and kept either at the temple or in the household Buddhist shelf or Butsudan. The priests are also called on to perform memorial services at regular intervals after death, each seventh day for forty-nine days, the first and other special anniversaries up to fifty and sometimes even one hundred years after death. A memorial anniversary often serves as an occasion for some civic-minded person to erect a useful monument in honor of the deceased such as a fire bell or a new temple structure. Buddhist views on taking life lead to memorial services not only for human beings but also for animals, so that collective memorial rites are performed for the souls of dead silkworms, and for the souls of insects killed in rice paddies.

Buddhist temples and their priests are supported wholly by their parishioners in contrast to orthodox Shinto priests and shrines which receive government subsidies. Thus Buddhism is a religion of the people serving to fill a social need in regard to matters of death and the after life.

Buddhist temples are always open and people are free to enter and make private prayers and vows at any time. The priests hold special services from time to time, and each temple has a few large festivals on certain days each year, attended for the most part by women, children, and old people. These recurrent holy days serve somewhat the same function as the more evenly spaced Sabbath of Christianity.

At New Year's time some Buddhist priests, as well as some Shinto priests, perform purification household ceremonies. Many people visit the temples of their family sect and the priests read sutras for the prosperity of the Emperor and the nation.

Spring Higan, an equinoctial holy week, is observed during the week of March 21. In some regions Zen followers visit the temple to reflect upon their sins and contemplate realistic pictures of hell. Religious lectures are given and Shinshū priests may perform collective memorial services for the ancestors of their parishioners.

April 8 is Buddha's Birthday, celebrated by visits to temples, especially those of the Zen sect where sweet tea (*amacha*) is prepared. The "tea" is placed in a wooden tub containing a small figure of Shaka over which is a framework elaborately decorated with fresh flowers to form a miniature temple. Visitors drink the sweet tea, dipping it out of the tub with tiny bamboo dippers. The liquid, having been poured over Shaka's body, becomes sacred and is believed by the devout to possess curative properties.

On June 15 there is a special memorial service, Segaki Kyō, and lectures at Zen temples. During the month of June there are also numerous local festivals in honor of Amida, Kwannon, and Jizō.

July 13–15 is the festival of Urabon. This period, popularly called Obon, is the time when souls of the dead are believed to return to earth. Family graves are cleaned, the family Butsudan is decorated and special offerings are placed before it. There are also special services at the temples. Until recently folk dances in honor of Bon were performed, the particular dances and accompanying songs varying from region to region. These dances were participated in by young people and the songs were often sexual in nature. With the general repression of all phallicism in Japanese religion during Meiji days, many Bon dances were suppressed but some towns and tourist centers still carry on bowdlerized forms.

Autumn Higan is observed during the week of the fall equinox, September 21. This is more important than Spring Higan and there are lectures at temples and visits to numerous local *dō* in some regions.

In the eleventh month a Sengo Kyō is held in Zen temples with special services for ancestors of temple members. Regular members may make gifts to the temple at this time in thanks for the services of the priests in caring for the souls of their ancestors.

The twenty-second to twenty-eighth of the eleventh month is Goshōki, the week of the death day of Shinran, founder of Shinshū. It is marked by the giving of gifts to the temple by parishioners.

The Women's Buddhist Society meets two or three times a year at the local temple to hear lectures. Japanese men, urban and rural, seldom attend Buddhist sermons, but their wives and mothers may be regular attendants. Many college-educated men tend to be agnostic, with a tolerance toward the religious activities of their womenfolk but not themselves participating.

Buddhism is still the living religion of the masses in Japan. It is to Buddhist temples that people go to hear soul-comforting sermons and the most important household shrine is the Butsudan. While State Shinto is emphasized in schools and on state occasions, in everyday life and at death it is to the Buddhist priest and to the unofficial popular forms of Shinto that people turn for psychological solace and security. The political power of Buddhists priests today is not great, their influence being largely upon the old people, women, and children of families belonging to their sect. They are subject to conscription just as any other Japanese subject. Indirectly they are important, however, inasmuch as they serve to give the people comfort with their talk of Amida's paradise and so help the masses to bear the discomforts of this life—thus indirectly serving as a conservative force for the maintenance of things as they are.

RELIGION OF FAMILY AND HOUSEHOLD

A Japanese dwelling house is far more than a shelter against the elements and a place to sleep. Here the family may live for generations, the house and yard full of old landmarks of family history, the home itself a dwelling place not only for the living but also for the spirits of the dead. The kitchen houses not only the maidservant and her stove but also protective deities. On the ridgepole of the house moulder the dusty remains of ritual fan, fish, and hemp ceremonially placed there when the house was built to protect all inmates from harm.

The religious aspects of family and household are, as a rule, a mixture of Buddhist and Shinto elements and the particular beliefs and practices are looked upon as matters of household concern without regard to nice theological distinctions.

Butsudan and Kamidana

In nearly every house, often in the good room or *zashiki* near the *tokonoma,* is a sacred corner where may be found the Butsudan and the Kamidana. The Butsudan or Buddhist shelf is a more or less elaborately lacquered structure, its elegance depending on the wealth of the family, in which is enshrined the central deity of the Buddhist sect to which the household belongs. If Shinshū, it might be either an image or scroll painting of the savior, Amida. Here also may be found wooden *ihai* or ancestral tablets bearing the priest-given posthumous names of deceased family members. Near the Butsudan may be hung photographs of the deceased family head and his wife.

Before the Butsudan every morning the family members, one by one as they arise, ring a small brass bell, bow, and recite the prayer of their sect. This simple morning ritual is of great importance to many people in giving them a feeling of having begun the day in the right way.

The housewife fills the small offering cups with rice and tea for the ancestral spirits and on special occasions a small cup of wine may be placed before the spirits of the ancestors. In the event of a wedding or a funeral, the doors of the Butsudan are open, symbolizing participation by the ancestral spirits in the family ceremonies.

Occasionally one may come across families, especially those of Shinto priests and some *samurai* families in Kagoshima, which do not have a Butsudan, regarding themselves as "pure Shintoists." Christian households also lack the Butsudan. But such households are exceptions to the general practice and even in these there is usually some substitute procedure for paying respects to the ancestors and symbolizing their presence at family ceremonies.

If there are some houses which lack a Butsudan, there are almost none lacking a Kamidana or Shinto god shelf. This is usually a plain unpainted wooden structure, a miniature Shinto shrine. The Kamidana usually contains a sacred paper talisman from the local shrine and a *taima* from Ise. In front of it is placed a cup or ceremonial wine jar for offerings to the deities represented. The Butsudan represents family unity, the Kamidana local group unity through the shrine talisman and participation in national unity through the Ise *taima*. In many ordinary families the bow at the Butsudan includes respects to the Kamidana, but in some families, especially those of high *samurai* origin, village officials, schoolteachers, and army officers, the head of the house may clap his hands Shinto style and bow particularly toward the Kamidana separately from his rites before the Butsudan.

Portraits of the imperial family are usually found either near the Kamidana or in the *tokonoma*. There are no special rites in connection with such portraits. (It is a popular American misapprehension which would make of the Japanese Emperor a supernatural figure. Divinely descended, yes, but not himself a deity.)

Ebisu and Daikoku

Two popular household deities of good fortune and general prosperity are Ebisu and Daikoku. In rural areas figures of these friendly gods are kept on a shelf high on some post in the kitchen. By way of an offering a green leaf or flower in season is kept in a bamboo vase beside them. In towns and cities, Ebisu and Daikoku serve as the patron deities of business and a plaque with their smiling faces hangs somewhere in most shops and stores— more as a traditional good luck sign than because of any faith in their powers.

Other Household Deities

In some regions a bamboo vase containing flowers in season may be seen by the entrance of country dwellings. These are for the sun, Nichirin-san. Similarly flowers are often kept by the kitchen stove for the deity of the stove, Kama-no-kamisama, and by the well for the water god, Suijin-san. Such simple observances symbolize the importance of sun and stove and well in the life of the average Japanese peasant.

In the yards of older landowning families there is usually some stone or shrine in honor of the spirit of the land—Kōjin or Jinushi. This attention is paid him in order that he may not bring harm to members of the household, just as land and water spirits receive special Shinto rites on the breaking of new land or the building of new bridges. Sometimes some other deity such as Jizō may be found in a houseyard, serving as a family protector. Hotels and *geisha* houses often have such a shrine, usually to Inari.

The doorways of many houses and barns have numerous paper talismans pasted on them to protect inmates from accident and disease. These have been purchased from shrines visited or from itinerant religious pilgrims. At New Year's time the household may receive a general purification by a local Shinto or Buddhist priest or from some visting mountain priest.

Attitudes and practices in connection with these aspects of religion in the household vary considerably. Most people, especially the women, observe the rites of Butsudan and Kamidana, but faith in paper talismans and purification ceremonies is stronger in rural than in urban regions and few if any are to be found in upper-class city families.

The Crises of Life

Related to household and family religion are ritual observances in connection with the various crises of family life—birth, marriage, and death.

A few days after a birth a naming ceremony is held at which the midwife and a few close relatives attend. Special rice cakes are offered by the *tokonoma* and the name may be chosen in a ritual manner involving the use of a Buddhist rosary. If the child becomes ill, the name may be changed on the advice of the healing priest.

At the end of the first month the child is taken by its mother and one or two relatives to visit the local Shinto shrine where the priest performs a brief ritual. Various birth tabus on food and work are now lifted from the mother and the child itself has been introduced to the patron deities whose good will allowed him to be born and to survive his dangerous first month of life.

When a young man leaves home to go to the barracks or overseas, he may visit the local shrine or sacred mountain to obtain a charm to protect him from harm while he is away. His mother may make a vow to the shrine or temple deities to do certain things in return for their protection of her child while he is away. In towns and cities departing soldiers may be given thousand-stitch belts to protect them from harm. These are belts, often made by members of some Women's Patriotic Association, in which one thousand persons have taken a stitch.

Since marriage is primarily a family affair, no priest is called in (except at the recently developed Shinto ceremonies). The ritual drink exchange between bride and groom (*sansankudo*), however, is usually performed before the Butsudan, the doors of which are kept open for the occasion.

In the event of sickness the gods may be called upon and the ailing person or some relative may visit a near-by *dō*, temple, or shrine to pray for recovery. In most regions there are priests whose principal income is from rituals performed to cure the sick. However, most sophisticated urbanites call a doctor.

It is at funerals that religion really enters, and even the agnostics of the family are usually buried according to Buddhist rites. The chief source of income for many Buddhist priests is from funerals and memorial services.

The dead are buried or cremated, according to local custom, but in the larger cities cremation is now required by law. Burial customs vary widely from region to region, but in general there is first a farewell ceremony and meal held in the home of the deceased followed by a brief ceremony at the grave side. Close kin are expected to assist in dressing the corpse and to participate in the funeral ceremony itself, requirements which are often most painful for younger members of the family who are suffering emotionally from the loss of mother or father, brother, sister, or child. Within the bosom of the family tears may be freely shed on such occasions, though to strangers one must put up a smiling front.

According to Shinshū belief, the souls of those with faith in Amida go to the Western Paradise. According to Zen, death is but another step in one's existence, the ultimate goal being nirvana, a state of selfless enlightenment. Many young men have no faith in either heaven or hell except as it exists within oneself.

From this brief description it can readily be seen that sacred beliefs and practices play a larger part in the daily life of a Japanese than in that of the average American. Perhaps the most important influence of religion in Japanese life is in the home, where daily rituals are performed and in which are enshrined not only the spirits of the family ancestors but numerous protective deities as well as the sacred Shinto talisman from Ise. This predominant role of the sacred in everyday life is in part due to the long history and broad peasant background of Japan.

Religion and the Local Community

In order to understand fully the religion—the body of sacred ritual and belief—of a society it is also necessary to understand the social and economic life of that same society because the sacred beliefs and practices of a people are a function of their whole economic and social organization. Because of this fundamental fact we can never learn the nature of a religion simply by a perusal of the sacred texts, i.e., written words, torn from their social context; nor will a life of Buddha and a study of his original teachings in 500 B.C. tell us much of the nature of religion in contemporary Japan.

Nations with large peasant populations lay more stress on seasonal change and aspects of the environment important to agriculture than do the people of, say, the United States. Every month, almost every day, has its own special occupations for the Japanese peasant. A reflection of this periodic recurrence of agricultural pursuits is the periodic recurrence of festival days. These festival days are regulated by a lunar calendar, and most of the important ones occur on the fifteenth of the lunar month—the time when the moon is full, a fine occasion for groups to come together for a celebration of some deity and day, for drink and good fellowship.

The basic and all-important product is rice, and there is a deity, Inari, associated with rice, fertility, sex, and good fortune. Rice and rice wine form the commonest offerings to the gods.

Things may be of negative as well as of positive social value. Wind can destroy paddy rice if it comes at the wrong time, rivers can flood and cause damage. Thus we find a special wind day in the festival calendar, and the destructive power of the river is recognized in a river god, Kawa-no-kamisama, who is regarded as, on the whole, malevolent.

The festival calendar in Japan is thus filled with a series of holidays in honor of various deities and aspects of the environment, a reflection of the agricultural base of the people and their traditional religious practices. The names of the deities are not important—whether they are what is called Shinto or Buddhist is of interest only to the culture historian. The significant thing is that they mark the different seasons of the peasants' year, that by what they are associated with and the type of offerings given they reflect in a ritual manner the things of greatest social value to the community.

Furthermore, the annual ceremonies in honor of each deity serve as periodic occasions for the individuals of the community to unite in a common ceremony, renew their sense of social solidarity in common ritual, followed by genial sociability. The individual's beliefs become expressed again, and by the repetition are kept alive. The individual again becomes conscious of his dependence on his fellows, on the one hand, and gains renewed vigor from the social contact, on the other. He goes back to his daily work with an added zest for life.

To illustrate these points, the deity Jizō may be taken as an example. Historically Jizō is a Buddhist deity, the one who guides children's souls through Hades. But his traditional role as a guide and protector of children is only one of his many aspects. He serves, for instance, as a protector of crossroads, entrances to villages, and other dangerous places. Some houses have images of Jizō by their entrances as protectors. Occasionally such households are said to have such images not for protection but as an aid to sorcery. Thus Jizō's supernatural powers may be turned toward either good or evil. At weddings in some rural regions young men of the neighborhood may bring an image of Jizō into the banquet hall, accompanied by ribald jests and demands for wine. In this context Jizō is said to keep the bride from running away to her home. Certain particular images of Jizō are regarded as good for curing certain diseases, especially earache, and receive prayers and offerings from the sick in this connection. But most interesting of all, images of Jizō are frequently found in hamlet god houses.

The neighborhood god house or *dō* serves as a play place for children, a sleeping place for wandering beggars and pilgrims, and a place of meeting for young people in the evening. The *dō* is no mere empty structure, for the presence of an image or deity makes it an inhabited building, a dwelling. Thus mothers feel it is a safe place for children; a lone pilgrim does not feel utterly alone when he sleeps there. This, then, is one important function of the *dō*— a public building where children may play or adults stop for a visit or a night's rest—a familiar homely little building looked after by the local group and housing a deity. The *dō,* in a sense, represents the hamlet.

Another expression of this is the annual celebration. Different neighborhood groups in the hamlet are responsible for looking after the *dō* celebration each year. During the day of the festival the group in charge serves tea to visitors and exchanges gossip. Someone from each house in the hamlet comes during the day to make an offering to the deity and to drink tea, and some time during the day, or in the evening under the full moon, there is a general gathering of neighborhood people to drink together. Thus once a year the local group renews its social solidarity by means of the local *dō* festival.

Jizō, then, as a particular named deity, is irrelevant. The use of some sacred object to mark crossroads and dangerous places reflects the society's recognition of these places as traditional sources of potential harm, hence requiring some preventive measure. A home is directly important to the family and indirectly to the community, and every• dwelling is protected by deities of various kinds—some have statues of Jizō. Certain families suspected of black magic are supposed to have some shrine to the evil dog spirit, and Jizō is one of the many forms such a shrine may take. Again, at marriage, Jizō is simply one of several aspects of the ritual recognition of the importance of marriage to the community. As to Jizō *dō,* the significant thing about this aspect of religious life of the local community is the way in which the god house serves to give expression to the social unity of the local group. There are many other festivals which serve the same or similar functions. Some involve Buddist deities, some Shinto, but both serve the same ends.

The religious system and festival calendar in Japanese community life at the local level serve, then, these functions: (1) through the offerings and beliefs surrounding the deities involved, i.e., in the belief and ritual concerning them, both individual and collective, they reflect things of social value to the community, such as rice, wind, sickness, and health; (2) as common centers for the local group and through the periodic ceremonies they serve to maintain the solidarity of the local group and to keep alive the common sentiments and beliefs by having them recurrently expressed; (3) through faith in local deities and ritual practices the individual gains psychological security.

In Japan there is, however, another whole body of belief and ritual in addition to the local deities, shrines, and community ceremonies, namely, ancestor worship. This is closely associated with

Buddhism—ancestral tablets are often kept in the local Buddhist temple; a Buddhist priest performs the rituals at funerals and memorial services.

The significant thing about ancestral worship is that it concerns the immediate family and the extended family, rather than the community or local group, One of the most important, and in the nature of things inevitable, events in family life is the death of the house head—an event which necessitates a complete rearrangement of social relations within the household. The son who was formerly subservient to the head is now himself head and takes over both the privileges and the responsibilities of head of the house. The widow goes up in status on the death of her husband, and her voice carries more weight in family affairs. All in all, the death of a house head is a break and a shock to the smooth functioning of the immediate family.

In parts of rural Japan there is an interesting dichotomy which manifests itself at a funeral. The local group, the neighborhood, comes to the aid of the stricken family by assisting in the funeral preparations, calling the priests, digging the grave. The extended kin group, on the other hand, assembles from far and near to mourn and participate in the funeral rituals. There is here a recognition of two separate social groups, one based on geographical nearness and the other on kinship, each group affected by the death and each responding to it, but doing so separately.

In addition to the funeral, a means of giving continuity to the family life and lessening the break caused by death is through the concept of the head becoming a spiritual, but nonetheless real, ancestor to whom duties of filial piety continue to exist and who continues to serve as a unifier and strengthener of family ties. Ties with the ancestors are maintained daily through offerings to the tablets and periodically through an annual ceremony participated in by the whole extended family through offerings at the graves, memorial services, and visits among relatives. This is the period called Bon in the seventh month when the ancestors are believed to come back to earth for a short period. The Bon period serves to revivify the sense of family continuity through time from generation to generation. It is a special re-emphasis on the part of the descendants of a unity expressed daily in each home through offerings to the tablets.

Ancestor worship, then, serves to unite the kin group, to insure its solidarity; a solidarity based on blood relationship in contrast to the other aspects of popular religion which serve to unify the local group, the group based on common territory. It also is important in providing the individual with a sense of personal security, even in the face of death.

CHRISTIANITY

Christianity first came to Japan with the landing of St. Francis Xavier at Kagoshima in 1549. The new religion gained considerable influence until the fatal Shimabara Rebellion and the decision of the Tokugawa that it was dangerous to the state. It was then rigorously suppressed until religious freedom came again after the Restoration. When this occurred a number of families in the Nagasaki area declared themselves as of the Christian faith, having maintained their beliefs throughout the two centuries of suppression, a remarkable example of the power of religious faith in Japan. (A similar event occurred in southern Kyūshū where for some time Shinshū was ruthlessly suppressed by the local daimyō, only to go underground till better days.) This record should give pause to zealous advocates of suppression of Japanese traditional custom and belief by an army of occupation.

During the nineteenth and twentieth centuries Christian missionaries have worked in Japan, but their success in making converts has not been great. Today there are about 350,000 Christians, less than half of 1 per cent of the total population of the country. Some of these few have been men of note, however, such as Kagawa.

An important contribution of the Christian missions has been in the field of education and health. Some of the first missionaries, such as Hepburn, were doctors, and from the start many of the new propagators of the faith laid as much emphasis on "good works" as on conversion to particular creeds. Dōshisha in Kyoto, a co-educational institution of university grade founded in 1875, is an example of such a mission school. This school played an important role in Japanese educational work for many years before the present war. Other schools and colleges founded and maintained by missions included Aoyama Gakuin, Rikkyō Daigaku, and Meiji Gakuin in Kobe. Two girls' colleges of note are the Tokyo Women's Christian College and the Kobe Girls' College. Mission groups early took the lead in the education of women in Japan and in the field of kindergartens. St. Luke's Hospital in Tokyo is an outstanding medical contribution of the Christian missions.

The Roman Catholic Church, as well as Protestant sects, has been active since the Meiji restoration. The nucleus of the Catholic Church in Japan was the group of 3,700 villagers around Nagasaki which had secretly professed Christianity during the years of persecution. The Catholics maintain a number of schools, sisterhoods, and monastic orders. The total number of Catholics is estimated at 90,000. Partly as a result of Axis ties and partly in connection with the occupation of the Philippines, the Japanese government made overtures to the Vatican and now has a formal diplomatic representative in Vatican City.

When the new missions were established in Japan, even before the old anti-Christian edicts were repealed, there was some feeling that Christianity might become an important religious force sweeping the country. But a reaction against it soon set in because of antiforeign sentiment, the unequal treaties, and a suspicion of Christianity's cosmopolitanism and its effect on the loyalty of Christian converts. The influence of Christianity has not been in converts but in the introduction of Western concepts of education, health, and public welfare. Not only have Japanese schools and hospitals been influenced by the examples of mission institutions but some urban Buddhist and Shinto sect churches have taken up welfare work and even instituted young people's church schools and adopted other techniques familiar to Christian churches.

Japanese Christians are often very strict and fundamentalist—giving up drinking and smoking and strongly censoring frivolities such as *geisha* parties. Such people are sometimes shocked to discover that Western non-missionary Christians not only may smoke and drink, but also may engage in sharp business practice and even participate in ruthless warfare.

Of recent years most of the mission churches have become self-governing institutions independent of overseas mission boards and since 1940 all remaining overseas ties were severed as a result of pressure from the government.

ISLAM

There is a handful of Moslems in Japan, not all of whom are Japanese, but the government has given the religion official recognition and mosques have been erected in Tokyo and Kobe. This special interest on the part of the government is largely political in nature, a gesture to win the friendship of Moslems in China and more recently in Southeast Asia and India.

Chapter IX

Culture Patterns

TRADITIONAL BEHAVIOR PATTERNS

EVERY society is characterized by its own peculiar etiquette and patterns of behavior. In old settled cultures such as those of France or Japan, these behavior patterns are generally more clearly defined than in a newly organized society like the United States, where we are still working out our social order.

In Japan there is a proper and an improper way of doing everything. Even a poor Japanese farmer or worker knows just what behavior is to be expected of himself and his various friends in any ordinary social situation. It is an ignorance of these customs and the motivations behind them that causes so many casual visitors to the Orient to misinterpret actions and get themselves into frustrating impasses which they tend to blame on native stupidity or cussedness. The same overt action in two societies may mean two quite different things, just as two similar sounding words in two different languages may have different meanings. In English "go" is a verb, in Japanese it is the name of a game; in Western culture one waves to a person to bid farewell, while in Japanese a wave of the hand means "come here." These are simple examples which rarely cause confusion, but there are others, more complex, which are less well comprehended, such as the use of a go-between, or the Japanese smile.

Group Action and Group Responsibility

As has already been noted, Japanese culture stresses group values in contrast to individual ones. The Japanese is taught to act in behalf of his family or his nation rather than himself. In the Japanese ideology individualism is a selfish sin.

One aspect of this pattern is a tendency to avoid individual responsibility for actions so that even in government, administrators tend to act only after consultation with, and agreement of, a council. There is no vote on an issue and no majority and minority report. It is considered more important to reach a unanimous and compromise decision, and if this cannot be done the dissenting members may resign. This is true not only of Cabinet ministers and army officers but also of village headmen and other representatives of particular small groups. In family matters the head of the house has authority over its members, but in the upper classes all important family matters such as selling family property are decided by a meeting of the Family Council. It is notable that in high government circles important decisions are made not in the administrator's name but in that of the Emperor, i.e., the nation.

In rural life the spirit of cooperation and group work is strong, and such group activity is usually carried out without any permanent administrative chief. Whoever is in charge—of hamlet matters, of a cooperative group, of neighborhood affairs—holds office for a limited period, the responsibility then shifting to another member of the group. In the national government no one man stands out as responsible government leader for very long at a time—different leaders appear as prime minister, but none becomes a permanent dictator.

There is indeed a definite fear of accepting full responsibility for actions involving many people and there is also a strong sanction against it in high places. A man holding high place in some organization responsible for an unpopular policy lives in grave danger of assassination. At lower levels the sanction is critical gossip which can be equally effective in removing a too presumptuous individual.

The Go-Between

The Japanese lay great stress on smooth relations among members of a community. Every effort is made to avoid open hostility and face-to-face actions which might lead to argument and the consequent embarrassment of one or the other party. This involves the concept of face—personal self-respect and prestige—so important in the Orient. To disagree point-blank with a guest over a cup of tea would be rude in the highest degree—hence the tendency for polite agreement with most comments made even though they be inconsistent one with another. On more important occasions such as a marriage or a business deal, where some disagreement is inevitable, embarrassing face-to-face relations are avoided by means of a third party or go-between. Thus whenever negotiations are to be undertaken involving such things as purchase, marriage, or appeals to higher authority concerning a grievance, a man does not go directly to the person with whom he is to deal, but rather operates through a go-between. This contrasts with the American pattern of behavior in similar situations, of negotiating directly with the responsible persons involved, a method of direct negotiation alien to Japanese tradition.

A marriage, which is primarily a social and economic relationship between two families, involves a good deal of careful investigation of family backgrounds for leprosy, tuberculosis, criminal records, and general moral character. Such investigations, if made directly, could easily lead to embarrassment and "loss of face" by one or another of the families concerned. This is avoided by a go-between who serves to maintain relations between the families during the critical period. The go-between also, incidentally, has face to maintain. If the boy and girl involved in the wedding decided to go about together publicly before marriage, the go-between would lose face since they would be short-circuiting his elaborate negotiations.

In business dealings where direct bargaining would be unseemly, Japanese employ the services of a broker or business go-between. He may receive a commission from both parties for his services—from one for getting a high price, from the other for having reduced the price.

In the field of administration and the presenting of people's grievances to higher officials, group representatives may serve as go-betweens, and if unsuccessful they may resign their office. A town or city mayor, for instance, is the go-between for his community in its relations with the prefectural and national governments.

In the employment of servants it is usually best to work through a go-between in Japan. And a servant is likely to resign on a moment's notice if his employer causes him to lose face by openly accusing him of some error in front of other people. For a servant to tell his master he is resigning because he doesn't like the work or because he has an offer of a better job elsewhere would be to cause loss of face to his employer, so he may give illness as the cause of his no longer working. The wise employer will understand and begin looking for another servant or offer to raise the wages.

Not only is it desirable to operate through a go-between in negotiating important social, business, and political arrangements; it is also essential to operate in a roundabout way in dismissing an employee for inefficiency or dishonesty. Once the employer decides that his employee must be dismissed, he then must decide on a way to allow him to resign without too much loss of face among his associates. If this is not done, the employer or administrator may discover that he is not only rid of the man he wished to dismiss but that the whole office force has resigned in sympathetic protest. More than one American businessman in Japan has learned this lesson the hard way.

Group Solidarity and Loyalty

The Japanese emphasis on group solidarity involves the duty of loyalty to one's group, so that the individual will traditionally defend the interests of his employer, of his family, and of any other group of which he is an active member. The Japanese government and army today stress loyalty to the nation through personal loyalty to the Emperor as the supreme duty of all Japanese citizens. The most famous of Japanese historical dramas, *The 47 Ronin,* is a tale of great personal loyalty to the memory of a feudal lord.

A corollary to these two traditional behavior patterns in Japanese society—group responsibility and face saving—is that an individualist is regarded as selfish and antisocial. American democracy is looked upon by many Japanese as a society full of stress and strain due to its many members who—to the Japanese way of thinking—regard their own individual welfare to be more important than that of their family or their country.

These concepts of loyalty, group action, and avoidance of face-to-face embarrassment have grown up in Japan as a result of two influences: (1) a long national history, especially the 250-year period of feudalism and peace which ended in the nineteenth century; and (2) the influence of Confucian ethics on Japanese thought. The American concept of rugged individualism comes in part from the frontier and pioneer tradition of a newly settled nation. Japan, on the other hand, has a long cultural history during which time traditional patterns of social relations have become stabilized. In such a society, an individualist and a man who acts in an unexpected manner is criticized as upsetting the social equilibrium. Americans have a tradition of liberal individualism from

Puritan and Huguenot Protestant origins and from such philoso-
phers as J. J. Rousseau. The Japanese, by contrast, have the philosophical traditions of Confucianism with an emphasis on family
loyalty, and propriety in human relations.

Ideal of Self-Discipline and the Attainment of Success against Great Odds

In the traditional emphasis on overcoming odds in achieving
success, Japanese and American society come somewhat closer
than in the first three national traditions. The Japanese school-
boy, for instance, is taught the story of how Abraham Lincoln
rose to greatness from humble beginnings and how he walked
miles to borrow a book. Many Japanese heroes are men who
rose to greatness by hard work and from humble beginnings.
Today the Japanese look upon their nation as a nation which
began the struggle for power in Asia with a handicap, coming
upon the scene after the industrialized European powers had
already carved out colonial empires and spheres of influence in
Asia.

Associated with the ideal of achieving great ends by overcoming handicaps is the Japanese ideal of frugality and self-discipline.
This is perhaps a reflection of the frugality of Japanese daily life
in homes with little by way of material comforts. Zen Buddhism,
popular in Japan, stresses mental discipline. The Japanese army
is spartan in all its phases, and the conscript is soon taught the
virtues of an even greater self-discipline and frugality than he
knew at home.

These twin ideals of self-discipline and success against odds are
symbolized in the paper carp flown on Boy Day—the carp that
swims upstream and which does not wriggle when laid out under
the fish knife.

The emphasis on self-discipline and propriety in Japanese life
is related by some to the occasional breakdowns whereby Japanese go off the deep end emotionally—e.g., the massacre of

Koreans in Tokyo during the 1923 earthquake and the rape of Nanking in 1937. But such an easy correlation ignores similar outbreaks among Occidentals—e.g., the Detroit race riot, or an American lynching party.

Ritual Cleanliness

When arriving at a Japanese inn or a Japanese home, the guest must remove his shoes before entering, and soon after arrival is expected to bathe. Almost everyone in Japan—even a poor worker or rural peasant—takes a daily bath. (The deep Japanese bath, it has been noted, is a purely Japanese development different from anything in the rest of Asia or the West.) A small infant soon learns to respect cleanliness and avoid dirt so that all a mother has to say to her child in order to make him drop something is "batchi!" or "kitanai!"—"dirty!"

The whole basis of Shinto ritual is one of cleansing one's self, body and soul. Before entering a Shinto shrine one must wash one's hands and rinse out one's mouth. Before the priestly ceremony begins, each participant presents a sacred branch at the altar as a symbol of a pure and sincere soul.

The ritual aspect of this Japanese emphasis on cleanliness may also be seen in the sharp contrast between custom in regard to a Japanese home or temple and that in regard to buildings of Western style in Japan. In a Japanese home or inn or temple, where it is etiquette to remove footgear before entering, the interiors are spotless, but in a train or a railway station where shoes are not removed, the floor may be littered with trash.

Exchange of Gifts and Services

The principle of reciprocity in social relations finds expression in Japanese culture in the practice of gift exchange. Whenever one makes a formal visit to a relative or neighbor on some special occasion such as New Year's or a wedding, one bears suitable gifts and in exchange one will receive not only food to eat but also food to take home. A gift is made in exchange for any favor received or help given. While a gift made in payment for a favor received need not be returned, any gift which is brought spontaneously must be acknowledged by a return gift later.

The most formal type of gift exchange occurs at weddings, where there is a carefully calculated exchange of value for value. Because the bride is coming into the family with her dowry, the groom's family presents elaborate gifts (silk *kimono,* etc.) at the engagement ceremony. The gifts of wine, rice, fish, footgear, tea, and rice cakes brought by the bride on the wedding day are returned in kind and in the same amount by the groom's family. There are traditional types of gifts for different occasions—at a naming ceremony, for instance, one takes a set amount of cloth for the baby's *kimono,* to a sick person one takes food, to a funeral rice or its equivalent value in money. A list is usually kept of people who bring gifts to a wedding or a funeral so that in the event of a wedding or a funeral in the guest's family later one can return in kind.

When a man is conscripted and is leaving for the army, friends call on his family bearing gifts. Gifts are also taken by guests invited to the farewell banquet given by the man's family. When the soldier returns home he brings souvenirs to all those who brought going-away gifts.

Gifts are usually brought in a special gift box or wrapped up in a kerchief. The container in which the gift is brought is never returned to the caller empty, but some trifle, such as matches or paper handkerchiefs, is put inside. Each gift must be tied with a special paper cord (*mizuhiki*): gold and silver for wedding gifts, black and white for funerals, and red and white for all other occasions. There are three different ways of tying the *mizuhiki* to suit the three different uses listed above. In addition to this, a *noshi* is always placed on the upper right side of the gift. This *noshi* consists of a colored or patterned paper folded in a special manner (usually about two inches long) with a narrow strip of sea ear (abalone) inserted in the middle.

Certain types of behavior accompany the giving and receiving of gifts—the donor always apologizes for the insignificance of his gift, the recipient always protests and insists that it was not necessary to bring a gift. Such protestations are purely formal, and to ignore the proper etiquette involved would cause serious offense.

Exchange is not limited to gift giving, but also applies to favors such as helping one another at rice harvest or in funeral arrangements. At banquets drinks of rice wine are exchanged between host and guest and between guest and guest. A speech by the host must be replied to by the guest of honor.

To refuse the proffer of a gift is to insult the giver, but to accept it involves the obligation of some suitable return at a later time. In the field of government administration this can create complex problems, and Japanese law prohibits civil servants from accepting gifts from persons under their direct jurisdiction. In practice this prohibition is limited to clear-cut cases of bribery, and it would be a stiff-necked official indeed who would refuse a banquet in his honor or gifts of local arts and crafts.

The exchange principle sets a pattern for behavior. For instance, when a person gives a farewell party, he invites relatives and neighbors and such other people as he wishes to ask or feels he should. Later, only the people who have been invited to this farewell make farewell gifts and come out to bid farewell on the day of departure. Once the situation is out of the ordinary and this general pattern is upset, confusion may set in. This was well demonstrated at the end of a village study made by the writer and his wife. At the end of the year it became known that we were leaving our belongings in the village and giving them away because we did not wish to sell anything. Since we were leaving for good, there could be no exchange so that as a result there was much grabbing and begging for things, and all the usual politeness and decorum that usually accompanies gift exchange was lost.

The Japanese Smile

Lafcadio Hearn, one of the first Occidentals to discover that similar overt acts mean different things in Japan and in the United States, once wrote an essay on the subject of the Japanese smile. Because Japanese etiquette requires a smile where European calls for a long face, the Occidental calls the Japanese heartless, and the Japanese thinks the Occidental crude.

It is a cardinal article of Japanese etiquette that a guest or a superior should not be troubled by one's own private and selfish worries. This means that if an honorable guest calls on one when one's wife is seriously ill in a back room, one must not trouble the guest by mentioning the fact but on the contrary must make the guest happy with light talk and a treat of wine. Or again, if a close relative has died and one wishes to be excused from work for a day or so to attend the funeral it is proper to announce the death to one's employer with a smile.

On the other hand, within the bosom of one's family or even in the presence of old friends, it is quite permissible to give vent to one's feelings and even to weep freely.

If one's employer or superior reprimands one, such a reprimand must be accepted with a smile. On the other hand, if such reprimand is made publicly, the employee, having "lost face," is very likely not to show up for work the next day. To talk back or show anger on the spot is improper, but it is quite proper not to continue to work for a person who so forgets himself as to embarrass another person publicly. No notice is necessary and the only way to resume relations would be through a go-between.

Suicide (*Seppuku* or *harakiri*)

There is no religious sanction against suicide in Japan, and it is not considered a sign of moral weakness or degradation. On the contrary, there are circumstances under which the courage to take one's own life is essential to the honor of the family name.

In feudal times a sentence of *seppuku* or self-destruction was considered more honorable than that of death at the hands of an executioner. Wives of *samurai* had as part of their dress a short dagger with which to commit suicide in the event of threat of personal dishonor. As is well known, Japanese soldiers are told that the only honorable course in the face of defeat and capture is suicide.

A man who regards himself as responsible for some tragic error may commit suicide. There have been cases of police officials who have committed suicide as the result of a relatively minor confusion in regard to arrangements for the Emperor's progress through the area of their jurisdiction. This type of suicide rarely occurs among high government or military officials.

Another motive for suicide is that of protest. A man who feels some act to be very wrong but who sees no way of changing it may commit suicide at the doorstep of the man he holds responsible in order to draw attention to the wrong. Such a suicide occurred before the American Embassy in Tokyo at the time of the American Exclusion Act. This type of suicide is intended to embarrass the person against whom the protest is made.

Still another form of suicide is the rather mystical one involving a desire to follow in death some beloved leader. The last famous example of this was when General Nogi took his life after the death of the Emperor Meiji.

In all these types of suicide it is clear that the individuals must have considerable will power and be in a state of high rather than low morale. They are not the acts of men at the end of a down-hill moral degeneration. However, in peacetime none of these forms of suicide is common. Most suicides in Japan are prosaic self-despatchings as the result of poverty, or some social or moral impasse such as the joint suicide of a young couple whose parents will not countenance a marriage. The suicide rate for the nation in the 1930's was just a little above that of the United States and below that of France.

Seeing and Not Seeing

There is in Japanese etiquette a general avoidance of socially perceiving things which one is not supposed to see. If a caller comes and the room needs cleaning up or the host must dress, the guest may be asked in by maid or daughter and while he sits waiting, the husband or wife in dressing or preparing some food may pass through the room or within physical vision of the guest, but he takes no notice till host or hostess comes in and bows and formally greets the guest, at which time they socially perceive each other for the first time. Similarly, at a shrine where a group of worshipers is already present, a newly arrived person first bows and finishes his ritual before greeting any of the others and before they notice him.

Lack of physical privacy in the home makes it necessary to provide for privacy by social fiction. Thus two or three members of the family may carry on quite separate occupations in the same or adjoining rooms, a child may be asleep, a wife sewing and talking to a neighbor, and the husband smoking his pipe—each socially oblivious of the activities of the others.

Trains and hotels are homes by proxy so that it is quite proper to dress and undress, to eat meals and in general behave as one would at home. It is a familiar sight on a Japanese train to see a man change his clothes en route without thought of retiring to a washroom for privacy. People not of the "household" are not expected to take notice unless formally invited and recognized. This is in contrast to behavior on the street, where it is socially tabu to eat anything and where if one passes an acquaintance one must bow and exchange greetings.

Another example of this same general pattern is to be found in the Japanese theater where property men, dressed in black, step out on the stage during an act to change scenery—they are not to be noticed and in accordance with Japanese tradition they do not interfere with the progress of the play or the playgoer's willing suspension of disbelief.

Nudity

In native Japanese culture there is little prudery about nudity or sex as such, and in rural areas children in playing house may imitate their parents not only in sweeping and cooking but also in love-making. On the other hand, when adult, one should restrict all love-making to the privacy of one's room and it is improper for husband and wife even to hold hands or exchange loving remarks in the presence of others.

If circumstances require it, as in rural areas and some public bathhouses, people may undress and slip into the bath in the presence of strangers. The said strangers are expected to take no notice. It may also be noted that Japanese bathers, even if no one of the opposite sex is present, always preserve essential modesty by holding a towel in such a way as to conceal ultimate nakedness. In general nudity is an informal state and etiquette requires proper dress when receiving guests. A man or woman working about the house on a hot day with few clothes on will always slip on a *kimono* before receiving a caller.

Understatement

A disarming and, to a Westerner, misleading social habit of Japanese is their custom of understatement. When speaking to a guest, a hostess belittles the food she serves, a husband belittles his wife's abilities or his son's intelligence. One must never praise one's own things or immediate relatives to a guest for this would be unseemly boasting. It would be a serious error to accept such humble protestations at face value; on the contrary the guest in referring to the quality of the food, the ability of the wife, or the intelligence of the son is duty bound to speak with honorifics.

The inverse of this pattern is to be found in Japanese nationalist dogma whereby patriots freely state that the Japanese nation is superior to all other nations of the world. The difference here is that in one case a man is speaking of himself as an individual and in the other of the more impersonal state of which he is a member.

Understatement or suggestion rather than exposition is also a characteristic of Japanese art and poetry—a few lines rather than a detailed landscape or tedious narrative. This is true even of country folksongs, as for example the following:

> My lover's heart
> And the wind—
> Where will they stop?

Notes on Etiquette

There are many other rules of behavior which require that things be done in a prescribed manner. For instance, there are special expressions to be used when greeting people on different occasions and at different times of the year. There are special expressions to be used when one returns home and informs one's family that one has returned, and special ways of answering these expressions. Before eating it is proper to say *itadakimasu* (I partake) and after finishing *gochisōsama* (I have eaten well). Similarly there are formal ways of commencing a social letter according to the months or seasons of the year, e.g., in spring (April) one would write: "The cherry blossoms are in their fullest splendor . . ." or in autumn (November): "The falling leaves beat against the window pane and wild geese wing their way (across the sky)."

There are prescribed ways for serving food. One's behavior, dress, and manner of sitting must conform with the occasion. On formal occasions certain stiff postures are assumed and everyone remains in that position until the host proclaims that guests should "be at ease." On the other hand, there are very informal postures, such as stretching out on the floor in hot weather or sitting around almost naked, which are, also accepted and are quite proper in their place.

Almost all social occasions demand the serving of tea. A guest is always served tea when he arrives and tea is served at the end of all formal banquets. Storekeepers and businessmen serve tea to customers and callers and even in administrative offices business matters will be discussed with a visitor over a cup of tea. The tea is green tea, taken without cream or sugar, and generally served with pickle or cakes which vary in quality according to the occasion.

In Japan when two people greet one another they bow, whereas in this country we shake hands. This reflects a general Oriental pattern of culture where bodily contact in public, especially between the sexes, is bad form. (To hug or kiss in public is shocking to conservative Japanese, a sure sign of Occidental depravity.)

The bow is also a mark of respect. The socially inferior bows more profoundly than his superior when they meet. The shrine worshiper bows to the gods before and after his prayer. When a subject bows toward the Emperor's portrait at a public meeting or on entering a schoolyard he is not "worshiping" the portrait but showing his respect for the highest ranking personage in the land, just as when Americans salute the flag they are showing respect for rather than worship of that symbol.

This brief summary of Japanese behavior traits, while of some value in predicting how particular Japanese may behave under certain circumstances, does not provide a magic explanation for Japanese aggressive warfare any more than a similar summary of national behavior traits would explain why the United States once attacked Mexico, the British took on an Empire, or the French swept over Europe under Napoleon. The Japanese under the Tokugawa maintained internal and external peace for over two centuries, while such aspects of her culture as child training, group responsibility, and the family system have been more or less constant during both the peaceful and aggressive phases of her history. It is necessary to look to various socio-economic causes, such as industrialization and European colonization in Asia, to explain the complex phenomena of modern wars. Behavior patterns help to predict how individuals of a given culture behave in a particular social context; they neither cause, nor can they "explain," why nations go to war or remain at peace.

Chapter X

National Attitudes

BACKGROUND

ATTITUDES of Japanese toward various foreign powers and the development of nationalism are largely based on a combination of Japan's feudal history, geographical position, and recent industrial development. As an island nation threatened in the past from the Asiatic mainland by an unsuccessful attempt at invasion by the Mongols in the thirteenth century and caught unprepared and defenseless against Perry's warships in 1853, Japan has stressed naval strength ever since she came out of her period of isolation.

A realization of the nation's weakness in the face of an industrialized West in the nineteenth century gave the nation's leaders a powerful desire for national unity and security. On the home front a program was undertaken to modernize the political structure and industrialize the economy—both as a means of gaining strength and as a means of getting rid of the unequal treaties forced upon her at this time. State Shinto was adopted as an ideological balance wheel during the period of rapid political economic change. Looking abroad and noticing that strength was best demonstrated by armies, Japan greatly strengthened her national defenses and built up a powerful army and navy. Attempts of Western powers to restrict her naval power on a ratio of three to America's five and Britain's five has been one of the arguments Japanese militarists have used to show Japan's need to become completely independent of and fortified against the Western powers. National policy has also been determined by the urge of a newly industrialized nation to gain control of sources of raw materials and markets.

In 1876 Japan tried out on Korea what the United States had successfully tried on Japan—diplomacy backed by the "big stick" to produce a treaty to open ports for trade. Conflicts with China developed over the internal affairs of Korea, whose own government was anything but strong. In 1891 Russia began building the Trans-Siberian Railroad and extending her interests in the Far East. A glance at a map will show why Japan felt her national sovereignty endangered by this whole uncertain situation so close to home. In 1894 Japan attacked China through Korea, defeating her in 1895. By the treaty of Shimonoseki China ceded Formosa to Japan and agreed to recognize the independence of Korea. Furthermore, by the terms of the treaty the southern part of Manchuria was to be ceded to Japan, but three European powers—Germany, Russia, and France—interfered and forced her to give up this territory, Russia later taking over Manchuria as a sphere of influence. This example of European interference in what Japan regarded as her own affair the Japanese have never forgotten.

Because of a common fear of Russia, Japan and Britain formed an alliance in 1902 which lasted nineteen years. As Russia extended her power east, the inevitable clash came in 1904 ending in another victory for Japan—much to the surprise of the rest of the world. In 1914 Japan entered the Great War on the side of the allies and had the pleasure of winning from Germany her scattered possessions in Asia and a mandate over those in the Pacific. During this war Japan presented her "21 demands" on China for special rights which would have given Japan virtual control of that country's economy—but again the Western powers interfered. At the Washington Conference Britain gave up her alliance with Japan partly as a result of American pressure.

In 1931 came the invasion of Manchuria, the establishment of Manchoukuo, and Japan's self-righteous resignation from the League of Nations. The rest is familiar history—growing economic barriers against Japanese overseas trade, the China War beginning in 1937, and finally the Greater East Asia War in 1941.

This brief recapitulation of history should provide a few clues to an understanding of some of Japan's attitudes toward various foreign countries. From the Japanese point of view, the nation was in a very precarious international position in the nineteenth century; at the same time the growing industrialization of the nation was causing difficulties both at home and abroad. Japanese financial interests, like those of the British before them, favored free world trade—but as Japan rose in power she found tariff walls growing, and increasing restraints on access to raw materials. The population having doubled with industrialization, the nation faced another crisis in the world depression of the 1930's similar to that of the 1850's. The financial interests and the advocates of political expansion became one in the creation of the puppet state Manchoukuo.

ATTITUDES TOWARD THE GOVERNMENT— NATIONALISM

Most people, be they American or Japanese, French or German, regard themselves, their culture, and their form of government as being superior to those of other nations. The Japanese attribute their own superiority to the possession of a unique indomitable and moral spirit. This "Japanese spirit" found expression in old Japan in the phrase *Yamato damashii* and today is often called *Nihon seishin*; another aspect of the Japanese spirit finds its expression in the *samurai* code of Bushidō.

Kōdō, the Way of the Emperor, is a recent political doctrine which harks back to a supposed remark of the Emperor Jimmu concerning *hakkō ichiu,* the eight corners of the world, which the Japanese should bring under one roof. The War Office has of recent years taken up the idea that Japan has a mission to wipe out injustice and inequality from the world by extending to it the divine rule of the Japanese Emperor.

Kokutai, a broad mystical concept of "Japanese national polity" which combines the "best features" of *Kōdō* and *Bushidō,* is still another form Japan's nationalism takes. National Shinto, for instance, is called *Kokutai* Shinto. The Japanese Spirit (*Yamato damashii, Nihon seishin*) is interpreted by Japanese as a manifestation of *Kokutai.*

The methods by which national unity is stressed in the school system have already been noted. Because of Japan's relatively homogeneous ethnic background, concepts of blood and soil find ready acceptance.

An example of the effects of Japanese concepts of nationalism on individual action is the suicidal dash of three Japanese soldiers carrying a long bomb into a barbed wire fence holding up a Japanese advance at Chapei in 1932. The men succeeded in clearing the way but all three were blown to bits. The "Human Bombs" were publicized and honored for their heroic patriotism and a statue of them carrying out their mission now stands in Tokyo. Schoolchildren are taken in groups to salute the statue and receive edifying talks from their teachers on this supreme example of *Yamato damashii.*

Other less honored examples of nationalist action are the political assassinations by rightist groups of national figures whose policies are regarded as being not sufficiently patriotic.

Bushidō and *Kōdō* are manifestations of a nationalistic revivalism which is in part at least a reaction against the unsettling flood of Western influences on Japan since Perry's day. This reaction has taken the form of a dislike of the West and a searching of the nation's past for ideal virtues. The acts of Western nations, such as interference in Japan's Asiatic activities, the denial of racial equality at Versailles, and the United States Exclusion Act, have only enhanced these mystical nationalist philosophies.

As with religion, so with nationalism, one may ask, who believes what? Some degree of nationalism—or to call it by another name, patriotism—is found in all Japanese. Among higher government officials including the military, as well as among the higher ranking businessmen, there is little misunderstanding of the Emperor's role in government. While they may be sincere in their belief in the Emperor's long line of ancestors and in his position as head of the state, they recognize also that his actual power is slight. They are themselves constantly engaged in political manipulations for power, part of which consists in "capturing the Emperor." This does not mean, however, that such a concept as *Kōdō* is not sincerely believed in by some military officers and nationalist writers and scholars.

A man such as the late Mitsuru Toyama not only believed in Japan's divine mission, but also believed Western nations to be corrupt, materialistic, and insincere in their foreign policies. A student of political science, on the other hand, who has studied abroad may have a more objective attitude in comparing the governmental structure of Japan with that of other nations.

On the whole, the mass of the people are but little concerned with such mystical concepts as *Kōdō* or the theology of State Shinto, though there is little in them to which they would object. This is similar to the situation in nineteenth-century England when only a few statesmen and writers such as Kipling actively concerned themselves with the righteousness of the white man's burden, while most Englishmen passively took for granted the general colonial expansion of the nation.

The white-collar worker and technician groups, although vocationally educated, have had little chance to study political and sociological phenomena, and as a group probably accept at face value the Emperor's supremacy in the state, as well as many of the ideological by-products of Japanese nationalism such as State Shinto. Dissatisfaction with the government takes the form of criticism of big business interests or other special cliques for misusing financial or political power.

The workers, even though the policies of the militarists have forced them to curtail their standards of living, probably include few persons who are not enthusiastic in their profession of Japanese nationalism. The labor organizations of the twenties have been either suppressed or transformed to become part of the structure of the new national unity. This has occurred because of the special circumstances of the Japanese industrial situation. Japanese trade-unionism, like so many other aspects of modern Japan which have been called by Western names, was never really like European or American trade-unionism. As already pointed out, relations between Japanese employers and workers have always had in them a good deal of the feudal tradition, workers being loyal to employers and employers feeling a paternal responsibility to workers. Because of these attitudes the alterations suffered by trade-unionism when it was imported into Japan were great. Furthermore, the group of extreme militarists now in control, although of different shades of opinion, generally abhor communism, particularly because of its relationship with Japan's old enemy, Russia. Yet they are decidedly anticapitalist themselves, so that their program has had a definite appeal to the anticapitalist elements in the country. The address made by one of the February, 1936, rebel officers to a street crowd demonstrates this point (as quoted in Wilfred Fleisher's *Volcanic Isle*) :

Why should we fight in Manchuria to protect the interests of the capitalists, the Mitsuis, the Kawasakis, the Morimuras and others? . . . Manchuria was all right in the beginning, but now it is the hunting ground of the capitalists who are exploiting it for their own profit. . . . We are for loyalty to the Emperor and elimination of the evil statesmen who stand between the people and the Emperor.

Thus it was not difficult for an early socialist leader to later identify himself with the younger army leaders in advocating a form of national socialism.

Farmers, while quite sincere in their attitudes of patriotism, are but little concerned with the finer points of nationalist theology. They are engrossed in the realities of making a living from the soil and inclined to remain rather unimpressed by doctrines from the city whose relevance to their economic life is not immediately apparent. The patriotic societies which include peasant or farmer in their titles are usually organized in actuality by urbanites or small-town men of some middle-class group which has suffered as a result of economic developments.

Most Japanese are sincere in their attitudes of reverence for the Emperor and of pride in race and culture, but there have been dissenters from the national ideology in the past, and the super-patriots, while they have had a very favorable set of attitudes to manipulate, have also had to encounter widespread skepticism. All Japanese value formal correctness highly and are trained from birth to conform externally, regardless of inner feelings. To them, frank self-expression, which we tend to praise, would be regarded as selfish rudeness. The typical Japanese reaction to differences between appearance and reality is to accept and use the discrepancies without attempting to debunk them. It is therefore necessary to avoid the too easy assumption that attitudes in Japan are as unified and as sweepingly nationalistic as the public behavior of many Japanese seems to indicate. Within the framework of custom and loyalty to the Emperor violent struggles for power between factions take place, and thousands of lesser folk in the ranks of civil service and business are perfectly well aware of the secular realities of political and economic motives of action.

ATTITUDES TOWARD FOREIGN PEOPLES

Any generalizations about Japanese attitudes, especially those about attitudes toward specific foreign peoples, are subject to numerous exceptions. Nonetheless, it is desirable to make some few such generalizations if for no other reason than to point out that such attitudes do exist and that Americans are not the only ones who look askance at strangers.

While Japanese regard themselves as superior people, they have a certain respect for some Occidentals because of the fact that so many aspects of the Japanese industrial revolution were adopted from them in recent decades. At the same time this very borrowing has led to a reaction against the West in the ideological field, and to some Japanese patriots all foreigners are evil. This point of view has traditional sanction in the old Tokugawa attitude that foreigners were not to be trusted and therefore should be kept out of the land of the *kami*.

At the bottom of the hierarchy of non-Japanese are the native peoples of the Pacific Islands and of Asia—the Ainu, the Formosan aboriginals, Micronesians, and Malayans. On a level above these native peoples in Japanese opinion are the Koreans and the Chinese. On the third level are the Russians, and above them, but somewhat below the Japanese themselves, come other Westerners —Americans, Englishmen, Frenchmen, Germans.

Native Peoples

The typical attitude of a Japanese toward Asiatic and Pacific "natives" such as the Formosans or the Micronesians is that they are a simple people who require supervision to prevent their injuring either themselves or others. A fatherly benevolence is combined with an exploitative attitude, making Japanese colonial administrators anxious to provide certain rudimentary benefits of civilization such as schooling, some medical care, and in general enough instruction in civilized ways to produce useful peaceful populations; but, at the same time, these colonial governors are willing to suppress any revolt with the utmost violence and to see the native peoples exploited economically and as labor.

In Formosa much of the interior is still occupied by preliterate tribesmen, many of whom were formerly headhunters. The Japanese have enclosed these people in a stockaded fortified zone around a vast inland area and through the years they have narrowed the zone and pushed back those natives who have been unwilling to adopt farming and life in the "civilized" portions of the island. Occasional violence by tribesmen has met with full-scale military punitive expeditions resulting in the massacre of hundreds of the natives. On the other hand, Japanese policemen assigned to the aboriginal areas have been expected to function not only as police but also as doctors, teachers, and councilors to the natives. Thousands of the aboriginals have been moved from the mountains to the lowlands and set up as "civilized" farmers, so that they have abandoned their own way of life and have become workers useful in various Japanese enterprises.

In occupying the Philippines, Malaya, and the East Indies the Japanese took with them this same general point of view. The Indonesians were "liberated" from the Dutch, but the Japanese were concerned, just as the Dutch before them, with changing their "lazy" ways, and fitting them into the Empire's total economy. This did not necessarily mean harsh treatment, but rather a desire to reorient the native from Holland to Japan. Even in the Philippines during the Japanese occupation, the Manila government felt called upon to exhort the people to give up their degenerate ways as inculcated by Americans, tighten their belts, and work hard for the good of an "independent" Philippines.

Koreans

There are over a million Koreans in Japan proper, mostly unskilled workers. This fact, taken together with Korea's position as a subordinate part of the Japanese Empire, affects Japanese attitudes toward Koreans. Having been encouraged by industrial concerns to emigrate to Japan because they will work for less than native Japanese, Koreans occupy much the same position in Japan as recent migrants in certain American industrial areas—i.e., they are resented by older native workers and are looked upon as dirty foreigners with low standards of living, morality, and honesty. As a submerged minority group they are subject to being made scapegoats in time of crisis. A striking demonstration of this occurred during the 1923 earthquake, when many Koreans were massacred on the basis of rumors about a Korean uprising against the Japanese.

The Chinese and China

The Japanese attitude toward the Chinese is ambivalent: there is considerable respect for Chinese culture, but it underlies a rather general disdain for the Chinese as people. Japanese scholars and most well-educated Japanese recognize the tremendous cultural debt owed to China and accord old China a high place for her achievements in art, literature, and philosophy.

This respect for Chinese culture is, however, directed toward the past, and modern China is thought of as being a country of corrupt, spiritually deficient people who do not have any unified sense of nationality. China is regarded as incapable of self-government by many Japanese. To an American this attitude seems like an easy rationalization of the Japanese desire to exploit the Chinese, but this is too simple an explanation. The Japanese are as sincere in regarding the Chinese as inferior as they are in their belief in themselves as the chosen people, and many believe that Japanese control and organization of the Asiatic continent will benefit not only Japan but also the Chinese.

Formosan Chinese are officially called "Taiwanese," the Manchurian Chinese, "Manchukuoans." Government officials and probably also the Japanese man-in-the-street tend to regard these emigrants from China proper as somewhat inferior to the Chinese in the homeland—perhaps because the admiration for Chinese culture is not carried over to them. Official policy is to "Japanize" the Formosan Chinese despite the fact that a general prejudice prevents their being given the better professional and administrative jobs.

Russians and the U.S.S.R.

Japanese attitudes toward Russia and the Russians are conditioned by the old imperial rivalry of the two countries in northeast Asia, the Russo-Japanese War, and the Japanese fear and dislike of Soviet political organization.

Because Japan succeeded in her war against Russia in 1905, Japanese for many years despised the military prowess of the Russians and largely for this reason have regarded the Russians as somewhat inferior to other Westerners. The performance of Russia in the first World War and the complete collapse of the old imperial organization served to strengthen these views. This attitude still prevails among many Japanese, although Japanese leaders have learned in a series of border clashes along the Siberian frontier that Russia is no longer weak in a military sense.

The imperial rivalry between the two countries has made the Japanese extremely suspicious of Russian intentions for decades. In recent years, these suspicions have manifested themselves in exceedingly strict surveillance of all Russians entering Japan and in the intricate diplomatic maneuverings concerning such matters as the Chinese Eastern Railroad, the boundaries of Manchoukuo, oil concessions in Sakhalin, and fishing concessions in Russian waters.

The recently abrogated neutrality pact between Russia and Japan did not destroy Japanese fear and suspicion of Russia. In spite of these antagonisms, there has existed an uneasy interdependence between the two countries in the form of oil and fishing concessions and a mutual desire to avoid open conflict. This interdependence may also stand Japan in good stead when Russia voices her plans for Asia at the peace table.

The United States

The Japanese have had a variety of attitudes toward the United States, and their feelings toward us are perhaps more complicated than toward any other nation because of the frequent and varied contacts between Americans and Japanese. Japanese attitudes have ranged from extreme admiration to profound dislike for the United States and her people. The admiration arises from America's leadership in bringing Western techniques to Japan and from the willingness of many Americans in Japan to recognize the Japanese as worthy people. American aid in the industrialization of the country, the generous response of this country in sending aid to the victims of the 1923 Tokyo earthquake, and the fact that many Americans in Japan acted less arrogantly than other Europeans have contributed to this friendship. In addition, many Japanese have relatives in this country from whom they have received favorable reports on conditions here (and also complaints about discriminatory treatment). Many Japanese have received part of their education in the United States. American missionaries, although their efforts to replace the Japanese gods with a supreme alien deity have been disliked, have contributed much in the way of educational and welfare activities which have been appreciated.

The dislike, rooted in a general antiforeignism, has arisen from American racial discrimination and our official condemnation of Japanese national expansion, and more recently, our economic sanctions against the country. The role of Perry and other American naval officers in forcing the doors of Japan has also contributed toward these hostile attitudes.

The position of America as the chief rival of Japan for Pacific power is an important factor influencing the opinions of Japanese nationalists, who wished to alter the Pacific *status quo* in their favor. Until the present war many Japanese regarded Americans as decadent, soft, and incapable of translating their enormous resources into effective military action. Early Japanese victories in the South Pacific doubtless reinforced this general point of view. The behavior of American tourists in Japan, with their love of luxury and ready spending of enormous sums of money, also helped in the spreading of this conviction.

An important set of influences which have produced dislike of Americans are those associated with our own assertions of superiority such as the 1924 Exclusion Act, which the Japanese have resented intensely.

However, America has many friends in Japan as has been shown even in crisis situations when the Japanese government has been whipping up anti-American sentiment. For example, at the time of the bombing of the *Panay,* the American Embassy received many expressions of sympathy as well as monetary contributions, large and small, from private citizens acting on their own behalf to show their friendship for this country. One Japanese woman even went so far as to visit the American Embassy and to cut off her hair in the presence of the Ambassador's secretary, tie it with a ceremonial cord and present it to him, a traditional gesture expressing extreme regret and a desire to atone for a wrong. When Americans, after long residence in Japan, began leaving the country because of State Department orders, they found numerous Japanese friends sorry to see them go and exceedingly sympathetic with them as individuals and as Americans. It is significant that Japanese propaganda has had to stimulate hatred for America by playing up "selfish" American imperialism and "atrocities" of American soldiers.

Great Britain

The Japanese feeling toward the English is rather like that toward Americans, except that the dislike is perhaps more intense and the friendliness less marked. If America has been a major Pacific rival, England with her Asiatic empire has been a principal obstacle to Japanese expansion on the continent. Some British who have visited Japan have tended to act as though they regarded the Japanese as "just another Asiatic people," and this behavior has made them disliked as a group. To the militarists, the British base at Singapore, the Crown Colony of Hongkong, and British treaty rights in China have been particularly galling.

France

Direct contacts of Frenchmen and Japanese have been more limited than Japanese contacts with either Americans or Englishmen, and Japanese attitudes toward the French have consequently not been built up on the basis of so broad an experience. There have been, however, a number of highly sympathetic contacts (e.g., Pierre Loti's enthusiasm for Japan), and certain general similarities between the two countries (love of art, marriage by go-between, administrative centralization, a sharp division between peasantry and townsfolk) are appreciated by many of the better-educated Japanese.

Politically France lost prestige after the German invasion and the Japanese became convinced that the French were no longer to be considered as of real significance in Asiatic politics.

Germany

Germany provided a model for the Japanese constitution, and the Japanese army was originally built along the lines of the nineteenth-century German army; but Germany's military defeat in the World War left German prestige in Japan at a low ebb.

After the occupation of Manchuria, trade with Germany increased, and in other ways official relationships between the two countries became more cordial. Unofficially, this meant that many German nationals moved into Japan, especially during the past decade. With the signing of the Anti-Comintern Pact in 1936 and its later extension to a military alliance with Germany (and Italy) in 1940, Japanese leaders recognized not only the coincidence of Japanese and German interests in upsetting the *status quo* in Europe and Asia, but also the growing military might of the Germans.

The ordinary Japanese is not particularly fond of Germans and the middle-class Japanese with business or political ambition is perhaps somewhat inclined to resent them on the ground that they are, after all, Westerners; German officials who have come to Japan in recent years have tended to exhibit their racial bias in irritable ways and even the government is apparently suspicious of Germans in Japan so that although forced by recent political circumstances to allow them considerable freedom, it keeps close watch on their activities.

It is essential in considering Japanese attitudes toward Germany and the Germans to recognize that many similarities between events in the two countries during recent years exist not because Japan copied Germany, but rather because two nations with similar problems found similar solutions. As has been pointed out earlier, the centralization of the Japanese government has developed out of native Japanese traditions and was not imported from Germany. On the other hand, when close imitation has been appropriate to the Japanese situation, German ideas have been utilized. An illustration is the new block organization of the Imperial Rule Assistance Association which is similar to the Nazi party organization; but even here the German technique is neatly adapted to traditional Japanese patterns.

BELIEFS CONCERNING CAUSES OF THE WAR

The Greek historian, Thucydides, writing of the Peloponnesian War over 2300 years ago, thought it necessary not only to discuss the historical origins of the conflict but also to assess specifically both its real and supposed causes. Some of his remarks might well be applied to the present conflict: "The real cause I consider to be one which is formally most kept out of sight. The growth of the influence and power of Sparta [Japan] and the alarm which this inspired in Athens [America], made war inevitable. Still it is well to give the grounds alleged by either side, which led to the dissolution of treaties and the breaking out of war."

Americans are fairly well acquainted with the "grounds alleged" by the American Department of State—let us now look briefly at those alleged by the Japanese.

This can best be done by a series of quotations from men of differing social position in Japanese society. First we may listen to a middle-class businessman talking to a foreigner, Miss Helen Mears, during an interruption in a train trip for military maneuvers in 1935. Mr. Naka's words as quoted (with permission) from Miss Helen Mears' *Year of the Wild Boar* (pp. 152–153):

"Why are you having such maneuvers?" I asked. "Does Japan expect to be attacked?"

"Sa!" He pointed again. I could see a whole burst of white puffs as the plane circled. It was a solitary plane and I could not see much sense in what it was doing. Perhaps because I am not a military expert. "To be attacked?" Mr. Naka echoed. "*Sodesu.* Of course, yes, we will be attacked."

"By whom?" I asked.

He shrugged. "Who knows? Perhaps Britain. Perhaps America. Perhaps Russia. Perhaps all of you." He laughed.

I climbed back up into the vestibule, and Mr. Naka climbed up beside me. I said, "Why should America attack Japan?"

"To help Britain, naturally." Mr. Naka looked at me with

scant respect. As a woman, I would not be expected by a Japanese man to know much about international politics. I persisted, however; I wanted to know what the Japanese thought about this.

"To help Britain do what?" I asked.

"To protect her interests in China. To exclude Japan from trade with her Empire."

"And you think, to accomplish these things, America and Britain will attack you?"

"With force, perhaps not. With boycotts, and blockades, yes. I think it. All Japan thinks it. And when that happens, do you think we cannot fight to defend ourselves from such smothering? And if we fight, well perhaps we will be bombed." He laughed again.

I spoke very slowly. "If Japan is bombed, she will be to blame, won't she? After all, you started the bombing yourselves. You attacked the Chinese in Manchuria by force, and created Manchukuo by force. If you wished not to fear attack, you should yourselves avoid attacking others."

Mr. Naka shrugged. "You Western peoples are so virtuous. You forget that it was your people not the Japanese, who invented bombs and airplanes, and first used them in war. You forget that the interests which Britain wishes to protect in China and in her Empire were taken by force. We Japanese can see that the white races think aggression is wrong only if it is by a colored race against a white race."

I interrupted. "But if you are going to call your people a colored race, then the Chinese are colored too. And it is the Chinese whom you have attacked."

"No." Mr. Naka's emotion was rising so that he had some difficulty in keeping his voice level. "No! It is not the Chinese whom we attacked. We must have peace with China. We cannot survive without peace with China. But the national government of China is today as much a puppet government of Britain as Manchuria is the puppet of my country. We cannot trust the national government. We must be able to depend on the government of China for we are alone in the world, and we are at the mercy of you Western powers. We are encircled everywhere with enemies. We must be prepared. As our *Tenno* has told us, our crisis is now, and also in the future."

Mr. Naka was a businessman speaking in 1935. Let us now turn to the views of a Japanese intellectual talking to an American missionary, Mr. Mickle, in June, 1940, as reported in his privately issued *Letters From Japan*:

1. "The U. S. and Japan are now nearer war than they have ever been. But if war does come it will be entirely the fault of the U. S., for Japan has been leaning over backwards to please the United States."

2. "In Japan it is impossible to judge public opinion by reading the newspapers. When you read the papers here you must always read between the lines. Public opinion does exist in Japan but you find it in the conversation of small groups of friends and not in public expression."

3. "Why is the United States so selfish? You set up the Monroe Doctrine over there and yet you object to our doing the same thing here. You have all you want and need there and yet you want what we have here."

4. "Fundamentally the United States fears Japan because they believe the military party is running wild without any brakes on. But this is not true. Superficially speaking there is 'Ni-ju-Seifu' (dual government) in Japan—'structurally' there is—but mentally and spiritually there is none. For the military and the people cannot be separated. We recognize that our military saved us from western powers and they have become the heirs of the samurai and samurai tradition. Of course there are many elements in the military that are rotten to the core and they are not worthy of the honor of being the heirs of the samurai."

5. "If the United States places an embargo on Japan, our navy will go into the Dutch East Indies at once."

6. "Personally I am not averse to Germany winning the war, but the German people have certain mental and spiritual weaknesses."

7. "Liberalism is the result of economic security. Give the Germans and the Japanese economic security and they will become as liberal and tolerant as the English, French, and Americans. But even granting this to the Germans, it will take them generations to strengthen their mental and spiritual weaknesses."

8. "You Americans keep delivering moral lectures to us and reminding us of treaties, treaties, treaties. You are forever thinking in terms of treaties, statistics, curves. You are too pragmatic."

The views and intentions of the military are well expressed in the following remarks of Admiral Nakamura Ryozo (retired) writing in "Kokumin" about November, 1940 (as quoted by Mickle):

The crisis confronting Japan today is more grave than the one before the Russo-Japanese war, and if Japan should this time miss the chance of at once overcoming the difficulties confronting it, then Japan will never be able to realize the great ideal of "Hakko-Ichiu," or the Oneness of the Universe. Japan must strike at America as it struck at Russia. The firm resolve to fight against the United States must enter into the heart of every man in this country. Japan should on longer resort to politics and diplomacy in the contest with America. For Japan, America has taken the place of Russia 35 years ago, and now ventures to stand audaciously in the way of Japan's advance. Without fighting America Japan will not be able to accomplish the structure of the Greater East Asia mutual prosperity sphere, nor will it be able to settle completely the present China incident. America today is no longer a democratic nation, but an aggressor nation trying to conquer the world—. I fully realize that the burden imposed on Japan by the four years of conflict with China is a heavy one. Accordingly, Japan will not be able to win a victory over America simply by resorting to ordinary tactics or by showing a lukewarm determination. Rather, in the spirit of seeking a narrow escape with the odds ten to one against, and with the resolve to plunge into the very valley of death as being the only hope, Japan must now enter on her fight against America.

Into the context of these remarks the wording of the Imperial Rescript declaring war on the United States fits as neatly as a round peg in a round hole:

To cultivate friendship among nations and to enjoy prosperity in common with all nations has always been the guiding principle of Our Empire's foreign policy. It has been truly unavoidable and far from Our wishes that Our Empire has now been brought to cross swords with America and Britain.

More than four years have passed since China, failing to comprehend the true intentions of Our Empire, and recklessly courting trouble, disturbed the peace of East Asia and compelled Our Empire to take up arms. Although there has been reestablished the National Government of China, with which Japan has effected neighborly intercourse and cooperation, the regime which has survived at Chungking, relying upon American and British protection, still continues its fratricidal opposition.

Eager for the realization of their inordinate ambition to dominate the Orient, both America and Britain, giving support to the Chungking regime, have aggravated the disturbance in East Asia.

Moreover, these two Powers, inducing other countries to follow suit, increased military preparations on all sides of Our Empire to challenge us. They have obstructed by every means our peaceful commerce, and finally resorted to a direct severance of economic relations, menacing gravely the existence of Our Empire.

Patiently have We waited and long have We endured in the hope that Our Government might retrieve the situation in peace, but Our adversaries, showing not the least spirit of conciliation, have unduly delayed a settlement; and in the meantime, they have intensified the economic and political pressure to compel thereby Our Empire to submission.

This trend of affairs would, if left unchecked, not only nullify Our Empire's efforts of many years for the sake of the stabilization of East Asia, but also endanger the very existence of Our Nation. The situation being such as it is, Our Empire for its existence and self-defense has no other recourse but to appeal to arms and to crush every obstacle in its path.

In October, 1943, at the height of Japan's conquests in Southeast Asia, a diplomat, Foreign Minister Shigemitsu, answered an interpolation in the Diet as to Japan's war aims.

To begin with, the present great war is the greatest war of imperialism which America and Britain have undertaken to wage. That is to say, their plan is to dominate the greater part of the world as colonies and their devilish hands are stretched out not only to East Asia but also to Iran, Iraq, and Arabia. Moreover, these hands are stretched out over even North and South America, and America is attempting to strengthen the foundation of the construction of an American world empire.

Allied Objectives—Thus their war objectives are to egoistically and selfishly victimize the world for the sake of their own prosperity. In other words, the present war is a war which America and Britain brought about to try to obliterate Japan and East Asia by force of arms. But East Asia being the native land as well as the stronghold of the East Asiatics, we East Asiatics must defend this native land to the bitter end.

Survival War—If this opportunity is missed, the people of East Asia will no doubt for all time never be able to seize an opportunity for autonomy and independence. In this sense, the G.E.A. War is a sacred war for the survival of East Asia, and to defend the birthplace of the East Asiatics is the war objective of our country. Today, looking forward to the liberation of Asia and the revival of East Asia to the very end, East Asia, through the cooperative aid and in an atmosphere of friendly national sympathies is attempting to purify the world and to win through in this holy war. I believe this is the true figure of East Asia. . . .

Racial Discrimination—East Asia is not exclusive. Mutual wellbeing and a common prosperity in East Asia are a part and parcel of world peace. Any attempt at aggression against East Asia shall be firmly and decisively dealt with for the sake of defense of this part of the world. Anyone who understands East Asia shall receive unstinted welcome. More than that, East Asia aspires to establish cultural intercourse throughout the world, abolish racial discrimination, and free traffic, and thereby contribute to the promotion of world peace.

Grim War—Inspired by this lofty ideal we are determined to fight together to the last man. The war today is extremely grim. To us it is a war to protect our native land, East Asia, a war for self-existence. To the enemy it is a colonial war, a war for world domination. Seldom, if ever, has a colonial war, a war of aggression, a war against justice been won. As far as I know, the Opium War against China was the only exception. Today, Greater East Asia has been liberated. The East Asiatic Nations have attained their aspirations and are replete with hope for the future.— (Radio Tokyo, October 27, 1943)

Japanese attitudes have been discussed at some length because so little attention is generally given to them or they are quoted out of context and in such a manner as to appear ridiculous. Actually they are the natural products of Japanese history, recent development, and international contacts. It is desirable at least to know of their existence because as social attitudes they appear to a Japanese just as sound and are believed in just as deeply as are American beliefs that the United States does not favor aggression, or that Japanese are a homogeneous race of fanatical *samurai*. For these reasons these attitudes will be facts to reckon with in the postwar world. These social attitudes are related to national behavior, and they cannot be changed by empty threat or even by military force any more than the Southern States accepted the views or culture patterns which carpetbaggers tried to force upon them in the 1860's. National attitudes develop and change slowly as the structure of the society and its relations with other nations change and develop.

Tomorrow

IN this outline of the national structure of Japan special attention has been paid to the network of social relations which make up the nation. Such a presentation inevitably tends to bring out those aspects of the structure which serve to preserve national unity and continuity rather than those dysfunctional aspects which tend to disrupt national solidarity. Every society has lines of cleavage, but under normal conditions a strong tendency toward social solidarity prevents such lines of cleavage from developing far enough to split the society

The Japanese nation has no serious lines of cleavage between religious or ethnic groups as does, for instance, the United States. However, the growth of socioeconomic strains during the Tokugawa period led to drastic changes in the nation during the period of social readjustment in the second half of the nineteenth century and since 1919 new lines of cleavage have come into existence. One of these has been a tendency toward democratic socialism as the industrialization of the nation developed, a tendency which ran counter to the old traditional system of social classes and military rule. This dysfunctional situation was finally resolved in the 1930's by a surprisingly rapid development of national socialism whereby the traditional position of the military and the social effects of the new industrialism were—temporarily at least—resolved.

Japan is now engaged in the greatest war in her history, a war which must be producing changes in her national structure as fundamental as those which occurred immediately after the fall of the Tokugawa. Women, for instance, are being given for the first time higher education in science and are being called upon for civic activities in national and local women's associations which must inevitably lead to changes in their social role. On the battle front Japanese forces, for the first time in the nation's history, have had to fall back hundreds of miles before a foreign foe and at Guadalcanal the high command deserted hundreds of its men who died miserable jungle deaths. Such developments may lead to a cleavage between disillusioned enlisted men and civilians on the one hand and high army officers and government officials on the other. Other future developments in Japanese society will follow trends already established. The economic and financial structure of the nation, already well on the way toward nationalization and away from small-scale competing enterprises, will perhaps become completely socialized—at least in the field of natural resources, public utilities, and heavy industries.

In the field of government it is likely that the new regional organization of the country into eight economic regions will eventually take on many of the functions of the present prefectural governments. This is in line with a long-term trend toward centralization of administrative areas since feudal days and also makes possible the decentralization of certain activities formerly administered solely from Tokyo.

In the field of education the trend toward more vocational education and a longer number of years of public school will doubtless continue when the country recovers from the effects of the present war.

Shinto sects, as the most recent indigenous religious movement, may well expand at the expense of the older inert Buddhist sects. This is especially likely in the event of a serious military defeat, when the people will need some spiritual solace to make up for material loss.

Japan has had many civil wars in her history—the last one less than seventy years ago. It is safe to assume that, revolution, or no revolution, the Japanese national structure will undergo many fundamental changes in the next ten years. Among these changes may be not only the new social role of women and of the army, but also a new political role for the Emperor.

The role of the Emperor in Japanese government has varied greatly in different periods of Japanese history: during the Tokugawa period he was largely a ceremonial figure, all political power resting in the hands of the *shōgun*; during the Meiji period political power not only rested in the hands of the Emperor, but Meiji himself was active in the determination of national policy; and today, while the Emperor remains symbolically the center of political power, actual rule is in the hands of imperial advisers. The whole system of State Shino, with its emphasis on the sacred descent and infallibility of the Emperor, is a new development since Tokugawa times. It could be dismantled tomorrow, without seriously disrupting Japanese society, the Emperor being reduced to the role of the British King and Shinto priests left to make a living from voluntary contributions on the same basis as Buddhist and Sect Shinto priests.

The irony of the present situation is that the American government, apparently accepting the present role of the Emperor at Japanese official face value, permits no propaganda to Japan which might undermine his prestige; and in the event of an occupation of Japan, our military government officers will undoubtedly, in the name of law and order, repress any revolution which might affect the imperial position. Meanwhile, some Allied committee may decide to enforce a change in the Japanese government from without and in the attempt solidify the nation again in the name of a sacred ruler.

As a matter of fact, the existence or nonexistence of an Emperor in Japan has little to do with the basic causes of Japanese foreign policy. Once the country was superisolationist as a result of a number of political factors having little if anything to do with the existence of the Emperor. After 1868 the Emperor became the symbol of a new nationalism and so was a handy rallying point for the Japanese military, but these military could scarcely have gained the backing they did if internal economic developments and international rivalries and pressures had not played into their hands. In the future Japan may be isolationist, nationalist, or internationalist depending on circumstances, whether or not there is an Emperor on the throne. Germany managed to create new symbols to replace the Kaiser, and the same could easily occur in Japan. By a similar token, England, with a king, was extremely expansionist during her nineteenth-century industrial development period but today favors the *status quo* and international cooperation—still retaining the throne.

Whatever happens, it is safe to predict that future social developments in Japan will be in accord with Japanese history and culture—the form of Japan tomorrow can best be understood and predicted by its shape of yesterday.

Japan today is far and way in the lead of all Eastern Asia so far as education and literacy, public health, and industrialization are concerned. There is little doubt that much of this progress is due to the fact that Japan alone of all Asiatic countries has had complete and independent sovereignty in contrast to the colonial status of Malaysia and the economic domination of China by foreign powers. Her very leadership in Asia is one of the fundamental causes of the present war. In the years to come, when Malaysia and China become truly independent areas, they too will come of age in industry, education, and public health with their by-products of economic strength, big-circulation newspapers, and self-conscious nationalism. Such a coming of age will mean the final withdrawal of Europe and America from political and economic control in Asia. The question is, can the Western powers withdraw gracefully, thus making possible a future of friendly social and economic interdependence between all modern nations, or will they resist the new trend, thus laying the groundwork for a second war in East Asia?

Appendices

Appendix I

The Japanese Constitution
(Official Translation)

PREAMBLE

Having, by virtue of the glories of Our Ancestors, ascended the Throne of a lineal succession unbroken for ages eternal; desiring to promote the welfare of and to give development to the moral and intellectual faculties of Our beloved subjects, the very same that have been favoured with the benevolent care and affectionate vigilance of Our Ancestors; and hoping to maintain the prosperity of the State, in concert with Our people and with their support, We hereby promulgate, in pursuance of Our Imperial Rescript of the 12th day of the 10th month of the 14th year of Meiji, a fundamental law of State, to exhibit the principles, by which We are to be guided in Our conduct, and to point out to what Our descendants and Our subjects and their descendants are forever to conform.

The rights of sovereignty of the State, We have inherited from Our Ancestors, and We shall bequeath them to Our descendants. Neither We nor they shall in future fail to wield them, in accordance with the provisions of the Constitution hereby granted.

We now declare to respect and protect the security of the rights and of the property of Our people, and to secure to them the complete enjoyment of the same, within the extent of the provisions of the present Constitution and of the law.

The Imperial Diet shall first be convoked from the 23rd year of Meiji and the time of its opening shall be the date when the present Constitution comes into force.

When in the future it may become necessary to amend any of the provisions of the present Constitution, We or Our successors shall assume the initiative right, and submit a project for the same

265

to the Imperial Diet. The Imperial Diet shall pass its vote upon it, according to the conditions imposed by the present Constitution, and in no otherwise shall Our descendants or Our subjects be permitted to attempt any alteration thereof.

Our ministers of State, on Our behalf, shall be held responsible for the carrying out of the present Constitution, and Our present and future subjects shall forever assume the duty of allegiance to the present Constitution.

CHAPTER I

The Emperor

Article I.—The Empire of Japan shall be reigned over and governed by a line of Emperors unbroken for ages eternal.

Article II.—The Imperial Throne shall be succeeded to by Imperial male descendants, according to the provisions of the Imperial House Law.

Article III.—The Emperor is sacred and inviolable.

Article IV.—The Emperor is the head of the Empire, combining in Himself the rights of sovereignty, and exercises them, according to the provisions of the present Constitution.

Article V.—The Emperor exercises the legislative power with the consent of the Imperial Diet.

Article VI.—The Emperor gives sanction to laws and orders from them to be promulgated and executed.

Article VII.—The Emperor convokes the Imperial Diet, opens, closes and prorogues it, and dissolves the House of Representatives.

Article VIII.—The Emperor, in consequence of an urgent necessity to maintain public safety or to avert public calamities, issues, when the Imperial Diet is not sitting, Imperial Ordinances in the place of law.

Such Imperial Ordinances are to be laid before the Imperial Diet at its next session, and when the Diet does not approve the said Ordinances, the Government shall declare them to be invalid for the future.

Article IX.—The Emperor issues or causes to be issued, the Ordinances necessary for the carrying out of the laws, or for the maintenance of the public peace and order, and for the promotion of the welfare of the subjects. But no Ordinance shall in any way alter any of the existing laws.

Article X.—The Emperor determines the organization of the different branches of the administration, and salaries of all civil and military officers, and appoints and dismisses the same. Exceptions especially provided for in the present Constitution or in other laws, shall be in accordance with the respective provisions (bearing thereon).

Article XI.—The Emperor has the supreme command of the Army and Navy.

Article XII.—The Emperor determines the organization and peace standing of the Army and Navy.

Article XIII.—The Emperor declares war, makes peace, and concludes treaties.

Article XIV.—The Emperor declares a state of siege. The conditions and effects of a state of siege shall be determined by law.

Article XV.—The Emperor confers titles of nobility, rank, orders and other marks of honor.

Article XVI.—The Emperor orders amnesty, pardon, commutation of punishments and rehabilitation.

Article XVII.—A Regency shall be instituted in conformity with the provisions of the Imperial House Law.

The Regent shall exercise the powers appertaining to the Emperor in His name.

CHAPTER II

Rights and Duties of Subjects

Article XVIII.—The conditions necessary for being a Japanese subject shall be determined by law.

Article XIX.—Japanese subjects may, according to qualifications determined in laws or ordinances, be appointed to civil or military or any other public offices equally.

Article XX.—Japanese subjects are amenable to service in the Army or Navy, according to the provisions of law.

Article XXI.—Japanese subjects are amenable to the duty of paying taxes, according to the provisions of law.

Article XXII.—Japanese subjects shall have the liberty of abode and of changing the same within the limits of law.

Article XXIII.—No Japanese subject shall be arrested, detained, tried or punished, unless according to law.

Article XXIV.—No Japanese subject shall be deprived of his right of being tried by the judges determined by law.

Article XXV.—Except in the cases provided for in the law, the house of no Japanese subject shall be entered or searched without his consent.

Article XXVI.—Except in the cases mentioned in the law, the secrecy of the letters of every Japanese subject shall remain inviolate.

Article XXVII.—The right of property of every Japanese subject shall remain inviolate.

Measures necessary to be taken for the public benefit shall be provided for by law.

Article XXVIII.—Japanese subjects shall, within limits not prejudicial to peace and order, and not antagonistic to their duties as subjects, enjoy freedom of religious beliefs.

Article XXIX.—Japanese subjects shall, within the limits of law, enjoy the liberty of speech, writing, publication, public meetings and associations.

Article XXX.—Japanese subjects may present petitions, by observing the proper forms of respect, and by complying with the rules specially provided for the same.

Article XXXI.—The provisions contained in the present Chapter shall not affect the exercise of the powers appertaining to the Emperor, in times of war or in cases of a national emergency.

Article XXXII.—Each and every one of the provisions contained in the preceding Articles of the present Chapter, that are not in conflict with the laws or the rules and discipline of the Army and Navy, shall apply to the officers and men of the Army and of the Navy.

CHAPTER III

The Imperial Diet

Article XXXIII.—The Imperial Diet shall consist of two Houses, a House of Peers and a House of Representatives.

Article XXXIV.—The House of Peers shall, in accordance with the Ordinance concerning the House of Peers, be composed of the members of the Imperial Family, of the orders of nobility, and of those persons who have been nominated thereto by the Emperor.

Article XXXV.—The House of Representatives shall be composed of Members elected by the people, according to the provisions of the Law of Election.

Article XXXVI.—No one can at one and the same time be a Member of both Houses.

Article XXXVII.—Every law requires the consent of the Imperial Diet.

Article XXXVIII.—Both Houses shall vote upon projects of law submitted to it by the Government, and may respectively initiate projects of law.

Article XXXIX.—A Bill, which has been rejected by either the one or the other of the two Houses, shall not be again brought in during the same session.

Article XL.—Both Houses can make representations to the Government, as to laws or upon any other subject. When, however, such representations are not accepted they cannot be made a second time during the same session.

Article XLI.—The Imperial Diet shall be convoked every year.

Article XLII.—A session of the Imperial Diet shall last during three months. In case of necessity, the duration of a session may be prolonged by Imperial Order.

Article XLIII.—When urgent necessity arises, an extraordinary session may be convoked, in addition to the ordinary one.

The duration of an extraordinary session shall be determined by Imperial Order.

Article XLIV.—The opening, closing, prolongation of session and prorogation of the Imperial Diet, shall be effected simultaneously for both Houses.

In case the House of Representatives has been ordered to dissolve, the House of Peers shall at the same time be prorogued.

Article XLV.—When the House of Representatives has been ordered to dissolve, Members shall be caused by Imperial Order to be newly elected, and the new House shall be convoked within five months from the day of dissolution.

Article XLVI.—No debate can be opened and no vote can be taken in either House of the Imperial Diet, unless not less than one third of the whole number of the Members thereof is present.

Article XLVII.—Votes shall be taken in both Houses by absolute majority. In the case of a tie vote, the President shall have the casting vote.

Article XLVIII.—The deliberations of both Houses shall be held in public. The deliberations may, however, upon demand of the Government or by resolution of the House, be held in secret sitting.

Article XLIX.—Both Houses of the Imperial Diet may respectively present addresses to the Emperor.

Article L.—Both Houses may receive petitions presented by subjects.

Article LI.—Both Houses may enact, besides what is provided for in the present Constitution and in the Law of the Houses, rules necessary for the management of their internal affairs.

Article LII.—No Member of either House shall be held responsible outside the respective Houses, for any opinion uttered or for any vote given in the House. When, however, a Member himself has given publicity to his opinions by public speech, by documents in print or in writing, or by any other similar means, he shall, in the matter, be amenable to the general law.

Article LIII.—The Members of both Houses shall, during the session, be free from arrest, unless with the consent of the House, except in cases of flagrant delicts, or of offenses connected with a state of internal commotion or with a foreign trouble.

Article LIV.—The Ministers of State and the Delegates of the Government may, at any time, take seats and speak in either House.

CHAPTER IV

The Ministers of State and the Privy Council

Article LV.—The respective Ministers of State shall give their advice to the Emperor, and be responsible for it.

All Laws, Imperial Ordinances and Imperial Rescripts of whatever kind, that relate to the affairs of the State, require the counter-signature of a Minister of State.

Article LVI.—The Privy Councillors shall, in accordance with the provisions for the organization of the Privy Council, deliberate upon important matters of State, when they have been consulted by the Emperor.

CHAPTER V

The Judicature

Article LVII.—The Judicature shall be exercised by the Courts of Law according to law, in the name of the Emperor.

The organization of the Courts of Law shall be determined by law.

Article LVIII.—The judges shall be appointed from among those who possess proper qualifications according to law.

No judge shall be deprived of his position, unless by way of criminal sentence or disciplinary punishment.

Rules for disciplinary punishment shall be determined by law.

Article LIX.—Trials and judgments of a Court shall be conducted publicly. When, however, there exists any fear that such publicity may be prejudicial to peace and order, or to the maintenance of public morality, the public trial may be suspended by provision of law or by the decision of the Court of Law.

Article LX.—All matters that fall within the competency of a special Court shall be specially provided for by law.

Article LXI.—No suit at law, which relates to rights alleged to have been infringed by the illegal measures of the administrative authorities and which shall come within the competency of the Court of Administrative Litigation specially established by law, shall be taken cognizance of by a Court of Law.

CHAPTER VI

Finance

Article LXII.—The imposition of a new tax or the modification of the rates (of an existing one) shall be determined by law.

However, all such administrative fees or other revenue having the nature of compensation shall not fall within the category of the above clause.

The raising of national loans and the contracting of other liabilities to the charge of the National Treasury, except those that are provided in the Budget, shall require the consent of the Imperial Diet.

Article LXIII.—The taxes levied at present shall, in so far as they are not remodelled by a new law, be collected according to the old system.

Article LXIV.—The expenditure and revenue of the State require the consent of the Imperial Diet by means of an annual Budget.

Any and all expenditures overpassing the appropriations set forth in the Titles and Paragraphs of the Budget, or that are not provided for in the Budget, shall subsequently require the approbation of the Imperial Diet.

Article LXV.—The Budget shall be first laid before the House of Representatives.

Article LXVI.—The expenditures of the Imperial House shall be defrayed every year out of the National Treasury, according to the present fixed amount for the same, and shall not require the consent thereto of the Imperial Diet, except in case an increase thereof is found necessary.

Article LXVII.—Those already fixed expenditures based by the Constitution upon the powers appertaining to the Emperor, and such expenditures as may have arisen by the effect of law, or that appertain to the legal obligations of the Government, shall be neither rejected nor reduced by the Imperial Diet, without the concurrence of the Government.

Article LXVIII.—In order to meet special requirements, the Government may ask the consent of the Imperial Diet to a certain amount as Continuing Expenditure Fund, for a previously fixed number of years.

Article LXIX.—In order to supply deficiencies, which are unavoidable, in the Budget, and to meet requirements unprovided for in the same, a Reserve Fund shall be provided in the Budget.

Article LXX.—When the Imperial Diet cannot be convoked, owing to the external or internal condition of the country, in case of urgent need for the maintenance of public safety, the Government may take all necessary financial measures, by means of an Imperial Ordinance.

In the case mentioned in the preceding clause, the matter shall be submitted to the Imperial Diet at its next session, and its approbation shall be obtained thereto.

Article LXXI.—When the Imperial Diet has not voted on the Budget, or when the Budget has not been brought into actual existence, the Government shall carry out the Budget of the preceding year.

Article LXXII.—The final account of the expenditures and revenue of the State shall be verified and confirmed by the Board of Audit, and it shall be submitted by the Government to the Imperial Diet, together with the report of verification of the said Board.

The organization and competency of the Board of Audit shall be determined by law separately.

CHAPTER VII

Supplementary Rules

Article LXXIII.—When it has become necessary in future to amend the provisions of the present Constitution, a project to the effect shall be submitted to the Imperial Diet by Imperial Order.

In the above case, neither House can open the debate, unless not less than two-thirds of the whole number of Members are present, and no amendment can be passed, unless a majority of not less than two-thirds of the Members present is obtained.

Article LXXIV.—No modification of the Imperial House Law shall be required to be submitted to the deliberation of the Imperial Diet.

No provision of the present Constitution can be modified by the Imperial House Law.

Article LXXV.—No modification can be introduced into the Constitution, or into the Imperial House Law, during the time of a Regency.

Article LXXVI.—Existing legal enactments, such as laws, regulations, Ordinances, or by whatever names they may be called, shall, so far as they do not conflict with the present Constitution, continue in force.

All existing contracts or orders, that entail obligations upon the Government, and that are connected with expenditure, shall come within the scope of Art. LXVII.

Appendix II

Japanese Weights and Measures

DISTANCE AND LENGTH

Ri = 36 *cho* = 2,160 *ken*	= 2.44 miles
Ri = (marine)	= 1 knot
Ken = 6 *shaku* = 60 *sun*	= 5.97 ft.
Shaku = 10 *sun* = 100 *bu*	= 0.99 ft. (1 *shaku* cloth measure = 1.25 ordinary *shaku*.)

LAND MEASURE

Square *ri* = 1,296 sq. *cho*	= 5.96 sq. miles
Cho = 10 *tan* = 3,000 *tsubo*	= 2.45 acres

QUANTITY, CAPACITY, AND CUBIC MEASURES

Koku = 10 *to* = 100 *sho*	$\begin{cases} = 47.95 \text{ gallons (liquid) U.S.A.} \\ = 5.12 \text{ Bushels (dry) U.S.A.} \end{cases}$
Go = (10th of a *sho*)	
Koku (capacity of vessels)	= 10th of a ton
Koku (timber)	= about 1 cubic ft. × 10
Koku (fish)	= 40 *kan* (in weight)

WEIGHTS

Kwan (*Kan*) = 1000 *momme*	= 8.27 lbs. avoir.
Kin = 160 *momme*	= 1.32 lbs. avoir.
Momme = 10 *fun*	= 0.13 oz. avoir.

MONEY

Yen = 100 *sen* = 1000 *rin*	= at par $.498 (U.S.) (In 1941 the exchange value was $.235.)

Appendix III

Table of Japanese Year Dates

1st Year of Meiji	 1868	
2nd " "	 1869	
3rd " "	 1870	
4th " "	 1871	
5th " "	 1872	
6th " "	 1873	
7th " "	 1874	
8th " "	 1875	
9th " "	 1876	
10th " "	 1877	
11th " "	 1878	
12th " "	 1879	
13th " "	 1880	
14th " "	 1881	
15th " "	 1882	
16th " "	 1883	
17th " "	 1884	
18th " "	 1885	
19th " "	 1886	
20th " "	 1887	
21st " "	 1888	
22nd " "	 1889	
23rd " "	 1890	
24th " "	 1891	
25th " "	 1892	
26th " "	 1893	
27th " "	 1894	
28th " "	 1895	
29th Year of Meiji	 1896	
30th " "	 1897	
31st " "	 1898	
32nd " "	 1899	
33rd " "	 1900	
34th " "	 1901	
35th " "	 1902	
36th " "	 1903	
37th " "	 1904	
38th " "	 1905	
39th " "	 1906	
40th " "	 1907	
41st " "	 1908	
42nd " "	 1909	
43rd " "	 1910	
44th " "	 1911	
45th " "	 1912	
1st Year of Taisho	 1912	
2nd " "	 1913	
3rd " "	 1914	
4th " "	 1915	
5th " "	 1916	
6th " "	 1917	
7th " "	 1918	
8th " "	 1919	
9th " "	 1920	
10th " "	 1921	
11th " "	 1922	

12th Year of Taisho	....	1923
13th " "	....	1924
14th " "	....	1925
15th " "	....	1926
1st Year of Showa	....	1926
2nd " "	....	1927
3rd " "	....	1928
4th " "	....	1929
5th " "	....	1930
6th " "	....	1931
7th " "	....	1932
8th " "	....	1933
9th Year of Showa	....	1934
10th " "	....	1935
11th " "	....	1936
12th " "	....	1937
13th " "	....	1938
14th " "	....	1939
15th " "	....	1940
16th " "	....	1941
17th " "	....	1942
18th " "	....	1943
19th " "	....	1944
20th " "	....	1945

Appendix IV

Glossary

Aikoku Fujinkai. The government-sponsored Women's Patriotic Society.

Ainu. The Caucasoid aborigines of Japan, now found only in Hokkaido.

amacha. Sweet tea used at ceremony of Buddha's birthday.

Amaterasu-ō-mikami. Sun Goddess and divine ancestress of the Emperor.

Amida. Amitabha, an important Buddhist deity; the savior deity of the Shinshu sect.

Aoyama Gakuin. American missionary college in Tokyo.

Araki, General Baron Sadao (b. 1877). Former War Minister, onetime mentor of the Young Officers' group.

ashigaru. Foot soldiers (Tokugawa period).

aza. Small subdivisions of land.

baishin. Retainers of *daimyō* and *hatamoto* (Tokugawa period).

bakufu. The *shōgun's* government.

benshi. Man who interprets action of a motion picture; institution of *benshi* becoming obsolete.

Benten. Sarasvati, a Buddhist goddess of good fortune.

Binzuru. A Buddhist deity of healing.

Bon (Obon). Buddhist festival in July when the ancestral souls are said to come back to reside in the Butsudan for three days.

bugyō. Judicial officers (Tokugawa period).

buraku. Hamlet, subgroup within a *mura* or township.

Bushidō. The Way of the Warrior (the *samurai* code).

butsu. A general term for Buddhist deities.

Butsudan. Buddhist household shelf.

Chichibu, Prince (b. 1902). Younger brother of the reigning Emperor.

chokunin. Second rank of civil service.

chōnin. Townsman (a merchant).

chorinbo. Synonym for *eta,* a low caste.

Chōshu. The old name for Yamaguchi, a region noted for the number of military leaders it has produced.

Chūbu. Geographical term for the middle area of the main island.

chūgakkō. Middle school.

Daibutsu. Large statue of Buddha or Amida.

daigaku. University.

Daikoku. Buddhist deity of good fortune.

daikwan. Shōgun's district officer (Tokugawa period).

daimyō. Feudal lord.

Dainichi. Vairocana, a Buddhist deity.

Daisai-Jitsu. Grand (religious) festival days.

Daishi dō. Wayside god houses enshrining Kobo Daishi.

Dengyō Daishi (767–822). The founder of the Tendai Buddhist sect.

dō. Small neighborhood or hamlet god house, usually Buddhist.

Dōgen (1200–1253). One of the introducers of Zen Buddhism into Japan.

Dōmei. Semiofficial news agency with a monopoly on foreign news distribution in Japan.

Dōshisha. Mission school in Kyoto founded by Joseph Neeshima.

Ebisu. Shinto deity of good fortune, image often found in farm houses and on plaques in stores.

Eisai (1141–1215). One of the introducers of Zen Buddhism into Japan.

eta. Formerly a pariah group, lower than *hinin;* today a minority group but officially merged with the rest of the *heimin* or common people.

fu. Urban administrative area.

fuda. Paper talisman (Shinto).

fudai. Hereditary (loyal) vassals (Tokugawa period).

fudo. Japanese Buddhist deity.

Fujin Club. Large-circulation women's magazine.

Fukuzawa, Yūkichi (1835–1901). Pioneer educator of Meiji period.
furo (ofuro). Japanese bath.
Fusō Kyō. Mountain sect (Shinto).

geisha. Japanese song and dance girl; courtesan.
Genrō. Elder statesman.
Gensui Fu. Board of Field Marshals and Fleet Admirals.
gikai. The Diet.
go. A Japanese game somewhat similar to chess.
gochisōsama. "I have eaten well." The proper expression to use after having eaten.
gokenin (hatamoto). Shōgun's direct retainers below the rank of *daimyo* (Tokugawa period).
goningumi. Five-household group of peasants (Tokugawa period).
gōsha. District shrines.
gōshi. Rural *samurai.*
Goshōki. The week of the death day of Shinran, founder of Shinshū. From the 22nd to the 28th of the eleventh month.
gumbatsu. The military clique.
gun. The old county administrative unit; abolished as an official unit in 1926.
gundai (daikwan). Shōgun's district officer (Tokugawa period).
Gunji Sangi In. Supreme War Council.

Hachiman. Shinto deity of war, deification of the Emperor Ojin.
haiden. The outer, less sacred part of Shinto shrine.
hakkō ichiu. The doctrine of "eight corners of the world under one roof" based on a passage in the *Nihongi* and used by some Japanese nationalists as a justification for world rule by Japan.
Hambai Kumiai. Marketing Association.
han. Old feudal fiefs.
hannin. Fourth rank of civil service.
harai (oharai). A Shinto purification ritual.
hara kiri. Ceremonial suicide; *seppuku.*
hatamoto (gokenin). Shogun's direct retainers below the rank of *daimyō* (Tokugawa period).
heimin. Commoner; all Japanese except royalty and the hereditary nobility are now *heimin.*
hibachi. Portable charcoal heaters.

Higan (Spring). The week of the Spring equinox; a Buddhist holiday.

Higan (Autumn). The week of the Fall equinox; a Buddhist holiday.

hinin. A pariah group of the Tokugawa period.

Hirata Atsutane (1776–1843). Shinto scholar.

Hokkaido. The northern island of Japan.

Hokkeshū (Nichiren). A Buddhist sect founded by Nichiren.

honden. The inner, more sacred part of a shrine.

Hōnen (1133–1212). The founder of the Jōdo sect of Buddhism.

Hongwanji. The Shinshu sect of Buddhism, today divided into two branches—East and West Hongwanji.

Honkyoku. Pure Shinto sect.

Honshū. The main island of Japan.

Hossō. An early, minor Buddhist sect.

hotokesama. Buddhas; also the souls of the dead.

Ie no Hikari. The name of a farmers' magazine published by the National Cooperative Association.

ihai. Ancestral tablet, usually kept in family Butsudan.

Inari. God of prosperity and of good crops, patron of *geisha* and of prostitutes, a popular Shinto deity.

inkyo. State of retirement.

inugami. Dog spirit, usually malevolent.

inugami mochi. Witches by means of the dog spirit.

irori. Fire pit in country houses.

Ise Dai Jingū. Grand Imperial Shrine of Ise in Mie Prefecture.

itadakimasu. "I partake," the proper expression to use before eating.

Ito, Hirobumi (1841–1909). Meiji period governmental leader; one of chief writers of the Constitution.

Iwakura (1825–1883). Meiji government leader.

Iwasaki. One of the *zaibatsu*; family of the firm of Mitsubishi.

Iyeyasu. *See* Tokugawa Iyeyasu.

Izanagi. Shinto male creator deity.

Izanami. Shinto female creator deity.

Ji. A minor Buddhist sect founded by Ippen.

jijūchō. Grand Chamberlain.

Jimmu Kai. A patriotic society.

Jimmu Tennō. First "historical" ruler of Japan. (The orthodox dates are 660–585 B.C., but critical historians place his reign about five centuries later.)

Jimmu Tennō Sai. Anniversary of the death of Emperor Jimmu; a national holiday.

jinja (jinsha). Shinto shrine.

Jinushi. Land deity.

Jizō. Kshitigarbhi, a Buddhist deity.

Jōdo. A Buddhist sect founded by Hōnen Shōnin.

jogakkō. Girls' school.

jorō. Prostitute.

jūdō. A form of jujitsu.

juzu. Buddhist rosary.

Kagawa, Toyohiko (b. 1888). Christian leader and novelist.

kagura (okagura). Sacred dances performed at Shinto shrines.

kakemono. Scroll paintings, often hung in *tokonoma.*

kama-no-kamisama. Popular deity of the stove.

kami. A Shinto deity.

kamidana. Shinto god-shelf found in most Japanese households.

kampeisha. Government shrines

kana. Japanese syllable symbols.

kawa-no-kamisama. River god popularly believed to be dangerous.

kazoku. Noble class.

Kegon. A minor Buddhist sect.

Keio. Private university founded by Fukuzawa, Yukichi.

kempō. The Constitution.

ken. Prefecture.

kendō. The art of fencing.

kensha. Prefectural shrine.

kimono. Clothing.

King. Large circulation magazine.

kō. Mutual financial-aid society.

Kōbai Kumiai. Purchasing Association.

Kōbō Daishi (774–835). Buddhist priest and scholar, founded by Shingon sect.

Kōdō. The Way of the Emperor.

Kojiki. Record of ancient matters; recounts Japanese myths and history through the seventh century; oldest Japanese book extant (A.D. 712).

Kōjin. Spirit of the land.

282 THE JAPANESE NATION

koku. Measure of weight (4.9629 bushels).

kokuheisha. National shrine.

kokumingakkō. Elementary school.

Kokuryū Kai. Amur River Society (commonly translated as Black Dragon Society).

Kokutai. Japanese national polity.

Kompira. A Buddhist god of healing and happiness.

Konkō Kyō. Faith-healing sect (Sect Shinto).

Konoye, Prince (b. 1891). Former prime minister.

koseki. Family record kept in the administrative office.

kotatsu. A lattice-like wooden structure placed over a fire pit and covered with a quilt.

koto. A thirteen-stringed harp.

kōtōgakkō. Preparatory school.

kōtōkan. Higher officials, a collective term for *chokunin* and *sōnin* (second and third ranks) of civil servants.

ku. Ward; an administrative district.

kuchō. The head of a ward or *ku.*

kuge. Court nobility.

Kumaso. Aborigines of Kyushu.

kumichō. Neighborhood head (Tokugawa period).

kumigashira. Neighborhood head (Tokugawa period).

kunaidaijin. Minister of the Imperial Household.

Kurozumi Kyō. Faith-healing sect (Sect Shinto).

Kwannon. Buddhist deity of mercy.

Kwanto. Geographical area; the plain around Tokyo.

kyōkai. Churches or shrines of Sect Shinto.

kyūreki. Old lunar calendars.

Kyūshu. The large southern island of Japan.

machi. Town.

mamori (omamori). Shinto talisman.

Matsudaira. One of influential noble families.

Meiji Era. The era of the reign of Emperor Meiji (1868–1912).

Meiji Gakuin. A Christian school in Tokyo.

Meiji Jingū. A shrine where are enshrined the souls of the Emperor Meiji and his consort.

Meiji Setsu. Anniversary of the birth of Emperor Meiji (November 1).

metsuke. Secret agents (Tokugawa period).

Mikado. Gateway of Heaven; often used to indicate the Emperor.
miki (omiki). Sacred wine offered to Shinto deities.
Minseitō. Political party (dissolved in 1940).
miso. Soybean paste used in base of Japanese bean soup.
Misogi Kyō. Purification sect (Sect Shinto).
Mitake Kyō. Mountain sect (Sect Shinto).
Mitsubishi. Business form of Iwasaki family, one of the *zaibatsu.*
Mitsui. One of Japan's largest business families and corporations; one of the *zaibatsu.*
miya (omiya). Shinto shrine.
mizuhiki. A special paper cord used to tie gifts.
Momotarō. Hero of a Japanese fairy tale who is born from a peach and who brings wealth and happiness to his foster parents.
monbatsu. Collective term for politically active group of the nobility class.
Motoori Norihaga (1730–1801). Shinto scholar.
mujin. Mutual financial aid societies (same as *kō*).
mukakusha. Ungraded shrines.
mura. Village or township.

naidaijin. Lordkeeper of the Privy Seal.
Naikaku. The Cabinet.
nakōdo. Go-between.
Namu Amida Butsu (Namanda). Buddhist ritual prayer or chant.
nanushi (shōya). People's representative or mayor in a village (Tokugawa period).
narikin. Nouveau riche.
nekogami. Cat spirit, usually malevolent.
Nichiren (Hokkeshū). Buddhist sect founded by Nichiren (1222–1282).
Nichirin-san. Buddhist deity of the sun.
Nihon (Nippon). Japan.
Nihongi. Early history of Japan compiled in A.D. 720.
Nihon seishin. Japanese spirit.
Ninigi no mikoto. Grandson of Amaterasu ō mikami who came down to rule the earth during the age of the gods.
Nippon (Nihon). Japan.
norito. Shinto ritual prayer.
noshi. A necessary item when presenting a gift; consists of a colored

or patterned paper folded in a special manner with a narrow strip of abalone inserted in the middle.

nusa. Sacred wand and pompom of hemp and *sakaki* used in Shinto rituals.

o. An honorific; for words with honorific prefixes, look up under second letter; e.g., *okagura,* see *kagura.*

ōaza. The term for the old constituent *mura* when two *mura* have been joined into one.

Obaku. Subsect of the Zen Buddhist sect.

Oda, Nobunaga (1534–1582). A man who, from humble origins, rose to greatness by putting an end to the civil wars which had been devastating Japan for over a century; he paved the way for the Shogunate.

O-Daishidō. God houses enshrining Kōbō Daishi.

Ojin Emperor (201–310). Today deified as Hachiman.

Okinawa. The prefecture of the Ryukyu Islands; also people from this prefecture.

Ōkuma, Shigenobu (1838–1922). Founder of Waseda University and leader in Meiji Government.

Okura. One of Japan's large business families; one of the *zaibatsu.*

Ōu. Geographical region, northern Japan.

Rikkyo Daigaku. Christian university in Tokyo (formerly St. Paul's).

Rinzai. Subsect of the Zen Buddhist sect.

rōnin. Unemployed warriors (Tokugawa period). A masterless *samurai.*

Ryōbu-Shinto. A combination of Shinto and Buddhism.

Ryo Kumiai. Enterprises Association.

Ryūkyūs. Islands south of Kyūshū, formerly independent and today incorporated into Japan as Okinawa and Kagoshima prefectures.

sa! "Well!"

Saigō, Takamori (1827–1877). Meiji leader; later spearhead of revolt against the new government's policies.

Saionji, Prince (1849–1943). The last of the Genro or imperial advisers of the Meiji Era.

sakaki. Cleyera Japonica, a sacred tree (Shinto).

sake. Rice-wine.

samisen. A three-stringed lute.

samurai. Warrior (Tokugawa period)'.

Sangyō Kumiai. National Cooperative Association.

sankin kōtai. Alternative attendance at the capital of *daimyō* and other families (Tokugawa period).

sansankudo. Formal drinking of ceremonial wine at the marriage ritual.

Satsuma. The older southern province now called Kagoshima.

Seinendan. Young Men's Association.

seinengakkō. Young people's school.

seishin kyōiku. Spiritual training, especially as practiced in the army.

Seiyūkai. A political party (dissolved in 1940).

Sekigahara. Famous pattle in 1600 which finally gave the Tokugawa full rule of Japan.

semmin. Term used to include the outcaste groups of *hinin* and *eta* in Tokugawa period.

semmon gakkō. Professional and vocational colleges.

Senji Dai Hon-ei. Imperial Headquarters, an emergency organization which meets usually in time of war at the command of the Emperor.

seppuku. Ceremonial suicide, *hara kiri.*

Shaka (Oshakasama). Gautama Buddha.

Shakai-Taishūtō. Social Mass Party.

shi. City.

Shikoku. One of four main islands of Japan.

shimenawa. Ceremonial straw rope (Shinto).

Shingon Sect. Buddhist sect with headquarters at Mount Kōya founded by Kōbō Daishi.

shinheimin. New commoner, a derogatory term for the *suiheisha.*

shinjū. Double suicide.

'shinnin. Highest rank of civil service.

Shinran-Shōnin (1174–1268). Religious leader and reformer; founder of Shinshu sect.

shinreki. New calendar (Gregorian).

Shinri Kyō. Pure Shinto sect (Sect Shinto).

Shinshū (Shin Sect). Buddhist sect founded by Shinran-Shōnin, stresses salvation by faith in Amida.

Shinshū Kyō. Purification sect (Sect Shinto).

shintai. God body (kept in inner sacred part of Shinto shrine).

Shinto. The Way of the Gods, includes State Shinto, Sect Shinto, and popular Shinto.

Shinyō Kumiai. Credit Association.

Shōbo Tai. Firemen's Association.

Shochiku. Large motion-picture combine.

shōgakko. Elementary school.

shōgun. The temporal and military governor of feudal times. The title *Shōgun* or Barbarian Expeller was given by the Emperor.

Shōjokai. Young Women's Association.

Shōtoku Taishi (572–621). Prince of Soga family who gave imperial patronage to Buddhism.

shōya (nanushi). People's representative or mayor in the village (Tokugawa period).

Shufunotomo. Large-circulation women's magazine.

shuku-jitsu. Fete days.

Shūsei Ha. Confucian Sect (Sect Shinto).

soba. Noodles.

sōdesu. "That is so."

Sōnin. Third rank of civil service.

Sonnō Jōi. "Revere the Emperor, expel the barbarian." A slogan of the Imperial Restoration of 1868.

sonsha. Village Shinto shrine.

sōshi. Thugs.

Sōtō. Subsect of Zen Buddhism.

Sugawara, Michizane (845–903). Exiled scholar who remained true to the Emperor; today deified as Tenjin.

Suiheisha. A minority group (Eta).

Suiheisha Undō. Equalization or water-level organization of the Eta people to gain social equality.

Suijin-san. Buddhist water god.

Sumitomo. One of big business families or *zaibatsu.*

Sūmitsu In. Privy Council.

Susanowo-no-mikoto. One of the important deities born early in the age of the gods; the strong brother of Amaterasu.

tabi. Japanese socks fashioned like mittens.

taima. Ise paper talisman.

Taisei Kyō. Confucian sect (Sect Shinto).

Taisha Kyō. Pure Shinto sect (Sect Shinto).

Takahashi, Korekiyo (1854–1936). Finance minister who initiated new fiscal policies; assassinated in February 26 unrising.

tamagushi. Small branch of the sacred *sakaki* tree with strips of white paper (Shinto).

tanomoshi. Same as *kō.*

tatami. Straw floor mats, three by six feet, found in Japanese homes and temples.

Tendai Sect. Buddhist sect at Mount Hiei founded by Dengyō Daishi.

Tenjin. Deification of the scholar, Sugawara, Michizane; deity of scholars and schoolboys.

tenko. Annual military examination of army reservists.

Tennō Heika. The Japanese Emperor.

Tenri Kyō. Faith-healing sect (Sect Shinto).

tera. Buddhist temple.

To. The Tokyo administrative district.

tōfu. Bean curd.

Tōgō, Admiral (1847–1934). Commander of the fleet in the Russo-Japanese War which sank the Russian fleet in Tsushima Strait.

Tōhō. Motion-picture company.

Tōjō, Hideki (b. 1884). Prime Minister at time Japan attacked Pearl Harbor.

tokonoma. An alcove in Japanese home in which may be hung *kakemono.*

Tokugawa, Ieyasu (1542–1616). First of the Tokugawa *shōgun* (Tokugawa period).

tonarigumi. Modern neighborhood association for rice distribution and rationing.

tonya. Wholesale dealers.

torii. Gateway to a Shinto shrine.

toshiyori. Council of Elders (village counselors) (Tokugawa period).

tōsui. Supreme command.

Toyama, Mitsuru (1855–1944). One of leaders of Japanese reactionary groups, an adviser of the Amur River Society.

Toyo uke hime-no-kami. Food goddess, enshrined at Ise.

Tsukiyomi no kami. Moon deity, contemporary of Amaterasu and Susano-o.

tozama. Outside lord (Tokugawa period).

Uchida, R. Leader of Amur River Society (Kokuryūkai).
udon. Noodles.
ujigami (sama). Patron deity and deities of a community.
ujiko sōdai. People's shrine representatives.
Urabon (Bon). Festival in July. *See* Bon.

Waseda. Private university in Tokyo, founded by Okuma, Shigenobu.
Wang Ching Wei (1877–1944). The Japanese-sponsored head of the Nanking government in China.

yakuba. Village office.
Yakushi. Buddhist deity of medicine.
Yamagata, Prince A. (1838–1922). Leader in Meiji government; strong nationalist.
Yasuda. One of the big business *zaibatsu*.
Yasukuni Jinja. Shrine in Tokyo; it enshrines the souls of dead soldiers and sailors.
Yedo. Old name for Tokyo; capital of Tokugawa government.
yen. Japanese monetary unit; equivalent to about fifty cents at par, but worth about a dollar in domestic purchasing power in Japan.
Yoshiwara. Licensed quarter in Tokyo.
yuzu. A citrus fruit, part of household decoration at New Year's.
Yūzū. A minor Buddhist sect founded by Ryōnin.

zaibatsu. Influential members of big business class.
Zaigō Gunjin Kai. Reservists' Association.
zashiki. Parlor or good room of Japanese home.
Zen. Buddhist sect introduced from China by Yeisei and Dogen. Stresses self-discipline for enlightenment.

Appendix V

Selected Works in English on Japanese Society

GEOGRAPHY

Smith, G. H. and Good, D.—*Japan, A Geographical View*, New York, American Geographical Society, 1943. pp. 104. (A short, up-to-date survey; contains a good bibliography.)

Trewartha, Glenn Thomas—*A Reconnaissance Geography of Japan*, University of Wisconsin Studies in the Social Sciences and History, No. 22. Madison, University of Wisconsin, 1934. pp. 283. (An excellent one-volume study with numerous maps and illustrations.)

Trewartha, Glenn Thomas—*Japan, A Physical, Cultural and Regional Geography*, University of Wisconsin Press, 1945. pp. 607. (A broader more up-to-date study than the previous title.)

HISTORY

Asakawa, K.—*The Early Institutional Life of Japan, A Study in the Reform of* 645 *A.D.*, Tokyo, 1903. pp. 346.

Asakawa, K.—"Notes on Village Government in Japan after 1600," *Journal of the American Oriental Society*, Vols. 30–31 (1910–1911), pp. 259–300, and 151–216.

Aston, William G.—*Nihongi, Chronicles of Japan from the Earliest Times to A.D. 697*, London, The Japan Society, 1896. pp. xxii, 407 and 443.

Borton, Hugh—*Japan Since 1931—Its Social and Political Development*, New York, International Secretariat, Institute of Pacific Relations, 1940.

Brinkley, Frank—*A History of the Japanese People from the Earliest Times to the End of the Meiji Era* . . . with the collaboration of Baron Kikuchi, with 150 illustrations engraved on wood by Japanese artists; halftone plates and maps, New York, Encyclopædia Britannica, 1915. pp. xi, 784. (Valuable for its illustrations as well as its text.)

Chamberlain, B. H.—*Ko-ji-ki or Records of Ancient Matters* translated into English by B. H. Chamberlain. 2d edition. With notes by the late W. G. Aston, an index of names and places and bibliography of books on the *Ko-ji-ki* written since 1883, Kobe, J. L. Thompson and Co., London, Kegan Paul, 1932. pp. lxxxv, 495.

Hara, Katsuro—*An Introduction to the History of Japan*, New York, G. P. Putnam's Sons, 1920. pp. 398.

Honjo, Eijiro—*The Social and Economic History of Japan*. A survey written by a Japanese authority for English-speaking readers. Kyoto, Institute for Research in Economic History of Japan, 1935. pp. xii, 410.

Murdoch, James—*A History of Japan* . . . (3 volumes) . . . Vol I: *From the Origins to the Arrival of the Portuguese in 1542 A.D.* Published by the Asiatic Society of Japan, Kobe, *Japan Chronicle*, 1910. pp. viii, 667. Vol. II: *A History of Japan During the Century of Early Foreign Intercourse (1542–1651)* by James Murdoch in collaboration with Ison Yamagata. pp. viii, 743. Vol. III: *The Tokugawa Epoch (1652–1868)*. Revised and edited by Joseph H. Longford, London, Kegan Paul, 1926. pp. vxiii, 823.

Nitobe, Inazo, and others—*Western Influences in Modern Japan, A Series of Papers on Cultural Relations*, Chicago, University of Chicago Press, 1931. pp. xii, 532.

Norman, E. H.—*Japan's Emergence as a Modern State*, New York, Institute of Pacific Relations, 1940. pp. 254. (An account of recent industrial and political developments.)

Sansom, George Bailey—*Japan; A Short Cultural History*, New York, Appleton, 1931, 2nd ed., 1943. pp. xvi, 537. (An excellent one-volume history of Japan to 1868.)

Takekoshi, Yosoburo—*The Economic Aspects of the History of the Civilization of Japan*. 3 v., New York, Macmillan, 1930. (An extensive, somewhat disorganized work.)

Tsuchiya, Takao—"An Economic History of Japan," translated by Michitaro Shidehara, revised by Neil Skene Smith, edited with an introduction and notes by Kurt Singer, *Transactions of the Asiatic Society of Japan*, Second Series, 15 (1937). pp. xviii, 271. (A valuable Japanese study.)

ECONOMY

Allen, G. C.—*Japan: the Hungry Guest*, New York, Dutton, 1938. pp. 442. (An excellent introduction to Japanese social and economic organization.)

Allen, G. C.—*Japanese Industry: Its Recent Development and Present Condition*, New York, International Secretariat, Institute of Pacific Relations, 1939. pp. x, 124.

Buchanan, D. H.—Chapter on "The Far East" in *American Society and the Changing World*, by C. H. Pegg and others, New York, F. S. Crofts, 1942. pp. 601.

Mitchell, Kate Louise—*Japan's Industrial Strength*, New York, International Secretariat, Institute of Pacific Relations, 1942. pp. 94.

Nasu, S.—*Aspects of Japanese Agriculture*, New York, Institute of Pacific Relations, 1941. pp. 168.

Orchard, John Ewing—*Japan's Economic Position, the Progress of Industrialization*, with the collaboration of Dorothy Johnson Orchard, New York, Whittlesey House, 1930. pp. xvi, 504. (A standard work on the subject as of 1930.)

Russell, Oland D.—*The House of Mitsui*, Boston, Little Brown, 1939. pp. xi, 328. (A history of the rise of one of Japan's great financial houses.)

Schumpeter, E. B., editor—*The Industrialization of Japan and Manchukuo, 1930–1940*, New York, Macmillan, 1940. pp. 944.

Stein, Guenther—*Made in Japan*, London, Methuen, 1935. pp. ix, 206.

Uyehara, S.—*The Industry and Trade of Japan*, London, P. S. King, 1936. pp. 259.

Yano, T. and Shirasaki, K.—*Nippon, A Charted Survey*, Tokyo, Kokusei-sha, 1936. pp. 487. (A translation of a Japanese text which deals largely with economics.)

GOVERNMENT

Byas, Hugh—*Government by Assassination*, New York, Knopf, 1942. pp. 369.

Colegrove, Kenneth Wallace—*Militarism in Japan*, World Affairs Books, No. 16, Boston, World Peace Foundation, 1936. pp. 78.

Fahs, Charles B.—*Japanese Government: Recent Trends in Scope and Operation*, New York, International Secretariat, Institute of Pacific Relations, 1940.

292 THE JAPANESE NATION

Hozumi, Nobushige—*Ancestor-Worship and Japanese Law,* 4th revised ed., Tokyo, Maruzen, 1938. pp. xxxi, 198.

Kitazawa, Naokichi—*The Government of Japan,* Princeton, Princeton University Press, 1929, pp. 128.

Lory, H.—*Japan's Military Masters,* New York, Viking, 1943. pp. 245.

Quigley, Harold Scott—*Japanese Government and Politics, an Introductory Study,* The Century Political Science Series, New York, Century, 1932. pp. xii, 442.

Reischauer, Robert Karl—*Japan, Government, Politics,* New York, Thomas Nelson, 1939. pp. xiv, 221.

Takeuchi, Tatsuji—*War and Diplomacy in the Japanese Empire,* Chicago, University of Chicago Press, 1935. pp. xix, 505.

EDUCATION

Keenleyside, Hugh Llewellyn, and Thomas, A. F.—*History of Japanese Education and Present Educational System,* Tokyo, Hokuseido, 1937. pp. xiv, 365.

World Federation of Education Associations—*Education in Japan,* Tokyo, 1938, 2 vols. (A valuable collection of papers presented at the seventh biennial conference of the W.F.E.A. held in Tokyo in 1937.)

SOCIAL ORGANIZATION AND FAMILY

Bacon, Alice Mabel—*Japanese Girls and Women,* Boston, Houghton Mifflin, 1902. pp. 337. (An old but excellent study of Japanese women, early childhood training, and family life.)

Embree, John F.—*Suye Mura, A Japanese Village,* Chicago, University of Chicago Press, 1939. pp. xxvii, 354. (A study of a contemporary rural community, its social, political, economic, and religious organization.)

Embree, John F.—*Acculturation Among the Japanese of Kona, Hawaii,* Menasha, Wisconsin, 1941. American Anthropological Society, Memoir 59. (A study of a Japanese emigrant community with emphasis on changes in social structure of kin and neighborhood groups.)

Hearn, Lafcadio—*Japan, an Attempt at Interpretation,* New York, Macmillan, 1904. pp. v, 541.

Knapp, Arthur M.—*Feudal and Modern Japan,* Boston, J. Knight Co., 1897, 2 vols.

Mears, Helen—*Year of the Wild Boar*, Philadelphia, Lippincott, 1942. pp. 346. (A discerning study of modern Japanese society.)
Morris, John—*Traveler from Tokyo*, New York, Sheridan House, 1944. pp. 253.
Ninomiya, Shigeaki—"An Inquiry Concerning the Origin, Development, and Present Situation of the Eta in relation to the History of Social Classes in Japan," *Transactions of the Asiatic Society of Japan*, Second Series, 10 (1933), 47–152.
Sansom, Katharine—*Living in Tokyo*, illustrated by Marjorie Nishiwaki, New York, Harcourt, 1937. pp. 192. (Informal sketches by the wife of a diplomat.)
Wildes, H. E., *Japan in Crisis*, New York, Macmillan, 1934. pp. 300.

RELIGION

Anesaki, Masaharu—*History of Japanese Religion with Special Reference to the Social and Moral Life of the Nation*, London, Kegan Paul, 1930. pp. xxii, 423.
Aston, William G.—*Shinto, The Way of the Gods*, London, Longmans, Green, 1905. pp. 377. (A pioneer study with much first-hand observation.)
Cary, Otis—*A History of Christianity in Japan. Protestant Mission, Roman Catholic and Greek Orthodox Missions*, 2 v., New York and London, Revell, 1909. pp. 367 and 431.
Eliot, Sir Charles—*Japanese Buddhism*, London, Edward Arnold & Co., 1935. pp. 431. (A reliable, scholarly work on the subject.)
Eliseev, Serge—"The Mythology of Japan," *Asiatic Mythology*, pp. 385–448, translated from the French, London, Harrap, 1932.
Erskine, William Hugh—*Japanese Festival and Calendar Lore*, Tokyo, Kyobunkwan, 1933. pp. ix, 209.
Florenz, Karl—"Ancient Japanese Rituals," *Transactions of the Asiatic Society of Japan*, 27, 1 (1900), 1–112.
Holtom, D. C.—*National Faith of Japan: A Study in Modern Shinto*, London, Kegan Paul, 1938. pp. 329. (A comprehensive authoritative treatment.)
Holtom, D. C.—*Shinto and Japanese Nationalism*, Chicago, University of Chicago Press, 1943, pp. 173.
Iwai, Takahito—*The Outline of Tenrikyo*, Nara, Tenrikyo Doyusha, 1932. pp. vi, 319.
Kato, Genchi—*A Study of Shinto, the Reliigon of the Japanese Nation*, Tokyo, Meiji-Japan Society, 1926. pp. x, 255. (Includes comprehensive bibliography on Shinto.)

Nukariya, Kaiten—*The Religion of the Samurai, a Study of Zen Philosophy and Discipline in China and Japan*, Luzac's Oriental Religion Series, IV, London, Luzac, 1913. pp. xxii, 253.

Reed, John Paul—*Kokutai, A Study of Certain Sacred and Secular Aspects of* Japanese Nationalism, Chicago, Department of Sociology, University of Chicago Libraries, 1937. pp. 274.

Reischauer, August Karl—*Studies in Japanese Buddhism*, revised edition, New York, Macmillan, 1925. pp. xviii, 361.

Satow, Ernest Mason—"Ancient Japanese Rituals," *Transactions of the Asiatic Society of Japan*, 7, 2 (1879), 97–132, 4; 409–55; 9 (1881), 193–211.

Steinilber-Oberlin, Emile—*The Buddhist Sects of Japan, their History, Philosophical Doctrines and Sanctuaries*, with the collaboration of Kuni Matsuo, translated from the French by Marc Loge, London, Allen and Unwin. pp. 303.

Suzuki, Deisetz Teitaro—*Zen Buddhism and Its Influence on Japanese Culture*, The Ataka Buddhist Library, Vol. 9, Kyoto, Eastern Buddhist Society, 1938. pp. xii, 288 (One of several volumes by this authority.)

BIOGRAPHY AND AUTOBIOGRAPHY

Anesaki, Masaharu—*Nichiren the Buddhist Prophet*, Cambridge, Harvard University Press, 1916. pp. xi, 160.

Coates, Harper Havelock and Ishizuka, Ryugaku—*Honen, the Buddhist Saint. His Life and Teachings*. Translation, historical introduction, explanatory and critical notes, 2nd edition, Kyoto, Chinonin, 1925. pp. xciv, 955.

Dening, Walter—*The Life of Toyotomi Hideyoshi* (1536–1598), 3rd ed., with preface, notes and appendix by M. E. Dening, Kobe, Thompson, 1930. pp. vi, 323.

Eckstein, Gustav—*Noguchi* (1867–1928), New York, Harper, 1931. pp. xi, 419.

Falk, Edwin Albert—*Togo and the Rise of Japanese Sea Power*, with a foreword by Rear Admiral Bradley A. Fiske, New York, Longmans Green, 1936. pp. xiii, 508.

Fukuzawa, Yukichi—*The Autobiography of Fukuzawa Yukichi*, (1835–1901), translated by Eiichi Kiyooka, with an introduction by Shinzo Koizumi, Tokyo, Hokuseido, 1934. pp. xviii, 370.

Hamada, Kengi—*Prince Ito*, Tokyo, Sanseido, 1936. pp. 240.

Hino, Ashihei—*Wheat and Soldiers*, translated by Shidzue Ishimoto, New York, Farrar & Rinehart, 1939. pp. 191. (Narrative of a Japanese soldier in China.)

Ishimoto, Shidzue—*Facing Two Ways*, New York, Farrar & Rinehart, 1935. pp. 373. (Autobiography of a pioneer Japanese feminist.)

Noma, Seiji—*Noma of Japan*, New York, Vanguard, 1934. pp. 290. (Autobiography of a Japanese school teacher who became a magazine king.)

Matsui, Haru—*Restless Wave*, New York, Modern Age Books, 1940. 252 pp.

Sadler, Arthur Lindsay—*The Maker of Modern Japan, the Life of Tokugawa Ieyasu (1542–1616)*, London, Allen and Unwin, 1937. pp. 429. (Very detailed.)

Sakurai, Tadayoshi—*Human Bullets*, translated by Masujiro Honda and Alice Bacon, Tokyo, Teihei Publishing Co., 1907. pp. 250.

Sugimoto, Etsu—*Daughter of the Samurai*, New York, Doubleday, Page, 1925. pp. 314.

SPECIAL MAGAZINE ISSUES

The Annals, May, 1941.
Fortune, September, 1936.
Fortune, April, 1944.

YEARBOOKS

The Japan Yearbook.
The Japan Manchukuo Yearbook.
The Far East Yearbook. (This is the 1941 edition of the *Japan Manchukuo Yearbook.*)

These yearbooks provide useful summaries of various aspects of Japan such as education, formal government structure, public health, etc. Of recent years, because of censorship, the industrial sections are less valuable than others. Despite this drawback, the yearbooks provide much valuable source material on the country.

Index

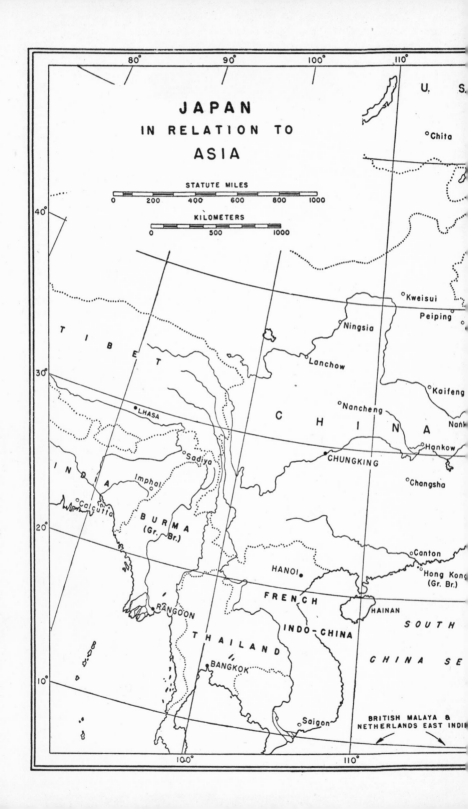